Louis Le Gear

Dr. Le Gear's stock book

Comprising a description of the general care, feeding and watering, stabling and breeding

Louis Le Gear

Dr. Le Gear's stock book
Comprising a description of the general care, feeding and watering, stabling and breeding

ISBN/EAN: 9783337141202

Printed in Europe, USA, Canada, Australia, Japan

Cover: Foto ©Lupo / pixelio.de

DR. LEGEAR'S STOCK BOOK

A COMPLETE, VALUABLE, INSTRUCTIVE BOOK
OF REFERENCE FOR ALL HORSE
AND STOCK OWNERS.

COMPRISING A DESCRIPTION OF THE GENERAL CARE, FEEDING AND WATERING, STABLING AND BREEDING, AND ALL THE DISEASES AND THEIR TREATMENT, OF STOCK IN TEXAS AND THE SOUTH. IT IS PLAINLY WRITTEN AND CONTAINS THE

LATEST AND MOST VALUABLE FORMULAS.

BY DRS. L. D. AND N. G. LEGEAR,

GRADUATES OF THE ONTARIO VETERINARY COLLEGE, TORONTO, ONTARIO; HONORARY MEMBERS OF THE ONTARIO VETERINARY MEDICAL SOCIETY; AND VETERINARIANS FOR "THE TEXAS STOCKMAN AND FARMER," SAN ANTONIO.

AUSTIN, TEXAS:
PUBLISHED BY THE AUTHORS.
1897

BEN C. JONES AND CO.
PRINTERS,
BINDERS AND ELECTROTYPERS,
AUSTIN, TEXAS.

Below is a voluntary testimonial from The Texas Stockman and Farmer Publishing Co., of San Antonio, Texas, who publish The Texas Stockman and Farmer, which is one of the best papers that is devoted to the live stock and farming interests of Texas and the Southwest:

THE TEXAS STOCKMAN AND FARMER,
San Antonio, Texas, August 3d, 1897.

To the Stock Growers and Farmers of Texas:

We have examined the advance sheets of the well-written and handsomely illustrated work devoted to the diseases and treatment of live stock in Texas and the South, and their proper care and breeding, to be issued shortly by Dr. L. D. LeGear and Dr. N. G. LeGear, veterinary surgeons, Austin, Texas.

This book is plainly and simply written, and will be of great value on every farm and ranch. Drs. LeGear are both graduate veterinary surgeons, and have built up a large practice in this State.

Dr. L. D. LeGear, for several years past, has been in charge of the veterinary department of this paper, and we have reason to know that he is one of the best posted men on diseases of livestock and their treatment in the South; hence it is that we take great pleasure in endorsing this work.

THE TEXAS STOCKMAN AND FARMER PUB. CO.,
Per Vories P. Brown, Editor and Manager.

Below is a clipping from the August 26th number of "The Texas Vorwarts," the largest and most widely circulated German weekly paper in the State, published at Austin, Texas, by Judge Schutze.

"We have read with great interest the manuscript of a book, very useful to the farmers and stock raisers, principally for such who reside in the State of Texas, or elsewhere in the South, and we can recommend same as a very valuable book. The book is edited by Drs. LeGear. It is indeed a stock book: complete, valuable, and instructive—a book of reference for all horse and stock raisers and owners. It furnishes an exact description of the general care of stock: its feeding, watering, stabling, and breeding. It treats on the diseases of stock, and their treatment in Texas and the South. The book is written in plain language, and contains the latest and most valuable recipes for the cure of the diseases of stock. The editors, Drs. L. D. and N. G. LeGear, are graduates of the Ontario Veterinary College at Toronto, honorary members of the Ontario Veterinary Medical Society, and veterinarians for "The Texas Stockman and Farmer," San, Antonio, Texas.

"JULIUS SCHUTZE, Editor and Manager."

INTRODUCTION.

After traveling about over Texas and the South for three years, practicing our profession as veterinary surgeons, and investigating the diseases and ailments peculiar to the domesticated animals here, we were very forcibly struck with this thought: "How greatly in need are the stock raisers and stock owners in Texas and the South of the proper information and instructions on the general care of stock, and their treatment while injured or diseased." This thought, with the request of hundreds of stock owners, stimulated us to the consideration of writing a general Stock Book, plainly written and profusely illustrated, by the aid of which every stock owner could treat the majority of diseases and ailments of his stock; and, best of all, learn how to care for them and keep them from becoming diseased. In offering our work to the public for sale, we think we have amply filled this want and demand.

Texas, with her 7,000,000 cattle, 2,000,000 horses, 2,000,000 hogs, and 4,000,000 sheep, can boast of being by far the greatest and best stock producing State in the Union; and then for her to be so nearly without veterinary skill, and plainly written veterinary books, shows the great need of a stock book of this kind on every ranch, farm, and in the house of every stock owner in the State. We find what few stock books there are in this country are either too old or are not written in a language plain enough for the ordinary citizen to understand. As veterinary science during the last few years has made such rapid progress in investigating the exact nature and more successful treatment of various stock diseases, therefore, a stock book at the present day is considered old and out of date if it is only five or eight years old. In writing this volume, we have taken special care and pains to write it in a very plain language, so that any one understanding the English language can read it understandingly. We have made special efforts to make all new treatments as plain as possible, and to give the very best formulas for the same. You will notice in the treatment of some of the diseases given in this book that we recommend Dr. LeGear's Celebrated Veterinary Remedies. These are a line of stock medicines, explained fully in this book, that we are manufacturing for the benefit and conveniences of the stock owner. They are put up in a very convenient form, and are cheaper than you can get formulas filled for the same diseases, and they can be had from your druggist, or your country merchant.

We are both graduate veterinary surgeons, having taken a full course of instructions, and graduated with high honors, from the Ontario Veterinary College, Toronto, Canada. In preparing this book, besides our veterinary skill, we have referred to the following noted modern veterinary writers: Robertson, Fleming, Chauveau, Strangeway, Liautard, Williams, Courtney, Armatage, Finley Dun, Special Reports of the Bureau of Animal Industry, and The American Veterinary Review. We have endeavored, as far as possible, to illustrate this book by using original, appropriate cuts, which we hope will be a great aid to all those who read it in understanding the various diseases and their treatment.

In conclusion, we wish to express a hope that this work may be favorably received by all into whose hands it may find its way, and more particularly the stock man and stock owners of Texas and the South.

DR. LeGEAR'S STOCK BOOK.

CHAPTER I.

FEEDING AND WATERING HORSES.

How often is the question asked, "How and when shall we feed and water our horses?" We shall endeavor to give, in as few words as possible, our opinion on this subject, which is endorsed by the best authorities in this country. Our remarks shall be confined to the driving horse, and the work horse and mule, not referring to horses at pasture. Over one-half the diseases of the digestive organs are caused by improper feeding and watering; therefore, this is a very important subject for all horse owners to consider.

The horse, man's most faithful and useful servant, since becoming domesticated has to depend on man for the feed he eats, the water he drinks, the freedom he gets, the air he breathes, the light he receives, and, in fact, his very existence is at man's will, to properly or improperly care for him. Considering the small size of a horse's stomach, it would lead one to the belief that he should be fed often and a small quantity at a time. Some of the large feeding stables in the North feed their horses grain four times a day, but we think three times is sufficient, but it should be done regularly, and at the same hour each day, if possible.

Hay, fodder, or whatever roughness is used, should be fed at night, when the racks can be filled up, and let them eat what they want, as they have all night for it to digest. This applies more particularly to driving horses, for if they are fed hay shortly before going on a drive their stomach and bowels are very distended, which makes it difficult and injurious to perform severe labor. Rapid and severe labor should not be performed on a full stomach. For such horses, food must be given in small quantities, and fed to them one or two hours before going to their work. One of the common errors of feeding, and one that produces more digestive disorders, is to feed too soon after a hard day's work. First give a few swallows of water, then some hay, and in about one hour give what water he will drink, and then his grain. By all means, feed sound, wholesome food, for damaged, inferior food is dear at any price.

The disproportion between the size of the stomach and the amount of water drank tells us plainly that the horse should always be watered before feeding, as the stomach holds but three and a half to four gallons. A series of experiments has proven this. A horse was given all the water he would drink and fed four quarts of oats, and immediately after eating them he was killed. On opening the stomach, it was found that nearly all the oats were in the stomach and undergoing the process of digestion. Another horse was watered and fed in the same way, and was killed one hour after eating the oats. In this case, it was found that nearly all the oats had left the stomach and were found in the bowels, thoroughly digested and undergoing absorption. A third one was given four quarts of oats, then given a bucket of water, and immediately killed. What a sad state of affairs was found. Nearly all the oats had been slushed out of the stomach by the water, and were found floating in the water in the bowels in an undigested state.

It is the same with all kinds of grain fed in this way. The grain which is washed out of the stomach by watering right after feeding not only passes out of the system only partially digested, but it gives extra work to the bowels, and weakens and overtaxes them. It can be plainly seen by the above that horses and mules should be watered before feeding, and not directly afterward.

Horses at work should be watered often, and a small quantity at a time; while standing in the stable, three times a day is sufficient. Nothing will refresh a horse, while driving on a hot day, like a few swallows of fresh water. It gives him new life and strength, and permits him to pursue his journey with much greater ease. On coming in, heated from a drive, a few swallows of water is beneficial to a horse, but all he will drink is dangerous. Water should be fresh, pure and wholesome. Impure water is the cause of many diseases of the horse. The quantity of grain fed should be regulated according to the size of the animal and the amount of labor he is required to do. Some horses are like some people—they can stand the violation of the proper laws of feeding and watering for a considerable length of time without experiencing or showing any inconveniences therefrom, but some day its effects will be plainly seen.

Sick animals should have a bucket of fresh, cool water before them all the time. The food for a sick horse should be very nutritious and easy of digestion. Bran mashes, either scalded or just wet with cold water; boiled oats; green grass, or green food of any kind; linseed gruel, beets, turnips, potatoes, etc., are all very good. Wheat bran is a very necessary article of diet for every horse owner to have about his stable. He should educate his horses to eat it, for it is very healthy to a well horse, and far more valuable to a sick one.

CHAPTER II.

STABLING AND GENERAL CARE OF HORSES.

This is a subject that is sadly neglected by a majority of horse owners in this country. Very few farmers, and a great many horse owners in the cities and towns, have what can be called stables for their horses; they have merely a lot and sheds, and, in fact, some don't have even a shed. These sheds, as a general thing, are cool, airy, and comfortable for summer, but are cruelly cold and disagreeable during the winter "northers." The horse, man's most faithful servant, needs comfort and protection against the cold and wet as well as man does. It is for the want of proper care and comfort that so many horses become affected with disease. These airy, cool sheds are the very best kind of stables for summer time in this country, but for winter we should have stables that we can close up to keep out the cold, chilly air, and give the animal a good bed of straw to lie on. How comfortable it seems to us when, during a cold "norther," we can close our doors and windows, and get into a soft, warm bed, provided with plenty of blankets to keep us warm. We should first see that our stock have a warm, comfortable place for the night, and then we can lie down and sleep with a clear conscience and an easy mind.

Stables should be kept clean and dry, and have plenty of ventilation and good light. Close, dark, poorly ventilated stables are very injurious to horses' eyes, and to their general health. Foul air should be allowed to escape through trap-doors or windows in the ceiling or top of the stable. The stalls should be large and comfortable, box-stalls being the best. The stall floor should be clay or dirt, and nearly level. A hard plank floor is injurious to a horse's feet and legs. The hay racks should not be too high; in fact, it is better to feed hay from the ground, which is the natural way for a horse to get its food. If racks are used, they should not be higher than the shoulder. The grain boxes should be in one end of the manger (rack). If the horse has a habit of throwing his hay out under his feet, nail a few slats across the rack. If he is a greedy eater, put a few cobble-stones in his grain box.

Horses, while working, should be groomed (cleaned with a curry-comb and brush) thoroughly once or twice a day. Use a fine-tooth curry-comb and a stiff brush, and thoroughly work all the dirt and dust out of the hair each time of grooming. It is claimed by some good authorities on this subject that the curry-comb and brush, well used, is worth half-feed. Good grooming keeps the skin clean and healthy, and makes the hair short, sleek and glossy. If your stable is cold, a blanket should be kept on your horse during the cold weather. It is very important and necessary that a street-blanket be had to put on your horse while he is standing in the cold. It is a cruel practice to hitch a horse in the street, either in the hot sun or cold wind, and let him stay for hours, as some do. If you have to hitch a horse out in a cold wind or storm, stand him with his tail to the wind. Don't be cruel and abusive to a horse. Be kind, but firm, to him, and he will obey you better than a hired servant. There is no excuse in working poor horses in a country like this, where so much grass and feed can be raised in abundance, with so little labor; and yet we often see poor horses and mules working to wagons with galled shoulders, and writhing under the whip of a cruel master. These are the farmers who have grassy crops and never get them cleaned out in time to receive the rain necessary to mature them. To prevent this cruel, barbarous treatment to stock, every town and community should form a humane society, whose object shall be the prevention of cruelty to animals. Texas has a law making it a misdemeanor to cruelly mistreat or abuse the horse, but it is not enforced.

Austin has formed a humane society, whose provisions are as follows, viz.:

"Article 786. If any person shall wilfully kill, maim, wound, poison, or disfigure any horse, ass, mule, cattle, sheep, goat, swine, dog, or other domesticated animal, or any domesticated bird, of another, with intent to injure the owner thereof, he shall be fined not less than ten nor more than two hundred dollars; and in prosecutions under this article the intent to injure may be presumed from the perpetration of the act.

"Article 787. If any person shall wilfully or wantonly kill, maim, wound, disfigure, poison, or cruelly and unmercifully beat and abuse any animal included in the preceding article, he shall be fined not exceeding two hundred and fifty dollars."

Let other cities, towns and communities follow Austin in this good work. Another cruelty inflicted on horses, which might be called a fashionable one, is high checking. This is practiced more extensively in the cities, where many a poor horse is checked up so high that he can't see his feet, nor even the ground he is walking on. Moderate checking is all right on short drives, but on long, country drives a horse should have the free use of his head. A practice that is cruel and needless is to let a horse stand hitched in the street with his head checked up too high. Always uncheck your horse if you can't let him stand ten minutes, as it rests him. Considerable attention should be paid to a horse's shoulders, neck and back, to prevent saddle and collar galls. Keep the collar or saddle clean and smooth, and see that they fit well. Sponge off the shoulders, neck and back on coming in from a hard drive, or day's work, with cold water, containing a little salt. This will toughen the skin and prevent galls.

A horse's foot is a very particular and wonderful mechanism, and it needs special care and attention, for the old adage is very true—"no foot, no horse." The foot should be cleaned out and washed every morning, to see whether a nail has penetrated it or a rock has become wedged under the shoe. Horses used entirely on the farm need not be shod only in exceptional cases—those of weak, tender feet. For road use, a horse needs shoes on to protect the wall of the hoof from wearing off too close, and to protect it from bruises it would likely sustain by being driven fast on hard, rocky roads. For general remarks on shoeing, read up on that subject under its respective heading.

Every stock man, stock owner and farmer, who is at all interested in stock raising and farming, should take one or more of the following stock and farm papers: "The Texas Stockman and Farmer," San Antonio, Texas; "The Stock and Farm Journal," Fort Worth, Texas; or "The Farm and Ranch," Dallas, Texas.

CHAPTER III.

BREEDING.

The breeding of horses is a subject that is sadly neglected by a great many breeders. Some men think if a mare can conceive and bring a colt, no matter how old, broken-down or crippled she is, she is just as good as a well-bred, sound, young mare. This is a very false idea. The law of like producing like is very plainly shown in breeding horses; therefore, if you wish to raise good colts, you must breed from sound parents. It is a profitable business to raise good horses, but common horses are raised at a loss. This is exemplified at the present time by the cheapness of the common horse, and the increasing demand and good price of good driving horses. It costs just as much to raise a common, scrub colt as it does a fine-blooded one; the only difference being in the cost of the sire. The first will sell, when four or five years old and broken to harness, probably for from $10 to $40, and the other will bring from $75 to $200.

Below is a portion of the paper prepared by Col. Henry Exall, of Dallas, and read before the Livestock Association of Texas at San Antonio, in March of this year. Colonel Exall is one of the greatest horsemen in Texas, and a good authority on this subject; therefore, we think his remarks will be interesting and profitable to all readers of this book:

"I will simply state that in my opinion, formed after the most careful investigation of the present status of the horse market, and the conditions surrounding the horse-breeding industry, that, at this particular time, no business offers greater returns, with the same degree of certainty, than the breeding and careful raising of a high class of trotting horse suitable for track and road purposes, having size, substance, good looks, good behavior and speed, ordinary or great, and the more the better. My reasons for this belief will be given very briefly:

"Breeding has been almost totally abandoned for the past four years, and it is estimated that there are not as many horses in the United States in 1897 as there were in 1890 by about 2,000,000, the decrease being proportionately much larger in the high grades of horses than in the cheaper and less desirable ones.

"Nothing but very high prices will stimulate the people to start to breeding again; and, when they do start, the scarcity of merchantable stock will be intensified by the number of mares that will be withdrawn from ordinary use and put to breeding. It will be at least six years after the breeding industry is well under way again before the colts, resulting from such breeding, will be old enough for general use.

"In the meantime, there will be a great scarcity of horses, and corresponding high prices.

"The great decline in prices in 1893-96 was, to a great extent, brought about by the fact that during the prosperous times, when horses were very high, thousands of parties, without any practical knowledge, rushed into the breeding business, using anything in the line of stallions and mares that was ever remotely related to anything that had trotted, paying no attention to size, good looks or soundness.

"In a great many instances, the stallions and mares upon so-called trotting farms failed to produce more than 2 or 3 per cent of horses that could be made to go in 2:30. Of course, this meant ruin and disaster whenever this character of stock was forced upon the market, as intelligent breeders would not buy them, and to the general public they were of no more value than the ordinary horses of the country.

"This indiscriminate breeding of trotters that could not trot and had very few other desirable qualities, very materially helped to increase the number of horses in the United States from about

11,000,000 in 1866 to about 16,000,000 in 1890. About this time the country began to feel the approach of an impending panic, money began to be scarce, and many parties who had other business interests to protect found it necessary to close out their horse business so as to concentrate their funds, and accordingly consigned their stock to the auction market.

"The decline in prices was precipitated and intensified by the fact that thousands of breeders all over the country, discouraged at the outlook and influenced to some extent by the example of others, unreasoningly, or in some cases from absolute necessity, consigned all their horses, regardless of condition or fitness for sale, to the auction markets. As no one at this time was buying breeding stock, the majority of these horses sold at ruinously low prices, and the very publishing of these low prices tended to keep up the panic and caused almost total abandonment of the horse-breeding industry.

"To-day, the condition is abnormal, and can not long remain as it is, to-wit, good horses ready for use are already scarce and bring remunerative prices in the chief markets of the country, but brood mares and immature young stock, the sources from which a future supply of merchantable horses must come, are abandoned and almost without price.

"With the dawn of 1897, a brighter future for the horse business is already in sight. The recent sales in New York, Lexington and Chicago have averaged almost double the prices realized in the same markets for the same class of stock one year ago.

"European parties, too, are active buyers at all sales in the United States now, and the recent winning of the greatest race ever trotted in the old world—the grand prize at St. Petersburg, Russia—by an American trotting mare, will give an increased impetus to the rapidly growing demand for high class American horses in Europe. This is evidenced by the fact that within the past ten days eighty-seven richly-bred trotting horses were sold in Lexington, Ky., to European parties, for the sum of $98,800, and shipped on the steamship Prussia to Vienna, Austria.

"The great success that has been attained by Woodburn and kindred farms is very largely due to the fact that they have persistently claimed that speed follows blood, and have insisted that their stallions and mares should be of the highest breeding. These are the only lines upon which very great success can be assured. The short, or half-bred, animal will occasionally produce speed, but not with uniformity. To reach the highest pinnacle of success, a breeder must determine that the choicest animals he raises are too good to sell and must be kept for breeding.

"If you will start with the best-bred ones that you can command, and intelligently grow and educate their offspring for a few generations, reserving always the best, we may yet produce not only the 2:00, but the 1:50, trotter on Texas soil, and I hope upon the Lomo Alto farm.

"When our colts have long lines of successful speed-producers on the side of both sire and dam—with size, substance, intelligence, docility and speed, that trot naturally and with little training—the type of the American trotter will be fixed, and the wealthy world will take at handsome figures all that we can raise. The breeder who will cause 500 bushels of oats and 10 tons of hay to produce a horse worth from $500 to possibly many thousands of dollars, instead of a horse worth from $25 to $100, will make a fortune for himself and set an example that should be worth millions to his countrymen."

In selecting a stallion or a mare for breeding purposes, see that they are of a kind disposition, good form, size and action, and free from all hereditary diseases, as heaves, roaring, ophthalmia, rupture, spavin, ring-bone, weak feet, curby hocks, etc. The colt may not be born with any of these diseases, but if the sire or dam is affected with one or more of them, the colt is liable to be born weak in those parts, and the disease is very liable to develop some time during its life.

CARE OF THE MARE.

A mare should have a certain amount of special care during the time she is carrying the colt. Regular, gentle work, and good feed, is to be preferred to no work and half feed. During the last two or three months of gestation, great care should be taken that the mare is not excited, pulled or run too hard, and should be kept away from the smell of fresh blood.

The usual time for a mare to carry a colt is eleven months, although it may vary between ten and twelve months. Time should be arranged so that the colt will come at a time when there is some grass, as the mare will do better when not confined to dry feed. The virgin mare, or one that has not had a colt for at least one year, should be bred when in season. The mare that has had a colt will be found in season (heat) on the eighth or ninth day, and should be served at that time. After serving the mare, the days for trial are the ninth after serving, the seventh after this, and the fifth after this again. Some commence again on the ninth day, and follow up as before, making forty-two days in all.

The mare and colt should be well fed and cared for. Moderate work, with good feed, will not, as a general thing, interfere with the colt's growth, but we think a mare has enough to do if she supplies the colt with sufficient milk for its growth and strength. If the mare is being driven, or doing farm work, the colt snould not be allowed to suck while the mare is hot, and the milk fevered. When the colt is about six or seven months old, it may be weaned, and should be turned into a good pasture away from the mare. To thrive and do well, the colt should be fed a little oats and bran once a day. If possible, keep your colts and horses away from barbed-wire fences, as it disfigures and ruins a large percentage of the horses in this country. Colts should be handled while young, if this is possible, and educated and trained like a child, and, when old enough to work, they can be taught to do so without much trouble. Colts can be broken to harness while yearlings, and driven lightly at the age of two; but it is better not to put them to hard work until about four years old.

CHAPTER IV.

HOW MEDICINES SHOULD BE GIVEN.

There are various ways by which medicines may be given to stock; but, as every horse owner, or stock man, isn't supposed to be a professional veterinarian, nor is he equipped with all the necessary instruments and appliances for treating stock, therefore, we will endeavor here to explain a few of the most convenient and useful ways by which medicines can be administered by any person competent of owning stock:

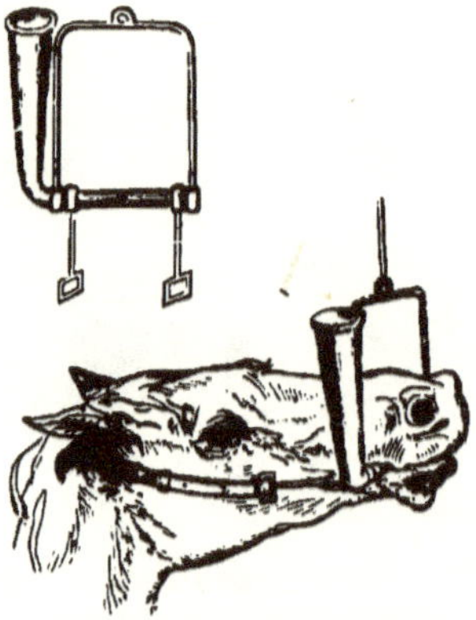

Fig. 1. Drenching Bit.

(1) BY THE MOUTH.—Medicines can be given by the mouth in the form of drenches, powders, balls, etc.

Drenches.—This is the most common and universal way by which medicines are given to animals. Drenches are to be given when the medicine is a liquid, and the dose large. Drenches must be given by the mouth, and never through the nose. Medicines given through the nose are very liable to irritate the nasal chambers, strangle the animal, and cause death—some times in a very short time. Water should never be poured through the nose to make a horse swallow. Do not rub, pinch or pound the throat, nor draw out the tongue, when giving a drench. These will not aid the horse to swallow, but are very liable to do much harm. When medicines are to be given as a drench, they should be put in enough water or oil to dissolve or dilute them. Medicines given not sufficiently diluted are liable to burn or irritate the mouth and throat. The most convenient way of giving a drench is by the use of the drenching bit (Fig. No. 1). The medicine is poured into the funnel at the side of the mouth, and it runs out of the little hole in the hollow bit that is in his mouth. By having the head slightly elevated, the horse will swallow the medicine without any trouble. The next best way to give a drench is to put on a bridle, with a straight, smooth bit. Tie a small rope or strap to each ring of the bridle rings, and pull the head up by this means. A loop may be made on the end of a rope large enough to go around the upper jaw, and back of the front teeth, and the head pulled up with the rope over a limb of a tree, or beam in the stable. Don't pull the head up too high, but just high enough so the medicine will not run out of his mouth. Use a smooth, strong, long-necked bottle, in which have the medicine. Pull the head up, and insert the neck of the bottle into the mouth from the side, and pour not over four ounces of the medicine at one time. Remove the bottle, and if the horse doesn't work his jaws, rub the roof of his mouth with your thumb, which will make him work his jaws and swallow. Be very careful, and don't let the horse crush the neck of the bottle between his jaw teeth. If he should break the bottle, or cough and strangle, let the head down at once. You may stand on a box or stool to give a drench.

Cows can be easily drenched by grasping the nose with the

thumb and middle finger of the left hand, and pouring the medicine down with the right hand.

Powders.—Powders are generally given mixed with damp feed, or dissolved in the drinking water. They should be finely powdered, and all bitter powders that are to be given in the feed should be scented or sweetened with a little powdered anise seed, fenugreen or sugar. They should never be put in the feed dry, but either mixed in a bran mash, dampened shelled oats, soaked shelled corn, etc. Those that are not bitter and are readily dissolved, can be given in the drinking water. Small doses of powders, such as our Condition Powders, can be put away back on a horse's tongue dry, with a long-handled spoon, without wasting them. Powders can also be given as a drench by being shaken up in one-half pint of water in a long-necked bottle.

Balls.—This is a means by which very few horse owners can, with any degree of satisfaction, give medicine to a horse. When a ball is properly made, it is about two inches long and three-quarters of an inch in diameter. Balls are frequently used by veterinary surgeons when they wish to give medicine that is extremely disagreeable or nauseating. They should be made up fresh and rolled into tissue paper before given. They should be made up with glycerine, vaseline, or soft soap. Gelatine capsules large enough for veterinary use are now made and are very useful and convenient for giving balls. The way balls are given is to grasp the tongue with the left hand, and with the right hand place the ball back on the root of the horse's tongue, and on letting the tongue go he swallows it. The mouth speculum (Fig. No. 9) may be used to open the mouth and prevent a horse from biting you while giving a ball. Don't shove a ball down a horse's throat with a stick, as you are very liable to injure his throat in that way.

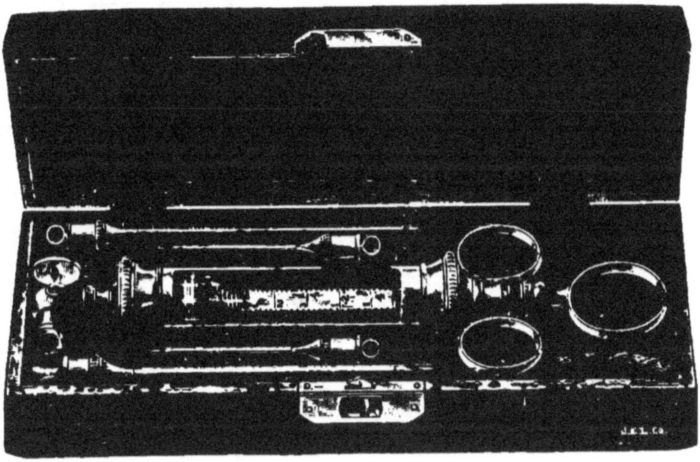

Fig. 2. Hypodermic Syringe.

(2) Under the Skin.—Medicines are frequently given under the skin by the use of a hypodermic syringe (Fig. No. 2). This is called the hypodermic (hypo., under; dermic, the skin) method of giving medicine. Such medicines as morphine, atropene, cocaine, eserine, pilocarpine, etc., are given in this way. Great care should be taken in giving these medicines in this way, because they are all poisons, and must be used with care. The needle should be perfectly clean, so as not to poison the animal. In the neck, or on the shoulder, is the preferable place to give medicine hypodermically.

(3) By Inhalation.—In certain head, throat, and lung troubles, inhalation of steam, containing a small quantity of such medicines as camphor, carbolic acid, turpentine, etc., is very beneficial. Chloroform and sulphuric ether are inhaled through the nose for anaesthetic purposes. To put a horse to sleep, use

pure chloroform; but with the dog, use two parts ether and one part chloroform.

(4) BY THE RECTUM.—Medicines are injected into the rectum to kill pin-worms found in the rectum, to stimulate the action of the bowels, and clean out the rectum. This is done with a large syringe or injection pump. Stimulating medicines and foods may be injected into the rectum, to be absorbed by the circulation, during sickness.

CHAPTER V.

ORGANS OF RESPIRATION (BREATHING).

The principal organs of breathing are the nostrils, nasal chambers, larynx, windpipe, and the lungs. Owing to the large size of a horse's soft palate, he can not breathe through his mouth, but must breathe through his nostrils entirely. The mucous membrane lining the nostrils and the chambers in a horse's head is very delicate and sensitive, and by a horse breathing through his nostrils exclusively explains why a horse catches cold, distemper, etc., so easily. The larynx is situated in the throat, and is the entrance to the windpipe. It becomes affected in the disease called roaring. The windpipe is the tube that conveys the air from the larynx to the lungs. It can be felt plainly in the front of a horse's neck. The lungs are the principal organs of breathing. They consist of two light, soft, spongy masses, one on either side, commonly called the "lights," being situated entirely in the cavity of the chest. On the outside, the lungs are completely covered by a thin, shining membrane, called the pleura, which also lines the chest cavity. The healthy lungs of any animal, after birth, will float on water, but will not before birth. It is in the lungs that the blood is purified—the oxygen in the pure air that the animal breathes comes in contact, as it were, with the impurities in the blood, burning it up, and converts it into a substance called carbon dioxide, which is thrown off from the lungs as a poisonous gas.

DISEASES OF THE ORGANS OF RESPIRATION.

CATARRH—COLD IN THE HEAD.

Catarrh, as meant in this article, is a discharge of fluid from the lining of the air passages of the head (nose).

Causes.—Sudden changes in the weather, exposure to cold and wet, badly ventilated stables, impure air, etc. The disease is mostly seen in young horses.

Symptoms.—The animal is duller than usual, and may or may not have a cough. The discharge, which is at first thin and watery, is usually from both nostrils, but soon becomes thicker and more abundant, and yellowish-white in appearance. It is liable to run into congestion of the lungs if the animal is put to work too soon. It usually runs a favorable course in from six to ten days.

Treatment.—The treatment for cold in the head is very simple, if taken in time; and usually terminates favorably. Protect the animal from the cold and wet by keeping it in a comfortable place, with plenty of fresh air. As a general thing, all the medicine that is necessary to give is our Condition Powder in one teaspoonful doses, morning and night, in bran mashes or other damp feed. If there is a cough present, bathe the throat well with our Liniment morning and night. Feed on soft, damp food. In very severe cases, if the animal is much weak, give the following:

Sweet nitre	1 ounce.
Alcohol	2 ounces.
Nitrate of potash	2 drams.
Water	1 pint.

Mix, and give as a drench twice a day until the animal is better.

Steaming the head by having the animal inhale the steam of hot water containing a little carbolic acid, camphor, or turpentine, is beneficial in bad cases. Apply our Liniment, and give our Condition Powders regularly until the cough and discharge from the nose entirely stops.

LARYNGITIS—SORE THROAT.

Laryngitis is an inflammation of the lining membrane of the larynx (the upper part of the windpipe). It is a serious affection, and very often causes the death of the animal.

Causes.—Are about the same as those causing catarrh: as, exposure to cold and wet, changes in the weather, draughts of cold air, giving certain irritating medicines, etc.

Symptoms.—About the first thing noticed is a cough, followed by a difficulty in swallowing, so that the water, and in some cases the food, is returned through the nose. The mouth is hot, and froth dribbles from it. Pressure on the throat causes a violent fit of coughing. The animal usually stands with his head "poked out." The membrane in the nose becomes red. The discharge from the nostrils, if profuse and coming away freely, is to be regarded as a good sign.

Treatment.—During an attack of sore throat, the horse should be laid off work, and fed on soft, easily digested food: as, bran mashes, chops, boiled oats, linseed meal, and, best of all, green grass, if it can be had. In ordinary cases, all the medicine necessary is Dr. LeGear's Liniment (see Appendix), well rubbed on the throat morning and night, and Dr. LeGear's Condition Powders, given in the feed morning and evening. The Liniment will draw the soreness out of the throat, while the Condition Powders will cure the cough and build up the animal's system. In very bad cases, the horse may be made to inhale steam from hot water, into which has been put a little camphor, carbolic acid, or turpentine. If there is much fever, ten drops of tincture of aconite may be given every four hours in a little water. One-half teaspoonful each of chlorate and nitrate of potassium may be given two or three times per day in the drinking water, or put on the tongue.

NASAL AND PHARYNGEAL POLYPI.

These are tumors, usually of a fibrous nature, situated in the air passages. They usually have a small neck, with a free expanded extremity.

Causes.—These growth are often the result of irritation of the membrane lining the parts, and often occur without any apparent cause.

Symptoms.—There is generally a discharge from the nostril on the affected side, which may be bloody. The breathing may become very difficult, even to such an extent as to cause the animal to fall down.

Treatment.—Make an examination, and if it has a small neck try to remove it with the ecrasure. If in the nose, you might be able to seize it with a pair of forceps and twist it off. The bleeding is often excessive, and there is always danger of the blood escaping into the lungs and causing death.

BLEEDING FROM THE NOSE—EPISTAXIS.

This often occurs in connection with other diseases, but may occur as an independent disorder.

Causes.—It may occur as a result of an injury, as a kick, blow, etc., causing rupture of a blood vessel in the nose. Sometimes severe exertion will also burst a blood vessel, while bleeding occurs at times without any known cause.

Symptoms.—The bleeding is almost always from one nostril only, and is never very serious—usually in drops.

Treatment.—Pour cold water over the face and head, or hang a bag with ice in it on the face. If necessary, plug the nostril with cotton wet in cold water. Of course only plug one nostril at a time. If this does not check the bleeding, give 1 dram acetate of lead dissolved in a pint of water, or give 1 ounce of turpentine in warm milk.

SPASM OF THE LARYNX.

Spasm of the larynx most commonly occurs amongst old horses, and is due in the majority of cases to cerebral (brain) disturbance.

Symptoms.—The attack is very sudden. In some cases a frothy spume issues from the nostrils; the breathing is very difficult, loud and labored; the animal staggers, struggles for breath, and finally falls.

Treatment.—Hypodermic injections of morphine, inhalations of chloroform, administrations of opium, etc., is the proper line of treatment. When due to cerebral disturbance give the following as a drench:

Bromide of potassa ....4 drams.
Water ....1 pint.
Mix.

CHRONIC COUGH.

It may exist without any apparent cause. It may follow laryngitis, and may be associated with chest diseases, indigestion, etc.

Treatment.—Carefully avoid the feeding of bad hay and oats, dusty food, etc., and give 1 dram of antimony twice a day for ten days; or give the following old reliable remedy:

Calomel ... .6 drams.
Digitalis ... .6 drams.
Camphor ... .6 drams.
Powdered opium ....6 drams.

Mix and divide into 12 powders, and give one every other morning before feeding.

CHRONIC CATARRH—NASAL GLEET.

This is characterized by a continuous discharge of a thick, white, or yellowish-white matter from one or both nostrils.

Causes.—The commonest cause is a neglected or badly treated cold, usually following those cases where the horse has been exposed, been over-worked, or has not received proper food. Other causes are: blows on the head and face, diseased teeth, tumors, fractures, or particles of food or other foreign bodies getting in the passages of the head.

Symptoms.—The discharge from the nose is at first white, soon becomes yellow, and sticks around the nostrils, but generally is not so sticky as the discharge of glanders. The lining membrane in the nose is reddened at first, but soon takes on a paler color, but has no ulcers. Slight enlargement of the bones of the face may be seen, and tapping the enlargement with the knuckles a dull dead sound is heard, indicating that there is matter beneath. In such cases the breathing may be affected. When the bones are diseased the discharge will have a disagreeable odor.

Treatment.—The treatment of this disease is very important, owing to the fact that animals affected with it (nasal gleet) are very liable to take the glanders if exposed to the contagion. Nasal gleet will not run into the glanders, but it weakens the animal's system and makes it very liable to take the glanders if exposed. If taken in time most of cases of this disease can be cured, but after it is let run on for several months it is then very tedious and hard to cure. It may be well to quarantine (remove it from other horses and mules) the animal for a few days and give large doses of blood tonics as the following:

Sulphate of iron .... 3 ounces.
Iodide of potassium .... 2½ ounces.

Mix, and make 20 powders, and give one night and morning in damp feed.

When the above are all given get the following prescription filled and give as directed:

Sulphate of copper .... 3 ounces.
Powdered nux vomica .... 2 ounces.
Powdered gentian .... 3 ounces.
Powdered anise seed .... ½ ounce.

Mix, and make 20 powders, and give one night and morning in damp feed.

Fig. 3. Trephine.

Sometimes a good blister applied to the face will be beneficial. If there is an accumulation of matter in the sinuses of the face the only relief will be the operation of trephining, which is done by boring into the head with a trephine (Fig. 3) and allowing the matter to escape. If the nasal gleet is the result of a diseased tooth, the tooth must be removed.

ROARING.

Roaring may be defined to be breathing with a loud and unnatural sound during violent exercise. Roaring in itself is not a disease, but it is only a symptom of disease. Wheezing and whistling are only different forms of the same disease, and both finally terminate in roaring.

Causes.—Roaring is caused by some obstruction to the free passage of air in the larynx (upper part of windpipe). Such diseases as laryngitis, distemper, etc., are liable to terminate in roaring. No doubt hereditary transmission has a great deal to do with it. Tight reining may be regarded as one of the causes of roaring, but, after all other causes are mentioned, it will be found that nine out of every ten well-established cases of roaring are caused by paralysis of the muscles of the larynx; the muscles of the left side are almost invariably the ones affected.

Symptoms.—The best way to test whether a horse is a "roarer" is to either make him pull a load rapidly up a hill or over a sandy road or soft ground; or, if he is a saddle horse, gallop him up a hill. After which the animal may be suddenly stopped, and by immediately placing the ear to the nose and throat, any unnatural sound may be heard. The above method of examination is to be recommended in all cases, as some cases of roaring are so slight as to be rather difficult to detect. In may cases, the characteristic sound can be heard at a distance. Another test is, to give exercise, then stand the animal by a wall, his head firmly held by an attendant. Now, with a whip make a motion as though you were going to strike the animal, when he will start forward very suddenly, and, if affected, will usually make the grunt peculiar to "roarers."

Treatment.—This disease, when once established, is incurable. But relief may be afforded by an operation called tracheotomy, by which a hole is cut in the front of the windpipe and a tube (Fig. No. 4) put in, through which the animal may breathe, and get sufficient air to undergo severe exercise without distress. This is a delicate operation, and should be undertaken only by experienced veterinary surgeons. Relief may be afforded if taken in time by giving 1 dram of iodide of potassium twice a day for two or three weeks. Sometimes, a good blister applied to the throat is beneficial. A "roarer" should never be used for breeding purposes, as the disease is very likely to be transmitted to the colts. In roaring, the disease is in the throat, and the horse has difficulty in getting enough air into the lungs for fast work, while heaves is an affection of the lungs, and the horse has difficulty in forcing the air out of the lungs.

TRACHITIS.

This is an inflammation of the lining membrane of the trachea (windpipe).

Cause.—It is generally due to the presence of some foreign body, or exists as a complication of sore throat.

Symptoms.—The breathing is somewhat labored, and on placing the ear to the windpipe a rattling sound may be plainly heard. There is usually a discharge from the nose.

Treatment.—Clip off the long hair over the course of the windpipe, and apply Dr. LeGear's Liniment, or put on a mustard plaster. Give, in each bucket of the animal's drinking water, 2 drams of chlorate of potash. Clothe the patient well, and keep out of draughts, and don't allow the animal to breathe very cold air.

BRONCHITIS.

Bronchitis is an inflammation of the lining membrane of the tubes which branch from the windpipe and carry the air to and from the lungs. It is more dangerous when the smaller tubes are affected.

Causes.—The disease may be caused by exposure to cold and wet, sudden changes in the weather, standing in draughts of cold air, improperly giving medicine—as, forcing it down, or giving it through the nose, a part of it passing into the windpipe, thence to the bronchial tubes, causing inflammation. A drench should never be given through the nose. Other causes are, breathing irritating gases and smoke, foreign bodies getting into the parts, etc

Symptoms.—At first, there is noticed a chill, quickly followed by fever. The animal usually stands, and has a somewhat dry, husky cough. On placing the ear to the chest, a rattling, or coarse, wheezing sound may be heard, indicating that the large tubes are affected; or a hissing or whistling sound, showing that the small tubes are the ones affected. A discharge from the nose soon follows, which, if yellow, may be regarded as a good sign; but, if it is of a reddish or rusty color, it is to be regarded as an unfavorable symptom.

Treatment.—Put the animal in a comfortable box-stall, free from draughts; cover the body with a blanket—light or heavy, according to the season of the year. Hand-rub the legs until they are warm, after which apply flannel bandages, from the hoofs to the knees and hocks. Don't fail to apply Dr. LeGear's Liniment (see Appendix) well over the side and front of chest, behind the elbow and shoulder blades, covering a large surface. Rub the Liniment in well every day. Put a tablespoonful of oil of turpentine in a bucket of boiling water, and make the animal inhale the steam. In bad cases, the steam should be inhaled every hour. Give as a drench three times per day the following:

Solution of acetate of ammonia	3 ounces.
Spirits of nitrous ether	2 ounces.
Bicarbonate of potassium	4 drams.
Water	1 pint.

Mix.

If much pain is manifested in drenching, you better not drench, but put in each bucket of drinking water, if the animal will drink, one tablespoonful of bicarbonate of potassium. If the horse won't eat, and seems weak, give the following drench every four or five hours:

Sweet nitre .... 2 ounces.
Alcohol .... 2 ounces.
Water .... 1 pint.

Mix.

If the bowels are constipated, give injections per rectum of warm water. Don't give a purgative; don't bleed.

HAEMOPTYSIS—BLEEDING FROM THE LUNGS.

Causes.—Bleeding from the lungs is often associated with congestion of the lungs, bronchitis, pneumonia, etc. Aside from these conditions the principal cause is the performance of some severe exertion when not in suitable condition; most commonly met with in trotting and running horses, and in those in fine condition.

Symptoms.—When the blood comes from the lungs the animal has a cough, and the blood is frothy and comes from both nostrils. The ear may be placed against the windpipe along its course, and if the blood is from the lungs a gurgling or rattling sound will be heard.

Treatment.—It is very seldom this trouble needs any internal treatment. If the blood is profuse and continues for any length of time, give:

Turpentine .... 1 ounce.
Raw linseed oil .... 8 ounces.

Mix, and give as a drench, and repeat in one hour if necessary.

One ounce tincture of iron may be given in one pint of water. Keep the animal quiet and in a cool place for several hours. If the coughing is severe, give 1 ounce tincture of opium as a drench in 1 pint of water.

CONGESTION OF THE LUNGS.

Congestion of the lungs is simply an excess of blood in the vessels of the parts affected. It may be considered as the first stage of inflammation.

Causes. — Congestion of the lungs in the horse is usually caused by being put to rapid work and severe exertion when the animal is not in a fit condition to undergo more than moderate exercise. Driving an animal while suffering from certain diseases, as simple catarrh, distemper, etc., keeping in damp, badly ventilated stables, impure air, draughts, etc., are all causes of congestion of the lungs. The disease runs its course within a period varying from 8 or 10 hours to several days.

Symptoms.—Most any intelligent person should be able to recognize a case of congestion of the lungs when caused by overexertion, as the history of the case is sufficient to point out the trouble. The animal is noticed to stand with his head down, legs spread out, breathing becomes very difficult, with flapping of the nostrils, cold sweats break out, and the ears and extremities soon become deathly cold, which is well marked during cold weather. If the pulse can be felt at all, it will be found to be quick and weak. The temperature gradually rises, there is trembling of the flanks, and by placing your ear to the sides of the chest the characteristic sounds (a kind of snoring sound) of congestion of the lungs are heard.

Treatment.—The treatment of this trouble should be prompt and energetic. Give some good diffusible stimulant as:

Sweet spirits of nitre	2 ounces.
Whiskey	4 ounces.
Water	1 pint.

Mix, and give as a drench, and repeat every two or three hours until the horse is not so distressed.

The animal should be well blanketed. The legs should be bathed with hot water and then bandaged with woolen bandages. Don't put the patient in a close stable, but allow plenty of fresh air. Instead of the above prescription, you may give 1 ounce of tincture of arnica in one-half pint of water every hour until relieved. Or turpentine, 1 ounce, may be given in one-half pint of new milk. Give the animal plenty of pure cold water and good, nutritious, easily digested food, as grass, boiled oats, bran mash, linseed meal, etc. After the alarming symptoms have passed off you may give:

Tincture ginger	1 ounce.
Tincture iron	2 drams.
Tincture gentian	2 ounces.
Water	1 pint.

Mix, and give as a drench every six hours for a couple of days.

Care should be taken of the animal for several days. During recovery give as directed Dr. LeGear's Condition Powders night and morning in damp feed for several days.

PNEUMONIA—LUNG FEVER.

This is inflammation of the lungs. Both lungs may be attacked, but, as a general rule, one lung only is afflicted, and that is usually the right one.

Causes. — Exposure to wet and cold, standing in draughts, neglected catarrh, etc., are among the causes to be mentioned. It may also be caused by irritating substances, as certain medicines, inhalation of smoke, and breathing the air of badly ventilated stables. Such diseases as bronchitis, laryngitis, etc., may terminate in pneumonia.

Symptoms.—At first the animal has a chill, which is generally overlooked. The breathing becomes quickened, and the animal hangs its head and has a very dull appearance. The mouth is hot, indicating fever, and has a sticky feeling. The pulse soon runs up to 80 or 100 or more per minute, and if the temperature is taken it will be found to have risen to 103 degrees Fahrenheit, or higher. There is usually a cough from the beginning. The temperature of the legs and ears is changeable—sometimes hot and sometimes cold. The discharge from the nose may be tinged with blood, while in others it has a mattery appearance. In this disease the ox usually lies down, while the horse always stands, usually with his head toward the stable door to get all the fresh air possible. By placing the ear to the side of the chest during the first stage of the disease a sound is heard quite similar to that made by rubbing a lock of hair between the thumb and fingers.

Flapping of the nostrils after a few days' illness is a very bad sympton; in such cases, usually in the course of four or five days, a brownish or rusty-colored discharge may be observed flowing from the nose; the eyes take on a peculiar stare, and the patient seems to be unconscious of everything going on around him. The pulse now becomes very quick and weak, body and legs deathly cold; the patient may lie down for a few minutes, then get up, stagger, fall, and rise no more. Death may take place in from three to twenty days.

Pneumonia is not a very fatal disease if taken in time and treated properly.

Treatment.—It is very necessary that the patient be kept as comfortable as possible, and plenty of fresh air allowed. If the weather is cool or cold, cover the animal with blankets. Rub the legs well, and apply woolen bandages to them to keep them warm. Give the horse plenty of cold water to drink, and his food should be nutritious and easily digested. If the fever is high and the pulse strong, give 15 drops of tincture of aconite every four hours as a drench in half a pint of cold water. The following should be given to keep up the animal's strength:

Liquor acetate of ammonia ....4 ounces.
Sweet spirits of nitre ....2 ounces.
Alcohol ....2 ounces.

Mix, and give 2 ounces every four hours in one-half pint of cold water.

One teaspoonful of nitrate of potassium should be put in the drinking water twice a day.

It is very necessary that applications be applied to the sides, such as Dr. LeGear's Liniment, well rubbed in on the ribs two or three times per day, or a mustard paste may be well rubbed into the hair and let remain. Blankets wrung out of hot water and applied around the chest are good. Don't give too much medicine in this disease. The great object is to keep the animal comfortable and keep up his strength with nutritious food and stimulants. If the horse don't eat much, raw eggs and new milk may be given with the medicine to keep up the strength. If the bowels are costive give enemas of warm water. When the animal begins to improve give him freely of Dr. LeGear's Condition Powders (see Appendix), which is a good tonic preparation to tone up the system and promote strength and a good appetite.

PLEURISY.

The chest cavity which contains the heart and lungs is lined by a thin, glistening membrane, called the pleura. It also covers the lungs. Inflammation of this membrane is called pleurisy.

Causes.—Pleurisy is caused by sudden changes in the weather, exposure to cold and wet, and by the various conditions which cause pneumonia. Other causes are impure blood, wounds of the chest-wall, broken ribs, etc.

Symptoms.—It begins with a chill, which soon passes off. The animal stands stiff, similar to founder, with the fore-legs as far apart as possible, and, when compelled to move, he grunts or groans with pain. The breathing is noticed to be done back of the ribs (by the abdominal muscles), while the ribs are kept as still as possible. On placing the ear to the side of the chest a kind of grating sound can be heard, caused by the dry pleural membranes rubbing against each other. But in a few days, possibly less, the animal stands apparently free from pain, and there is no grating sound in the chest; this is a sign that a fluid has collected in the chest between the layers of the pleura. Such a collection of fluid in the chest-cavity is called hydrothorax, or dropsy of the chest. A great amount of fluid may thus be collected, rendering the case a hopeless one, without any very well marked symptoms being observed. Besides these signs, there is a cough, an elevation in temperature, and pressure on or between the ribs gives rise to considerable pain.

Treatment.—The general care and comfort of the animal is to be about the same as in pneumonia. As there is generally a high fever, and a rapid, strong pulse, give 15 drops of tincture of aconite in one-half pint of cold water, as a drench, every four hours; or, the following prescription may be given:

Liquor acetate of ammonia	4 ounces.
Nitrate of potassium	2 drams.
Chlorate of potassium	2 drams.
Sweet spirits of nitre	1 ounce.

Mix, and give as a drench every six hours in 1 pint of water.

Dr. LeGear's Liniment should be rubbed in the sides of the chest two or three times per day; also, the sides should be bathed with hot water, and blankets applied. Mustard paste may be rubbed in once or twice. If there is severe pain, it may be relieved by giving the following:

Tincture of opium	1 ounce.
Raw linseed oil	8 ounces.

Mix, and give as a drench. If the bowels are constipated, give enemas of warm water freely.

During convalescence, give Dr. LeGear's Condition Powders (see Appendix) in the feed as a general tonic and appetizer; also, give 1 dram of iodide of potassium in the drinking water morning and night for ten days.

HYDROTHORAX.

This is dropsy of the chest; or, in other words, a collection of fluid in the cavity of the chest. This condition is a result of pleurisy, sometimes resulting from a very mild attack, and even in cases where the animal has had the best of care.

Symptoms.—The symptoms are plain: difficult, short and labored breathing, and flapping of the nostrils. The eye has a peculiar, glassy appearance. The pulse is weak and irregular. There is a heaving motion of the flanks. The animal stands persistently, and soon peculiar swellings appear in the limbs, and extend along the belly. Death usually results when a considerable quantity of water collects in the chest. Perhaps several gallons of fluid will collect in a few days, and seriously interfere with the action of the lungs.

Treatment.—The great aim in the treatment of this disease is to support the animal's system as best we can, so as to cause absorption of the fluid in the chest. This may be done by giving nutritious, easily digested food and stimulants. Two ounces of sweet nitre and six ounces of whisky can be given as a drench every two or four hours in one-half pint of water; or, alcohol, ale, wine, etc., may be given. Tapping the chest and drawing off the fluid with a suitable instrument can sometimes be done successfully by a qualified veterinary surgeon, but we will not recommend the operation here. Give two drams of nitrate of potassium twice per day, and the best of care must be taken of the animal all through, if a recovery is expected.

THUMPS—SPASM OF THE DIAPHRAGM.

Thumps, or spasm of the diaphragm, is generally thought to be a palpitation of the heart by inexperienced persons. It may be as well to state that the heart has nothing to do with it. There is a very important muscle (called the diaphragm, or midriff) in the body, which separates the chest-cavity from the abdominal (cavity which contains the bowels). Spasms or irregular movements of this muscular partition in the horse is called the "thumps." Thumps in the horse is the same as "hiccoughs" in man, although the peculiar noise is not always made in the throat of the horse, as in man.

Causes.—Fast driving, or violent exertion, if the animal is not in proper condition.

Symptoms.—The symptoms are very plain: the breathing is difficult, a thumping sound is heard, which affects the whole body, and is not confined to the region of the heart, but back of it. By placing one hand on the body at about the middle of the last rib, and the other one over the heart just behind the left elbow, it will be an easy matter to make a distinction between the thumping or jerking of the diaphragm and the beating of the heart.

Treatment.—The treatment should be the same as that given for congestion of the lungs. If not relieved, death usually results from congestion.

HEAVES—BROKEN WIND—ASTHMA.

Broken wind is a condition the nature of which is not very well understood. Many horsemen wrongfully apply the term to all ailments where the breathing is difficult or noisy. It is generally accepted to be a derangement of the digestive organs, characterized by difficult and peculiar breathing and the presence of a long, deep cough, known as "the broken-winded cough."

Causes.—Broken wind may be caused by improper feeding of some kind, or by a supply of bad food, or bulky or dusty food of any kind, the stomach being kept overloaded with the same. Severe exertion when the stomach and bowels are full has a tendency to cause broken wind—that is, when the system is in poor condition. A chronic cough from any cause is liable to run into heaves. Another cause, and a very reasonable one, is that the exciting cause of broken wind is due to an affection of a certain nerve—pneumogastric nerve, which sends branches to the lungs, heart, stomach, etc. It is claimed that coarse or indigestible food irritates the branches of these nerves, which supply the walls of the stomach, and this irritation is reflected or extended to the branches of the same nerves which supply the lungs, when the trouble known as broken wind follows.

Symptoms.—"Heaves" is easily detected by almost every experienced horseman. When you have once seen a well-marked case, you will always know it. The peculiar, bellows-like movements of the flanks, and walls of the belly, point out the ailment at once. But in mild or recent cases, the affected animal does not show the characteristic breathing unless freely exercised —running or pulling a heavy load. There is always a peculiar cough, which is difficult to describe—the sound is short, very deep, and something like a grunt. Indigestion is always present in these cases. The animal's appetite is depraved, as shown by a desire to eat dirt and soiled bedding, which he often prefers to the clean food in the manger. The stomach is liable to be overloaded with indigestible food. The abdomen may assume that form called "pot-bellied." The animal frequently passes wind, the odor of which is very offensive. Horses with round chests are said to be subject to heaves; and, in cases of long standing, the chest usually becomes rounder than natural.

Treatment.—Heaves is a disease, when once well established, that can not be cured. All we can do in such cases is to relieve the animal for the time being by giving certain remedies, and paying strict attention to diet. All the feed given should be free from dust, and of the very best quality. All hay, grain and dry feed should be dampened, and not very much hay or roughness given. It is well enough to give a pretty good feed of hay at night, but very little, if any, at noon and in the morning. Always water the horse before feeding, and not directly after. Strict attention to diet is a great thing in treating heaves. Cases of heaves have been cured by bringing horses from the East and North out West, and let them feed on the coarse prairie hay. Heavey horses are comparatively few in Texas to what they are up North. In the early stages, heaves can be checked, and in many cases cured, by the following:

Oil of tar	3 ounces.
Glycerine	1 ounce.
Fowler's solution of arsenic	3 ounces.
Fluid extract of belladonna	1 ounce.
Tincture of opium	1 ounce.
Raw linseed oil	3 ounces.

Mix, and give one tablespoonful every morning and night in damp feed.

Fowler's solution of arsenic given in one tablespoonful doses, night and morning, for two or three weeks, is sometimes very beneficial. Unscrupulous dealers often give some remedies to check the heaves for the time being, which are generally poisonous, but we will not mention them here, as we don't advocate any treatment or remedy that is not honest and fair.

DISTEMPER—STRANGLES.

Horse distemper is the common name by which the disease, "strangles," is known. It is a peculiar, eruptive fever of the horse, and is a disease that nearly every young horse becomes affected with. It is oftener seen among young horses and colts, but horses at any age may take the disease. It received the name, "strangles," from so many cases in the severe form nearly choking or strangling the animal by the formation of a large tumor in the throat. All cases of influenza, sore throat, colds, catarrh, etc., are called distemper by a great many horse owners.

Cause.—Distemper is a contagious disease, and where one case breaks out or is introduced into a herd of horses, nearly all are generally affected. During some seasons, it takes on a very dangerous and fatal form, while again it is very mild, the animals recovering without much inconvenience or loss of flesh.

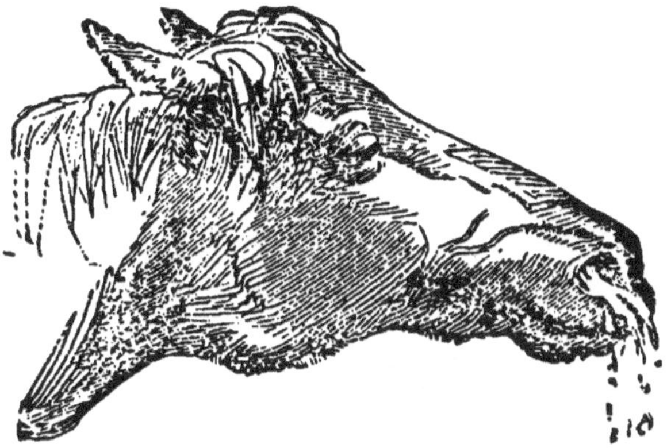

A Case of Strangles.

Symptoms.—Before the disease really breaks out, the animal is for a few days generally off its feed, weak, and languid, and easily exhausted. A slight cough may be noticed, and the animal shows some trouble in swallowing. In a regular case, there is noticed in a few days a swelling forming in connection with the throat, or under the lower jaw. These swellings may be small, or may become very large, making it almost impossible for a horse to breathe or swallow. The animal will have more or less fever, and in some cases becomes very weak, languid, and dull. In the irregular form of strangles, the swellings may form in the breast, in the groin, among the bowels, in connection with the liver, spleen, lungs, etc., and is a more dangerous form of the disease. The swelling in the throat may break, and run matter out of the nose, or down the windpipe, and cause strangulation of the animal. Distemper runs a certain course, its duration generally being from eight to twelve days, but it may last for several weeks.

Treatment.—As this disease has a certain course to run, there shouldn't be anything given to check it; but we should support the animal's system by giving soft, easily digested, nourishing food, and medicines to purify the blood. The animal should be protected from cold rains and "northers," and have comfort and good care generally. Give what fresh, cool water the animal will drink, into which dissolve 1 dram of chlorate of potassium, morn-

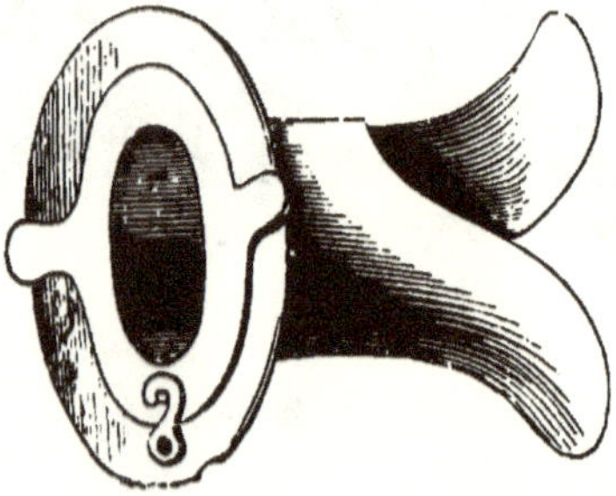

Fig. 4. Tracheotomy Tube.

ing and night. Also, give one teaspoonful of our Condition Powders, morning and night, to purify the blood, and keep up the animal's strength. Bathe the swelling in the throat two or three times a day thoroughly with our Liniment, to draw it to a head. It may be well to apply a hot poultice, and, after removing it, then apply the Liniment. As soon as the swelling becomes soft, it should be opened freely with a sharp lance, to allow the matter to escape. Syringe out the cavity with a weak solution of carbolic acid for a few days, and it will soon heal. Sometimes these swellings in the throat become so large that the horse can't breathe, and it becomes necessary to perform the operation of tracheotomy (putting a tube in the throat to breathe through. (See Fig. 4.) This is a very delicate operation, and we wouldn't advise any but a qualified veterinarian to perform it. Some people entertain the very foolish idea that a horse doesn't need any medicine or special care while he has the distemper. This is very wrong. It is not so much the distemper that is dangerous, but it is the other diseases that are liable to attack the body, while it is weak, and the blood bad from the distemper. So many horses that are not treated for the distemper are left with a chronic cough, catarrh, enlarged glands, thick wind, roaring, etc. It is true that a great many cases of distemper look very mild, but they are worse than they look, and all are bad enough. By all means, give your horse some special care and treatment, and, if you don't do anything else, give him some of our Condition Powders, night and morning, in damp feed, according to directions. We don't claim that our Powders are a specific for the distemper; in fact, there is no medicine that will check it, and keep it from running its course, without endangering the animal; but we do claim that they will purify the blood, strengthen the system, and help the animal throw off the disease. They are all the medicine that is necessary to give in the majority of cases.

PINK-EYE—EPIZÖOTIC CELLULITIS.

This is a disease of the horse that resembles influenza to a certain extent, but it is a distinct disease of itself. It is properly known as "Epizöotic cellulitis," as it is a contagious disease and affects principally the cellular tissues of the body.

Causes.—This disease is due to a contagion or germs that are carried in the air from sick to healthy animals. The germs will remain in the stable or sheds, where the disease has been, for a considerable length of time, and infect healthy horses or mules that are brough in there. The exact nature of these germs is not as yet thoroughly understood, but it is without any doubt an epizöotic (contagious) disease, as it has been known to spread over large districts in a short time.

Symptoms. — The first symptom that attracts attention is a watery discharge from the eyes, and a reddened or pinkish color of the conjunctiva (lining of the eye) is seen at the same time. The animal appears dull, has a weak pulse, and high temperature. The eyelids become swollen and discharge a white-colored matter. The legs become swollen and the swelling may extend along the belly. The bowels become constipated and the urine scanty. The body is hot all over, and the animal lays down most of the time.

Treatment.—As a general thing the treátment for pink-eye is quite successful, except in some very severe forms. Never bleed or physic an animal with pink-eye. Give 2 drams of nitrate of potash two or three times a day. Give the animal plenty of cold water to drink. If the animal is weak, give stimulants, as sweet nitre, whisky, etc. Keep the animal in a comfortable place, and give soft, easily digested food. If the bowels are constipated, give one-half pint of raw linseed oil as a laxative. Bathe the eyes well with water two or three times per day. Good care, a comfortable place, with fresh air and water and easily digested food, are of great benefit in this disease.

INFLUENZA—EPIZÖOTIC—LA GRIPPE.

This is a disease that attacks all the domesticated animals as well as man, and has been known for ages past. It is a contagious and an infectious disease, but during certain seasons and in certain localities it takes on a much more fatal form. There was a very serious and fatal outbreak of this disease in the United States druing the year 1872. It killed over 75 per cent of the horses and mules in many cities and localities. In some of the large cities not a horse could be seen on the streets for weeks at a time—all the teaming being done with oxen. This disease prevails nearly every winter and spring, but not in a very fatal form as a general thing. Nearly every person can remember, to their sorrow, how the *la grippe* raged all through this country among people last winter and spring. It is nearly the identical disease that attacks the horse, so you will know how to sympathize with your faithful servant the horse when he has the "grippe."

Causes. — It, without a doubt, originates from some atmospheric influence, and when once started spreads through the air and is caught by well horses coming in contact with sick ones. The germs or contagion may be carried on the clothing of people from one stable to another. A case is on record where the disease was conveyed three miles across water, either through the air or on the clothing of people, as no animals were taken on to the island for three months previous to the outbreak of the disease. It is seen more frequently and in a worse form in crowded, poorly ventilated stables, and it is more fatal in large cities than in the country. Colts and old horses are easier victims to the disease than middle-aged, healthy horses. One thing that makes influenza such a fatal disease is the other diseases that follow it, as pneumonia, bronchitis, rheumatism, heart troubles, etc.

Symptoms.—In the early stages of the disease there is general weakness, dullness, watery eyes, a watery discharge from the nose which turns to matter, a cough, etc. The pulse and temperature run up sometimes very high, and the animal loses its appetite. The symptoms, instead of improving in two or three days, as in catarrh or cold, get worse, and the animal becomes a great sufferer. The throat is sore, the cough is painful, the breathing labored and fast, and the animal shows all signs of weakness and soreness. These symptoms may continue on to death or they may abate in five or eight days and the animal begin to improve. Any of the complications, as lung troubles, kidney troubles, heart troubles, brain troubles, etc., may set in at any time.

Treatment.—Bleeding, physicing, or any treatment that has a tendency to weaken the animal should not be practiced. As the disease now appears, it is in a form that can generally be treated successfully. As it is a fever that has a certain course to run, we must adopt a form of treatment to help nature throw off the disease, and support the animal while the disease is running its course. We must never try to cut the disease short, as that is dangerous to the animal. Keep the animal in a comfortable place and allow plenty of fresh air and water and what easily digested food the animal will eat. If the weather is cold, blanket the animal, and hand-rub and bandage the legs. Give one dram of nitrate of potash three times a day, either in feed, drinking water, or put it on the tongue with a large spoon. Give this regular for two or three days, then give one dram of chlorate of potash three times per day for a few days. Give whisky, alcohol, and sweet nitre, to keep up the animal's strength. Bathe the throat well with our Liniment (see Appendix) twice a day to remove the soreness. Steaming the head by the use of hot water and a little carbolic acid is beneficial. If the bowels are constipated give one-half pint of raw linseed oil as a drench and give injections of warm water.

In mild cases our Condition Powders (see Appendix) is all the medicine that is necessary to give, and in all cases give our Powders after the severe symptoms have passed.

If any other disease sets in, treat it according to the treatment given in another part of this book.

CHAPTER VI.

THE DIGESTIVE ORGANS.

The principal organs of digestion are the teeth, stomach, and bowels. Mastication takes place by the teeth, which is the first step toward the process of digestion. A horse has 40 teeth, a mare 36, a cow 32, a dog 42, and a pig 44 teeth. The canine teeth, or tushes, are seldom developed in the mare. Cattle have no upper front teeth, there being nothing but a tough pad of gristle in the place of teeth. The teeth of a horse need a great deal of attention—far more than they get. A horse, dog and pig each have but one stomach, while cattle, sheep and goats each have four stomachs. The capacity of a horse's stomach averages three and a half to four gallons, a cow's from forty-five to fifty gallons, and the dog's one to three quarts. The length of a horse's bowels is about 100 feet, while a cow's is about 150 feet. The horse's bowels although shorter than a cow's are larger in capacity. It is estimated that three-fourths of the horses that die, die of some disease of the stomach or bowels, and in a majority of cases it is caused by faulty feeding or watering. Therefore, it is very important that every horse owner should have a thorough knowledge of the proper way to feed and water. Below will be found all the diseases of the digestive organs, briefly described.

DENTITION.

This covers the period during which the young horse is cutting his teeth—from birth to the age of five years. The horse experiences more difficulty in cutting the second, or permanent, teeth than with the first, or milk teeth. Too little attention is paid to the teeth of young horses by farmers and stock raisers. The mouths of all horses between the ages of one and five years should be frequently examined, to see if one or more of the milk teeth are not remaining too long, causing the second teeth to grow in crooked, in which case the first teeth should be removed by the forceps. During the time the animal is shedding a tooth, he may or may not eat well, often cuds his food, and wastes more or less of it The gums are found, on examination, to be red, swollen, and very tender. The irritation of the gums may extend to and involve the stomach and bowels, giving rise to constipation, diarrhoea, etc. Allow the animal to have soft food, of a laxative and nutritious character.

TEETH.

The teeth of a horse, the principal organs of mastication, are a very important part of his body, and should have proper attention when diseased or improperly shed. A horse has forty teeth, and a mare 36, the tusks being seldom developed in a mare. The teeth are of three classes, consisting of molars, or grinders; incisors, or front teeth; and tusks, or canine teeth. The horse, like other animals, is provided with two sets of teeth: temporary or colt teeth, and permanent or horse teeth. There are twenty-four temporary teeth, twelve grinders and twelve front teeth. The permanent teeth are forty in number, consisting of twenty-four grinders, twelve front teeth, and four tusks, except in mares, who seldom have fully developed tusks.

A colt, at birth, generally has twelve temporary grinders, and four incisors or front teeth—two above and two below, in the middle. The name for the two middle front teeth on each jaw is the nippers; the next two, one on each side of the nippers, the lateral incisors; and the outside ones, the corner teeth. At from six to nine weeks, a colt cuts its lateral incisors, and at the age of about nine months the corner teeth appear. The temporary incisor teeth differ from the permanent ones by being smaller in size, having a prominent neck, and much whiter appearance. The first permanent grinder, the fourth on the jaw, comes through when the colt is about one year old; and at about eighteen months old the second grinder, the fifth on each side of each jaw, comes through. At about two and one-half years of age, the colt sheds its nippers, middle front teeth, and the first two on each jaw of its grinders, and they are all taken place by permanent teeth. Between three and four years, the colt sheds its lateral front teeth, and the third temporary grinder, and they are taken place by permanent teeth; also, at about this age, the sixth permanent grinder comes through. Therefore, a colt, at four years of age, has a full set of permanent grinders. Between four and five, he sheds his corner incisors and gets the permanent ones, and at about this time the tusks come through, making a horse at five years of age have a "full mouth."

AGE OF A HORSE.

How to tell the age of a horse is something that must be acquired by practice, and not theory alone. Most any one can learn, by a little study and practice, how to detect the age up to six or eight years in most cases, but beyond this age is very much harder to tell accurately; in fact, no one can tell within one or two years after a horse has passed the age of ten years. If all horses had a uniform wear and growth of the teeth, it would be a great deal easier to tell the exact age, but different breeds of horses, and different kinds of food, greatly change the wear and shape of the teeth. Hard, gritty food wears the teeth much faster than soft food, free from sand and other gritty substances. A horse's teeth are continually growing and wearing off, no matter how old the horse. It is estimated that they grow one inch in about ten or twelve years.

By carefully reading over the remarks on "The Teeth," it can be easily seen how to tell a horse's age up to five years. By looking at the wearing surface of a horse's front teeth at five years old, you will notice a depression, called the cup or mark. It is by watching the wear and disappearance of this cup that we are enabled to indicate the age up to eleven or twelve years. At about six years, the cups will be worn out of the nippers on the lower jaw, and at seven years the cups will be worn out of the lateral incisors of the lower jaw; and at eight, it will disappear from the corner teeth of the same jaw. Therefore, at the age of eight, the wearing surfaces of the lower row are perfectly smooth; also, about this time there will be noticed a little hook-like projection on each of the upper corner incisors. At about the age of nine years, the cups disappear from the middle front teeth of the upper jaw; at about ten, they are worn out of the upper lateral incisors; and about eleven, they are all perfectly smooth. The foregoing is the general rule to go by, but, of course, there are certain cases that vary a great deal from that rule. There are certain signs and rules to go by to tell the age of a horse above twelve years, but they are not very reliable. The front teeth of a young horse are wider from side to side, but in an old horse they become wider from before backwards. Some dishonest dealers cup an old horse's teeth to make him look young, but this can be easily detected by looking at the general form and appearance of the teeth. A crib-bitter may be known by the peculiar appearance of his teeth, which are worn and broken off in front. In such a horse, it is hard to tell the age.

SHARP AND PROJECTING TEETH.

As a horse advances in age the teeth usually wear down in an irregular manner. This is better understood when we know that the grinders (molars) of the upper jaw do not come directly opposite to those of the lower jaw. Consequently sharp

Fig. 5. Dunn's Float in use on the Molars.

points are formed on the outer part of the upper molars, which lacerate and cut the cheeks when chewing the food, and similar points on the inner side of the lower ones, which cut and bruise the tongue. These ragged edges would not form if the upper grinders were directly opposed to the lower grinders. Horses' teeth should be examined occasionally to ascertain whether any such points are causing the animal any trouble. On passing the hand into the mouth the sharp and projecting points can be felt with the fingers, and on examining closer the tongue and cheeks are seen to be sore and lacerated. The mouth speculum, or balling iron (Fig. 8), may be necessary in some cases when it is desired to make a thorough examination of all the teeth. The animal eats but little, on account of the great pain caused by chewing his food, which is cudded and wasted to a great extent. Nor does the animal drive as well as usual, being slow to answer the rein, and may while traveling carry his head to one side, consequently being hard to keep straight in the road.

When these sharp projections are found, it is necessary to remove them. The best instrument for this purpose is a tooth-rasp (Fig. 6), after which the animal should be fed for a few days on soft food; nothing more is necessary unless the animal is run down in condition. If so, give one teaspoonful of Dr. LeGear's Condition Powders morning and night in damp feed.

Fig. 6. Tooth-Rasp or Float.

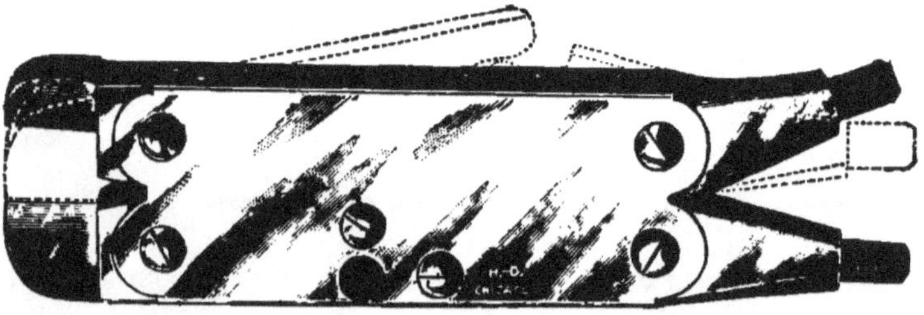

Fig. 7a. Haussmann's Lever Open Molar Cutters, for cutting off large, projecting teeth.

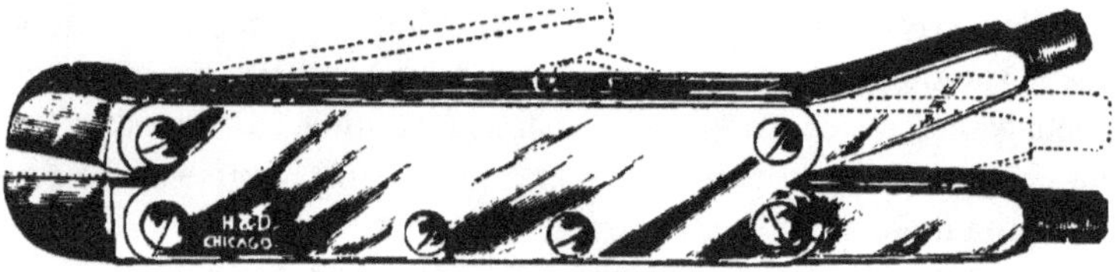

Fig. 7b. Haussmann's Lever Closed Molar Cutters, for cutting small, projecting teeth.

LONG PROJECTING TEETH.

This is a very common condition, and is found most common v in connection with the first grinder of the upper jaw, and the last grinders of the lower jaw. It constitutes quite a serious condition, and more especially is this the case when the sixth (last) grinder of the lower jaw is the one at fault. It gives rise to quidding of the food, imperfect chewing, loss of condition, etc. A projecting tooth is one that grows longer than the other teeth on account of the opposite tooth immediately over or under it becoming decayed or having been pulled out, consequently the tooth meeting with no resistance grows out longer than is natural, and causes much pain and irritation.

When a long projecting tooth is found, it becomes necessary to reduce it to a level with the other teeth. The best instrument for this purpose is a pair of molar cutters (Figs. 7a, 7b), after which file off the roughness with a tooth-rasp. Then feed the animal on soft feed for a few days, and in the course of ten days or a fortnight he will have improved to such an extent as to be hardly recognizable as the same horse. But at the same time don't fail to give in the feed Dr. LeGear's Condition Powders.

In all cases where horses "quid" their food, where they are slobbering, or where they show pain in chewing the food, shown by holding their head to one side, the teeth should be carefully examined.

DECAYED TEETH.

This is indicated by gradual decay or wasting away of the tooth-substance in small particles. It is quite a common condition, especially in connection with the grinders (back teeth), although none of the teeth are free from the trouble. Decay may commence in any part of the tooth. It is by no means as common in the lower animals as in man, on account of people eating so many sweets, etc., which have a bad effect on the teeth.

Causes.—Decayed teeth may arise from a great many different causes, but the most common cause is some injury to the tooth, caused by taking into the mouth with the food some hard substance, as a piece of iron, pebble, etc., which during the act of chewing comes into contact with the tooth, breaks its cover-

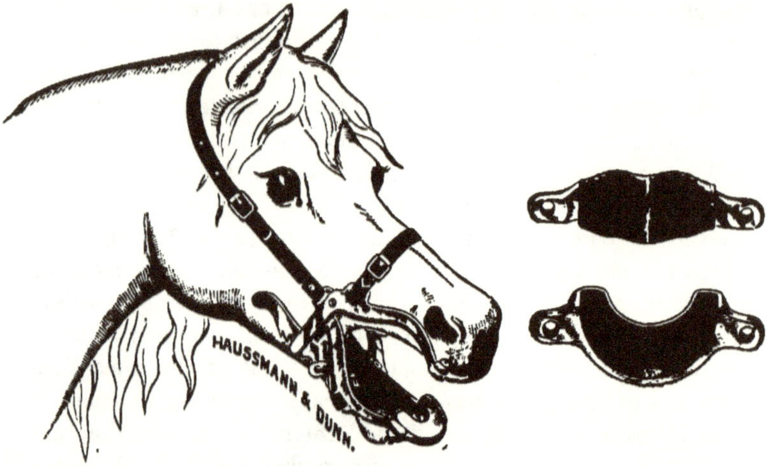

Fig. 8. Haussmann's Mouth Speculum, used to open the mouth for work on the teeth, and for examining the mouth.

ing, and decay quickly follows. A severe blow on the jaw might also produce decay of the teeth.

Symptoms.—It may be noticed that the animal has some difficulty in chewing his food, and frequently while eating stops and throws up his head as though suffering severe pain. While drinking cold water he may stop and hold the head to one side, etc. The above are general symptoms when the crown of the tooth is decayed. When the root of the tooth alone is diseased, the symptoms are quite different. Then a swelling appears on the face at the side the diseased tooth is on and directly over the decayed tooth. It is the prevailing idea among horsemen that if a horse has a swelling on his face they say he has "blind teeth." He may have blind teeth, but they seldom if ever injure a horse. Blind teeth, properly known as Wolf Teeth, are little peg-like teeth, situated one in front of each upper grinder, and are generally harmless. (See Fig. 9a, page 56.)

We often hear it said that "blind teeth" grow or come out through the bones on the face. That is an erroneous idea, and is as foolish as it is absurd. Such a thing never happens. What causes the swelling on the face is the matter which inflames the bone and causes it to bulge out. When the matter becomes abundant enough it will burst through the bone and skin and cause a running sore. When there is a cavity from the grinding surface of the tooth all the way up to the root, the matter will escape into the mouth and not form an enlargement. The above is regarding the grinders on the upper jaw. When the roots only of one of the lower grinders become decayed it forms an enlargement on the lower border of the jaw; in the same way the enlargement is formed on the upper jaw. If an enlargement is seen on a colt or right young horse it is generally due to the caps (colt teeth) not being properly shed. Very often the matter from a diseased upper grinder will break into the nostril instead of on the face, and forms a running at the nose of a very offensive smelling matter. If the crown of the tooth is decayed and the matter runs into the mouth you can smell a very offensive odor every time you open his mouth or put on the bridle.

Treatment.—As the art of filling teeth in the lower animals can not as yet be successfully done, the only remedy for a decayed tooth is to remove it. This is generally done by means of tooth forceps made especially for such work. Figure 9 is a pair of forceps for pulling the molars or grinders from horses. Figure 8 is a speculum for opening the mouth to see which tooth is decayed and where to place the forceps for its extraction. It is generally advisable to throw a horse for this operation. After the horse is secured, put on the speculum, grasp the tooth firmly with the molar extractor (forceps) and by using steady force you may be able to remove the tooth. Unless the whole tooth is decayed and loosened it will be found a big job to pull an upper grinder in most of cases. A little wooden block may be placed

Fig. 9a. Wolf Tooth Forceps, for pulling Wolf Teeth (blind teeth).

Fig. 9. Molar Extractors.

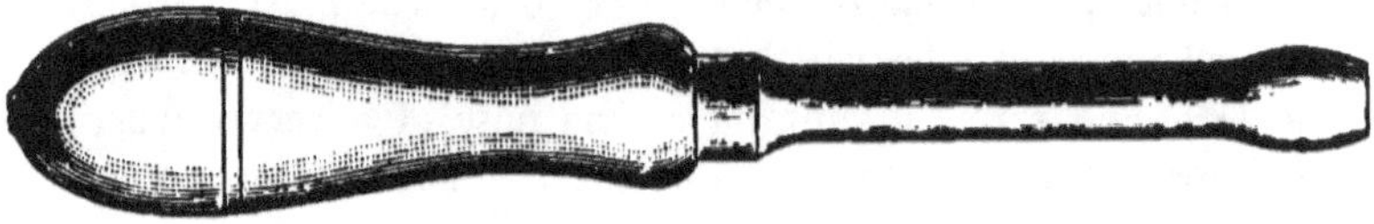

Fig. 10. Handle for Molar Extractors and Cutters.

on the sound teeth in front of the one to be pulled which will serve as a lever by which extra power can be obtained. If the crown of the tooth is decayed so there is no hold for the forceps, or if the tooth is implanted in the jaw too solid to be pulled, it may be removed by trephining and punching it out. This operation is done by cutting the skin on the face and exposing the bone over the roots of the teeth. Then bore through the bone by using the trephine (Fig. 3), and with a steel punch about three-eighths size drive the tooth into the mouth. If colts fail to shed their colt teeth, they should be pulled before they interfere with the growth of the permanent teeth.

PARROT MOUTH.

Parrot-mouth is a condition in which the incisors (front teeth) of the upper jaw project further forward than those of the lower jaw, and, when the mouth is shut, the upper incisors pass down in front of those in the lower jaw. A horse with this deformity does not do very well at pasture, for the simple reason that he can not gather sufficient grass to keep him in good condition. But, feeding from the manger, he does very well, except when fed on ear corn, in which case he experiences considerable difficulty in getting the grain off the cob. About all that can be done is to keep both the upper and lower incisor teeth shortened by means of the rasp (Fig. 6), to prevent contact with, and injury to, the soft tissues.

UNDERSHOT.

This is just the opposite from parrot-mouth. It is a deformity in which the under jaw is longer than the upper jaw; consequently, the front teeth do not meet. The only thing to be done is to cut or rasp off the front teeth when they get too long.

LAMPAS.

Lampas, or more commonly called lampers, is the name given to a swelling of the membrane covering the roof of the mouth just behind the front teeth. Animals between the ages of three and five years are most subject to it. On examination of the mouth, the gums and rings of the hard palate, just behind the upper front teeth, are found to be unnaturally reddened and swollen, the animal objecting very much to having the parts pressed upon, showing that the parts are very sore. Many horses have naturally very prominent gums, etc., but unless the parts are reddened, sore and tender, it is not lampas, although the parts are just as much enlarged as in a case of lampas.

Treatment.—Unless it is a genuine case of lampas, let it alone, as you will do more harm than good. Where the parts are inflamed and tender, with a sharp lance or a pocket-knife make several shallow cuts across the first two bars in the roof of the mouth. The cuts must be made in front of the third bar, and made very shallow, as you are liable to cut an important blood vessel. Under no conditions burn the parts with a red-hot iron, as this is cruel and barbarous to say the least. After bleeding in the mouth, apply alum water to the parts once or twice a day. There is nothing better, though, than Dr. LeGear's Healing Lotion for such purposes. Feed on soft feed for a few days, and lay the animal off work, if possible, as the presence of the bit in the mouth will keep up irritation.

APHTHAE—SORE MOUTH.

This is an inflammation of the mouth; the eruptions are usually seen about the lips and tongue.

Causes.—Irritating medicines, foods, or other substances, will produce it.

Symptoms.—There is a swelling of the parts, little blisters are formed, and the mouth is found to be hot and tender; the appetite is partly or wholly lost, and there is difficulty in chewing.

Treatment.—Change the food and give a laxative: as, raw linseed oil, 1 pint; powdered gentian, 2 drams; carbonate of soda, 4 drams; Mix, and give as a drench. Swab out the mouth with chlorate of potash, borax, or alum, about one-half ounce in a pint of water. Feed on soft food, as, bran mashes, chops, etc., and dampen all the fodder you give him.

PTYALISM, OR SLOBBERING.

This consists of an excessive secretion of saliva (spittle) from the mouth.

Causes.—It may be caused by irregular teeth, inflammation of the mouth or tongue, or by such medicines as mercury, lobelia, etc. Foreign bodies, as nails, wheat-chaff, and corn cobs, becoming lodged in the mouth, will cause it, as well as certain kinds of food.

Treatment.—Ascertain the cause of the trouble, and remove it. Change the food, and feed the animal some of our Condition Powders. Wash the mouth out with alum water in case of soreness.

CHOKING.

Choking is the name applied to the trouble where an animal gets some object, or portion of unmasticated food, lodged in the oesophagus (gullet). Cattle are more frequently troubled with choking than horses. Greedy eaters very often take too much into their mouths at once, and try to swallow it without properly grinding it; therefore, the food—a potato, an apple, a turnip, an ear of corn, a cob, shelled oats, or whatever it may be—becomes lodged in the gullet by being too large to pass into the stomach.

Symptoms.—The animal makes continued efforts to swallow, and may have spasms of pain while doing so. Slobbering at the mouth is abundant, and there may be coughing. If the animal attempts to drink, the water runs out through his nose. In cattle, there is always more or less bloating (accumulation of gas in the stomach). If the substance is in the throat, or lodged in the gullet between the throat and breast, it can generally be plainly felt from the outside. After the object has been lodged in the gullet for one or two days, swelling and inflammation sets in and causes great pain to the animal.

Treatment.—If the obstruction is in the throat, it may be worked out by pressing and kneading at it from the outside; or it may be removed with the hand, by passing it into the mouth; the latter being held open by the mouth speculum. If it is below the throat, a probang (Fig. 11) may be used to gently force

Fig. 11. Probang, used in choking, in horses and cattle.

it on into the stomach. The probang is a pliable leather tube, six feet long, with a knob on the end to press on the object. The probang is also hollow, through which a little oil can be poured for the purpose of softening the object and making it more easily moved. In place of a probang, a pliable whalebone whip may be used. Never run a broom-stick or hoe-handle down an animal's throat, for you will surely injure the gullet and kill the animal. A gag or speculum can be put on the animal to keep it from biting the probang. If taken in time, the probang, properly used, will generally relieve the animal in a few minutes; but, if let go until the gullet becomes swollen and inflamed, it is often a very difficult job to unchoke the animal. In cattle, you can let out the gas through the hollow probang by letting it remain in the stomach for a minute or two after the obstruction is removed. A probang is something that every town or community ought to have for the benefit of the public, where there is no veterinary surgeon. If the obstruction is lodged between the throat and breast, and can't be dislodged with the probang, it may be cut down upon and removed. This is a delicate operation, and seldom proves successful, except when performed by a qualified veterinary surgeon. The hole in the gullet must be tightly sewed up, also the muscles and skin, by separate stitches. An animal should be fed on soft, wet food for several days after a bad case of choking.

RESULTS OF CHOKING.

Choking may result in rupture, stricture, or dilalation of the oesophagus (gullet), but, as little can be done for these conditions, we will not describe them.

BOTS—LARVAE OF THE GAD-FLY.

Bots are of two kinds: the stomach bot, which infests the horse's stomach during development; and the fundament bot, which is found in the rectum (last gut), anus, etc.

It is surprising what erroneous ideas are entertained amongst most horse owners, and even some "horse doctors," about bots. As every obscure lameness in the foot is supposed to be in the shoulder, so when a horse is taken sick with abdominal pain, nine times out of ten it is laid to bots. If he turns up his upper lip, looks at his side, paws and rolls, or shows any uneasiness, it is taken as a sure sign of bots.

Bots as a rule are harmless parasites, seldom if ever producing any mischief, and they are found in the stomach of almost every horse that dies, sometimes in great numbers, adhering to its coats.

One of the best authorities on the subject is Cobbold, who writes as follows:

"The common gad-fly (Gastropilius equi) attacks the animal while grazing late in the summer, its object being, not to derive sustenance, but to deposit its eggs. This is accomplished by means of a glutinous excretion, causing the ova (egg) to adhere to the hairs. The parts selected are chiefly those of the shoulder, base of the neck, and inner part of the forelegs, especially about the knees, for in these situations the horse will have no difficulty in reaching the ova with its tongue. When the animal licks those parts of the coat where the eggs have been placed, the moisture of the tongue, aided by warmth, hatches the ova, and in something less than three weeks from the deposition of the eggs the larvae have made their escape. As maggots they are transferred to the mouth, and ultimately to the stomach, with food and drink. A great many larvae perish during this passive mode of immigration, some being dropped from the mouth and others being crushed in the fodder during mastication. It has been calculated that out of the many hundreds of eggs deposited on a single horse scarcely one out of fifty of the larvae arrive within the stomach. Notwithstanding this waste the interior of the stomach may become completely covered (cuticular portion) with bots. Whether there be few or many they are anchored in this situation chiefly by means of two large cephalic hooks. After the bots have attained perfect growth they voluntarily loosen their hold and allow themselves to be carried along the alimentary canal until they escape with the feces. In all cases they sooner or later fall to the ground, and when transferred to the soil they bury themselves beneath the surface in order to undergo transformation into the pupa condition. Having remained in the earth for a period of six or seven weeks they finally emerge from their pupal-cocoons as perfect dipterous (winged) insects—the gad-fly. It thus appears that bots ordinarily pass about eight months of their lifetime in the digestive organs of the horse."

It is very common to hear bystanders declare, when a horse is suffering from what is commonly called colic, "that the horse has the bots," and their suggested treatment is always varied and heroic. It is true, we have good reason to believe that they could cause serious trouble, as claimed by some veterinary surgeons, by blocking up the passages, but these instances are so rare that such cases are not seen in a lifetime. At post-mortem examinations, when the stomach is found to be ruptured, the opinion, frequently expressed, that "the bots have eaten through the stomach," is again a mistake. Bots seldom or never do this; the rupture is due to over-distention of the viscus with food or gases.

Bots may, and probably do, when in large enough numbers to be attached to the true digestive portion of the stomach, slightly interfere with digestion; the animal may not thrive, the coat stares, and emaciation may follow; but beyond this, with a few exceptions already noted, they are harmless. Even if they were the cause of the trouble, there are no medicines which will loosen them from their attachments and cause them to pass out of the body.

Treatment.—It is useless to give treatment in order to loosen the bots from their attachments, as they will go their allotted time, loosen themselves, and pass out in spring or early summer. Horse owners, noticing them in the manure, unhesitatingly say that his horse "has the bots."

WORMS. (INTESTINAL.)

Worms that infest the horse are of many kinds, and may be found in almost every part of the body, but the ones we shall refer to are found in the stomach and bowels. They are most common in young horses, especially those that are weak and unthrifty; or those that graze on low, wet or marshy pastures. We shall speak of but a few of the most common ones: First, the Lumbricoid, which infests principally the small intestines, is white or reddish in color, and measures from four to twelve inches in length. Some have been seen that were nearly thirty inches long. It resembles the common earth worm, being thickest at the middle and tapering at the ends. Second, the pin-worm, found principally in the large intestines, is another common variety of worms. It is a thread-like worm, and is but one or two inches long. The third variety is the tape-worm; and when once seen is easily recognized. It is white, flat, broad and jointed, and sometimes measures from twenty to thirty feet. Its head is found at the smaller end of the worm.

Symptoms.—The surest sign, and one that most people depend upon, is the passage of worms in the horse's dung. Other important symptoms are slight colicy pains, rubbing of the tail or rump, depraved appetite shown by eating dirt, licking the walls, and being particularly fond of salt; the horse becomes poor, does not shed his coat, is hide-bound and pot-bellied. Some place much dependence upon turning up of the upper lip; while others declare that when we see a dried whitish substance adhering around the anus, worms are present.

Treatment.—In preparing our Worm Remedy, we were very careful that we put in it medicines that would act on and kill all kinds of stomach and bowel worms; therefore, in ordinary cases, all that is necessary to give is one teaspoonful of Dr. LeGear's Worm Remedy (see Appendix) night and morning in bran mash or other soft, damp feed, for about ten days or two weeks. It is advisable to give bran mashes freely, as bran is a laxative and easily digested, and is beneficial in the treatment of worms. If in bad cases the Worm Remedy fails to rid the horse of all the worms, give the following physic after you have given the Worm Remedy for ten days:

Powdered Barbadoes aloes	6 drams.
Powdered ginger	3 drams.
Calomel	2 drams.
Turpentine	1½ ounces.
Raw linseed oil	8 ounces.

Mix, and give as a drench.

The Worm Remedy will kill the worms, and the above physic will drive them out. If pin-worms are present, it is well to give the horse an injection of warm water every day for four or five days, to which add one ounce of turpentine to every gallon of water. The turpentine has a tendency to kill the little worms lodged away back in the rectum. You may inject tobacco water instead of the turpentine. Our Worm Remedy is sure death to the worms, but perfectly harmless to the horse. It not only kills the worms, but it aids the horse's digestion, tones up his stomach and bowels, purifies his blood, and builds up his whole system in general

INDIGESTION, OR DYSPEPSIA.

Indigestion in the horse is similar to that in man. This is an age of dyspeptics in man, and would be, no doubt, in the horse were he fed on similar "dainties," prepared by the good wife to suit our highly cultivated tastes. Happily for the horse, that is not so! Indigestion may be applied to all those conditions, from any cause, where digestion is improperly performed, and not pronounced enough to produce colic.

The seat and causes of indigestion vary considerably in different horses, and may vary in the same horse at different times. One of the first things to examine is the teeth. If these are sharp, irregular or decayed, the food is improperly masticated (chewed), and taken into the stomach before there has been a proper admixture of saliva (spittle). Food in this condition is anything but fit for the organs of digestion to act upon. The bile (fluid secreted by the liver) may be deficient in quantity or quality; there may be lack of secretion of the pancreas; or there may be lack of perstaltic (worm-like) movement of the stomach and intestines, which is very essential to the passage of the ingesta. Other causes are, wintering on hard, dry hay or corn stalks, or any bulky or innutritive food; irregular feeding or over-feeding, though the latter is more liable to cause engorged stomach.

Symptoms.—It is characterized by an irregular appetite, which is often depraved: refusing food at times, and at others eating ravenously; his depravity is shown by eating wood, dirt, soiled bedding, or even his own feces; to-day the bowels may be loose and bad smelling, to-morrow bound; grain often passes whole in the dung. The animal loses flesh, the skin becomes hard and dry, and seems very tight (hide-bound).

Treatment.—If the teeth are sharp or irregular, have them rasped by a veterinary surgeon; if any are decayed, they must be extracted; if due to ravenous eating or bolting the food, compel it to be eaten slowly by spreading it out on a large surface, or by putting some rocks in the feed-box. Also, pay particular attention to the quality and quantity of the feed, and the time of feeding; examine the water supply, and see that it is given before feeding. Don't forget, the seat of trouble may be in the stomach, intestines, or other organs of digestion. To remove any irritation of the bowels, such as worms, undigested food, etc., give as a drench, linseed oil, 1 pint; oil of turpentine, 1 ounce; and follow with Dr. LeGear's Condition Powders, according to the directions on each box.

RUPTURE OF THE STOMACH.

Causes.—It is usually caused by the horse throwing himself down violently when the stomach is full of gas, food, etc., during an attack of acute indigestion, etc.

Symptoms.—The symptoms are never very positive, and in no case will you be able to state positively that rupture has taken place. Vomiting is a prominent symptom, which may take place before or after rupture does. The animal turns round, or walks in a circle, lies down, and sits upon his haunches after the manner of a dog; the eyes take on a peculiar stare, cold sweats break out, and death soon occurs.

Treatment.—Nothing in the way of treatment can be done for it.

FLATULENT OR WIND COLIC.

Flatulent or wind colic is also a very dangerous disease, unless relieved, and is characterized by an over-distention of gas in the large intestines.

Causes.—Among some of the principal causes of this form of colic are, coarse, inferior food, especially hay or corn that is sour or mouldy, imperfect mastication (chewing), owing to defective teeth, etc., and especially in old animals, whose digestive powers are impaired; sudden changes of food of any kind, too long fasting. crib-biting, etc., and, in fact, anything that produces indigestion may operate in causing flatulent colic.

Symptoms.—Quite similar to cramp colic, but not so suddenly produced. At first, the animal becomes uneasy, turns his head to one side and paws, generally throws himself down, and rolls; the pulse soon runs up, and the abdomen (belly) is seen to increase in size—becoming distended with gas. In a well-marked case, the ribs of the leanest horse can no longer be located. The pains are continuous, and the suffering of the poor animal now becomes very great. In addition, there is difficult breathing, profuse sweating, trembling, staggering gait, and, finally, if relief be not quickly given, death will very soon follow.

Treatment.—Whatever is done must be done quickly. Give at once Dr. LeGear's Colic Cure, according to the directions on each bottle. Give, frequently, injections per rectum of warm

Fig. 12. Trocar and Canula, used for tapping an animal in wind colic (bloating).

water, with a small quantity of common salt in solution. Gas escaping by the anus gives relief, and is to be regarded as a favorable sign; and at this time don't push remedies too far, as harm may result. Tobacco injections are highly useful in all forms of colic. If the above treatment fails to give relief, and the belly still continues to enlarge, recourse must be had to the operation of puncturing (tapping) the colon to allow the gas to escape. This operation must be done with an instrument for the purpose, called the trocar, and canula. Select a spot on the right, midway betwixt the point of the hip, the last rib and the lumbar transverse processes, plunge the instrument in, draw out the trocar, thus leaving the tube (canula) in for the gas to pass through. This operation must be performed before the animal gets too weak. This gives the animal instant relief, and, by the time the gas has all escaped, the animal ceases to suffer. The after-treatment consists of easily digested food in small quantities, tonics, etc. Dr. LeGear's Condition Powders will regulate and tone up the digestive organs, and prevent a return of the trouble. If the bowels are constipated, give the following:

Turpentine	$1\frac{1}{2}$ ounces.
Raw linseed oil	1 quart.

Mix, and give as a drench.

SPASMODIC OR CRAMP COLIC.

Spasmodic or cramp colic is a very common as well as a very dangerous disease of the horse, and is more commonly known as gripes, bellyache, etc. It is wholly of a spasmodic nature, and if not promptly relieved, will, in severe cases, run into inflammation of the bowels, causing speedy death.

Causes.—The common causes are a sudden change in the feed; drinking large quantities of cold water when in a heated or exhausted condition; indigestible food; foreign bodies, as nails or stones, in the bowels; driving a heated horse through deep streams; cold rains; draughts of cold air, etc., may cause it as well as other troubles.

Symptoms.—This form of colic is characterized by the suddenness of the attack. All at once the animal is suddenly seized, stamps and paws, and sometimes kicks as though he were trying to strike his belly with his hoof; he throws himself violently down, rolls from side to side, and appears to be suffering intense pain. After rolling a while he gets up, stands quietly for a few minutes, evidently free from pain, when he is suddenly seized again and goes through the same performances as before. As the attack progresses these intervals of ease become shorter and shorter, until the spasms are continuous or nearly so. Now the animal breaks out in profuse perspiration, continues to throw himself down, rolls violently, jumps up, drops down again, paws and strikes, and makes frequent attempts to urinate, but can not. Because he can't make water, those ignorant of the disease are sure to pronounce it trouble of the kidneys or bladder. It is no positive sign because a horse yields or sinks when pinched over the loins that it is kidney trouble.

During a spasm the pulse runs up; between spasms it rapidly decreases, till it is normal. Sometimes constipation is present; in others, diarrhoea. It is a bad sign to see diarrhoea in a severe case of colic.

It will be difficult in many cases to distinguish between colic and inflammation of the bowels, as the symptoms are quite similar.

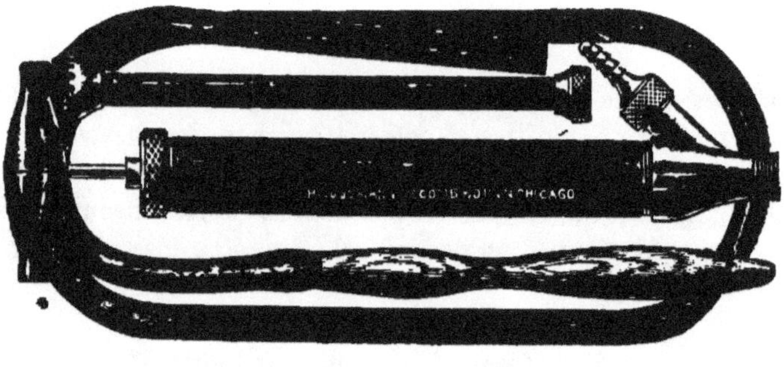

Fig. 13. Injection Pump, used to give injections into the womb, or rectum (lower bowel), of warm water, etc.

Treatment.—If taken in time it is a disease usually satisfactory to treat. Whatever plan of treatment is pursued, it must be prompt and energetic. As soon as possible a draught should be administered, the very best one being our Colic Cure. Dissolve half the contents of the bottle in a pint of water in a long-neck bottle, and give as a drench at once. If at the end of half an hour pain is still present, give the other half as you did the first. Besides this, give in a drench 1 pint of linseed oil as a laxative to clear out the intestinal tract, for, if any foreign substance is allowed to remain in the bowels it may cause another attack in a day or two afterwards. Also give injections per rectum (Fig. 13) of warm water containing a little soap and turpentine. Put the animal in a place where he can not hurt himself and allow him to roll as much as he wishes, as it gives him some relief. But don't put a man or boy on him and run him up and down the road. This is a cruel and dangerous thing to do. If the animal is still in pain after you have given two or three doses of our Colic Cure, inject under the skin with a hypodermic syringe (Fig. 2) 3 or 5 grains of morphine dissolved in one dram of water. Repeat it in one hour if necessary. If you haven't a syringe to put morphine under the skin, give as a drench in one-half pint of cold water 8 or 10 grains of morphine, and repeat in one hour if necessary. Inject one or two buckets of warm water into the rectum every hour. The following may be beneficial in some cases:

Chloral hydrate	1 ounce.
Sulphate of morphine	5 grains.
Water	1 pint.

Mix, and give as a drench. Repeat in one hour if necessary.

Never give medicine through the nose, as this is a dangerous and cruel procedure. Many a poor horse is killed by the ignorant owner pouring medicine through the nose.

CONSTIPATION.

Constipation is an undue accumulation of feces in the intestinal canal. It may be only a symptom of disease as well as being a disease of itself.

Constipation or costiveness is often witnessed in the horse, and more particularly in the foal. The colt should always get the first of the mother's milk, for, at first, this milk possesses laxative properties. Whenever the foal's bowels fail to act, and more particularly if there are signs of colicy pains, or straining, something should be done for it. In most cases it will only be necessary to give a few injections of soapy water per rectum and to introduce the finger through the anus to break down any hardened feces found there. If this fails to regulate the bowels, give from 2 to 4 ounces of castor oil, according to age. Linseed oil is also good for such purposes. Constipation in adult horses is generally due to long feeding on dry, innutritious food, lack of intestinal secretions, lack of exercise or water supply, derangements of the liver, etc. It may also follow indigestion, as well as other diseases, or any derangement of the digestive system.

Symptoms.—At first there may be a slight diarrhoea, which soon ceases. If any manure is passed, it consists of hard pellets, and perhaps covered with mucus. The animal is dull and sluggish, and shows abdominal pains in the usual way. He rolls and paws, but not in a manner so violent as in colic. A symptom often noticed, especially when in connection with the large intestines, is a tendency on the part of the animal to back his buttocks up against the wall or manger and press upon the parts. More or less protrusion of the rectum is noticed on acount of frequent straining while endeavoring to expel the feces.

Treatment.—In many cases a change to light, sloppy diet, as bran mash, etc., or a run at grass, is all that is required. If colicy pains are present a physic must be given:

Barbadoes aloes .... 6 drams.
Bicarbonate of soda .... 4 drams.
African ginger .... 2 drams.
Nux vomica .... 1 dram.

Powder, and mix into a mass with syrup or soap, and give as a ball; or dissolve the powder into a pint of water and give as a drench.

If the above does not move the bowels in from 24 to 36 hours, administer the following:

Raw linseed oil .... 1 quart.
Tincture of nux vomica .... 1 ounce.

Mix, and give in one dose as a drench. Repeat every six hours until a passage is effected.

If there is much pain the following anodyne mixture may be given every four hours if necessary:

Sulphate of morphia .... 8 grains.
Water .... 8 ounces.

Mix, and give as a drench.

When due to lack of intestinal secretions, give fluid extract of belladonna three times a day in two-dram doses, and a handful of epsom salts in the feed daily. Injections per rectum of soapy water should be freely employed to remove all hardened fæces from the rectum and colon. It may be necessary to remove the fæces with the hand every day for a week or two, if any paralysis of the rectum is present.

In all cases of constipation be sure to follow up with Dr. LeGear's Condition Powders, to tone up the stomach and bowels, to purify the blood, regulate the liver, kidneys, etc.

IMPACTION OF THE LARGE BOWELS.

This is a very common, as well as a very dangerous, bowel trouble, and usually results in death, unless promptly recognized and properly treated.

Causes.—Over-feeding on grain, on old, dry, hard hay, lack of water, want of exercise, lack of the watery secretions of the bowels, or paralysis of nerve-endings, etc.

Symptoms.—A slight abdominal pain, which may disappear for a day or two, to reappear with more violence. The manure passed is hard and dry. The belly is full, but contains no gas; he paws, and looks back at his sides. Soon the animal lies down, head and legs extended, occasionally raising his head to look toward his flank; he rises occasionally (from five to fifteen minutes), walks about the stall, looks at his sides, backs up against the stall, paws, and soon lies down again, in his former position. The bowels cease now to move at all. A horse may suffer from this trouble from one to three weeks, and then recover, but they seldom last over four or five days.

Treatment.—Give at once the following purgative:

Powdered Barbadoes aloes	1 ounce.
Calomel	2 drams.
Powdered nux vomica	1½ drams.
Powdered ginger	2 drams.
Water	1 pint.

Mix, and give as a drench.

If the bowels don't move in twenty-four hours, the above dose may be repeated, but not before that time. Give injections of warm water and soapsuds freely, to clean out the rectum. Give walking exercise, which may help the physic to act; also, allow the animal all the water he wants before it acts, but don't let him drink too much while physicing. The bare arm may be oiled and inserted up the rectum, and with the hand remove any dry feces that may be found. Inflammation of the bowels is liable to follow if relief is not given.

ENTERITIS, OR INFLAMMATION OF THE BOWELS.

Enteritis is an inflammation of the lining membrane of the bowels. It is in the lower animals, as well as in man, one of the most serious and fatal of all diseases, and a well-marked case in the horse is almost sure death.

Causes.—Among the many causes are, foreign substances in the bowels, as, sticks, stones, sand, etc.; irritant poisons, over-doses of physic, drinking impure water, or drinking cold water when in a heated condition, standing in draughts of cold air after sweating freely, etc. It may follow such diseases as colic, volvulus, diarrhoea, etc.

Symptoms.—At first, the symptoms are similar to those of colic and other painful bowel troubles. The horse walks about the stall, paws, lies down carefully, and usually rolls upon his back, and remains in this position for some time. There is a high fever, the temperature running up to 103 or 105 degrees Fahrenheit. The full, quick pulse, high temperature, continuous pain, which is increased upon pressure, position of the horse when down, coldness of ears and legs, etc., will enable you to tell a case of inflammation of the bowels. At a later stage of the disease, the pulse becomes weak and wiry. Now the eyes look blood-shot, and have a glassy appearance; the patient seems unconscious, and wanders about his stall, taking no notice of his surroundings. Soon there comes a period of quietness, which may be regarded as the turning point of the disease. If the pulse at this time begins to recover its tone, it may be regarded as a good sign; but, if the pulse is weak and running down, the body and legs cold, the mouth cold and clammy, the case may be regarded as hopeless, the symptoms shown indicating that gangrene (mortification) has set in. In some cases, the animal may live eight or nine hours after gangrene has set in, but death usually follows in an hour or so.

Treatment.—The treatment of enteritis is anything but satisfactory. You must endeavor to overcome the disease by giving medicine that will overcome the pain. For this purpose, give Dr. LeGear's Colic Cure (see Appendix) every half-hour until relief is obtained. Don't stop with one bottle, but keep giving as long as there is any hope of recovery. If it is a strong, fat animal, a good blood letting, from six to ten quarts, may be attended with benefit. Mustard, ammonia, hot water, etc., may be applied to the belly, to assist in relieving the pain. Give linseed tea, oatmeal gruel, starch water, etc., to drink. All foods that are in the least hard, dry, and indigestible, should be avoided. If, when the inflammation subsides, the bowels do not act, give walking exercise, and, if necessary, a dose of raw linseed oil. Feed lightly for a week or ten days, on roots, grass, bran mashes, etc., and keep rather quiet.

INTUSSUSCEPTION, OR INVAGINATION.

Intussusception, or invignation, is the slipping of one portion of a bowel into another portion, similar to a partially turned glove finger. The small bowels are the ones usually affected.

Causes.—Rather difficult to account for in many cases. It may occur from a severe attack of spasmodic colic, in which the animal throws himself down violently. It may also follow diarrhoea, inflammation of the bowels, or an injury, exposure to cold, etc.

Symptoms.—It is a trouble difficult to recognize. There are colicy pains similar to inflammation of the bowels, but not so violent, and are more prolonged. The pulse may vary from 45 to 100 beats per minute. There is also a peculiar sighing or catching of the breath. Sitting upon the haunches is a prominent symptom, and, when seen, death is almost certain within forty-eight hours from the beginning of the attack.

Treatment.—This trouble usually ends in death. However, a case may occasionally be cured. About all you can do is to try to allay the pain by giving our Colic Cure (see Appendix), in addition to which a dose of olive oil may be given. Keep the animal perfectly quiet. Sometimes the invaginated portion of the bowels may slough off and come away with the manure, and recovery take place. Injections of warm water per rectum should be freely used.

VOLVULUS, GUT TIE; OR, TWISTING OF THE BOWELS.

This condition consists in a portion of the bowels becoming twisted, or tied in some way or other.

Cause.—Similar to intussusception, such as violent abdominal pains, etc., will produce it.

Symptoms.—The symptoms of volvulus are about the same as intussusception.

Treatment.—Treat the same as for intussusception, which is generally useless.

DIARRHOEA.

Diarrhoea is just the opposite of constipation, and consists in the passage of an undue quantity of liquid feces. It is quite common amongst horses and cattle, and, in a majority of cases, is a symptom of some other disease, but also occurs as a separate trouble.

Causes.—Feeding on rich and succulent (juicy) food, when the animal is not accustomed to it, and over-doses of physic, which produces one of the worst forms of diarrhoea; drinking stagnant or putrid water, diseased condition of the teeth, eating irritating substances, etc., are among the many causes. Horses with long bodies, long legs, and narrow, flat sides are predisposed to scour, and are called "washy" by horsemen. Fast or road work aggravates the trouble, and, in fact, may cause it.

Symptoms.—It is easily recognized. There are frequent watery discharges, sometimes forced out in a violent manner, while in others it may be seen trickling down the legs. After each passage, there is quite often slight griping pains. In a day or two the pulse becomes quicker and weaker, the ears and extremities become colder than in health, and the animal gets weak and staggers in his gait. He has no appetite, but has an excessive thirst. If not checked, inflammation of the bowels may follow.

Treatment.—Try and find out the cause of it before you begin its treatment. If due to some irritant in the bowels, give at once one-half to one pint of linseed oil in a drench. Nearly every case of diarrhoea can be cured in a short time by giving from two to four tablespoonsful of our Colic Cure (see Appendix) every half-hour in one pint of water as a drench. Blanket the animal, and hand-rub and bandage the legs, to keep up the circulation. If, after you have given the Colic Cure for two or three hours, the diarrhoea still continues, then try the following:

Powdered opium	1 dram.
Powdered catechu	4 drams.
Prepared chalk	3 drams.
Water	1 pint.

Mix, and shake well, and give as a drench, and repeat in one hour if necessary.

Use the animal carefully in regard to feed and work for some time.

DYSENTERY—BLOODY FLUX.

Dysentery, or bloody flux, is an affection of the lining membrane of the bowels, characterized by thin, coffee-colored or bloody discharges, with a very offensive smell, and passed with much straining. It is seldom seen in the horse, but quite common among cattle.

Causes.—Foreign bodies in the bowels, such as sand, poisonous substances, etc., will cause it. It also arises from grazing on low, wet lands, drinking impure or stagnant water, etc. Diarrhoea of long standing may terminate in dysentery.

Symptoms.—The most prominent symptom is the thin, bloody discharge from the bowels, with a disagreeable odor; and on examination it may be seen to contain shreds of mucus membrane (lining membrane of the bowels). Griping pains with loss of appetite are early symptoms. There is a high fever, the pulse is quickened, and the patient has a great desire for water. The strength rapidly fails, the flanks present a hollow appearance, the coat dry and hot, and unless relieved death soon follows.

Treatment.—This is a very dangerous and fatal disease. More horses die that become affected with it than recover. Give 8 ounces raw linseed oil and 1 ounce of laudanum as a drench. The oil is soothing to the bowels, and the laudanum quiets the pain and checks the discharge. We know nothing better in this disease than our Colic Cure, giving four tablespoonsful every two hours in 1 pint of cold water. This preparation (Colic Cure) will quiet the pain, stimulate the animal, and has astringent properties to check the discharge. Strictly pure cool water must be allowed. Perfectly sound, easily digested food given in small quantities to eat. If the above remedies fail, the following may be given:

Powdered opium	1 dram.
Powdered catechu	3 drams.
Tincture ginger	1 ounce.
Tincture aconite	20 drops.
Water	1 pint.

Mix, and shake well, and give as a drench. Repeat in four hours if necessary.

One pint of water containing 1 ounce of laudanum may be injected into the rectum two or three times per day. If the animal improves, he then needs a good course of tonic powders, and there is nothing superior or cheaper than Dr. LeGear's Condition Powders.

DISEASES OF THE LIVER.

Diseases of the liver are very rare, and they are very hard to diagnose when they do take place. A horse has no gall-bladder, which is one reason he seldom has any liver derangement. Diseases of the liver are more frequently seen in the Southern country than up North, but they are rare here. The bile, in the horse, as soon as it is secreted, is emptied right into the bowels, and not stored in the gall-bladder, as in man and other animals. The liver is the largest secreting gland in the body, weighing, in the horse, 10 or 12 pounds. It secretes the bile and gets rid of certain effete materials from the system. Bile acts as a laxative, stimulating the peristaltic action of the bowels. In derangement of the liver there is generally constipation, and clay colored feces; also jaundice (yellow appearance of the mouth and lining of the eyes), which shows that the bile is not being secreted from the blood.

INFLAMMATION OF THE LIVER.

We will here give a brief description of this trouble, as some reader of this book may be benefited thereby. It is seen more in horses that are fed high, and have very little to do. It may be caused by feeding highly on stimulating food during the hot weather. Injuries on the right side over the liver may cause inflammation.

Symptoms.—There may be dullness. and more or less abdominal pain; the animal laying down on the left side most of the time. Constipation, clay-colored feces, if any be passed, and the urine is high colored and scanty. Pressure on the right side just back of the last rib may cause pain. The lining of the eyes and mouth are of a yellow color. The appetite may be impaired or entirely lost.

Treatment.—Give the following physic:

Powdered Barbadoes aloes	6 drams.
Calomel	2 drams.
Ginger	2 drams.
Water	1 pint.

Mix, and shake well together, and give as a drench.

If this does not work on the bowels, repeat it in 30 hours. A good mustard paste should be rubbed in well over the region of the liver on the right side of the animal. If the animal will eat, feed moderately for sometime. Give our Condition Powders regular for sometime. A run at grass is an excellent thing after the acute stages of the disease have passed.

JAUNDICE—THE YELLOWS.

This can not be considered as a disease of itself, but is due to some disordered condition of the liver. It is caused by the retention and absorption of bile into the blood. It can be detected by looking at the eyes, nose and mouth, when it will be seen that these parts are yellowish, instead of the pink color of health. The urine is dark colored, the dung is of a dirty gray color, and constipation is mostly present.

Treatment.—Give a physic as recommended for inflammation of the liver. Calomel in 2-dram doses may be given every day for three or four days. Feed lightly on light food, as grass, green food, bran, oats, etc. Give our Condition Powders night and morning for two weeks, after the bowels have been thoroughly opened with a physic.

There are a few other troubles that the liver is liable to, such as Rupture of the Liver, Cirrhosis, Gall-Stones, Worms in the Liver, etc. They are so seldom met with and so hard to detect that we will not attempt here to give an account of each.

Diseases of the Pancreas and Spleen (melt) are so rare, or their symptoms are so little understood, that we will not attempt to give any of them here. The spleen becomes enlarged in certain diseases, as in Texas Fever in cattle, but diseases of the spleen are very little understood.

RUPTURE—HERNIA.

Ruptures are quite a common occurrence among young animals. The most common place for it to appear is at the umbilicus (navel), and in the scrotum (bag). Although animals at any age are liable to rupture from direct injury, such as kicks, rolling on sharp objects, goring from cattle's horns, etc., the injury may not be severe enough, or the instrument sharp enough, to break through the skin, but a breach is made in the muscles, which lets a portion of the bowels come through the opening against the skin, puffing out, forming a swelling or enlargement.

Symptoms.—The indication of rupture at the navel is a soft, puffy swelling, varying in size from a pecan to that of a man's head. It is generally somewhat smaller than a man's fist. In pressing upon it, a little hole can be plainly felt, through which the protruded mass comes. Rupture at the scrotum can be detected by the increased size of the bag, generally at one side. Ventral hernia, or rupture caused by an injury, can be detected by the sudden appearance of a soft, puffy swelling in the region of the belly. On examining it, a breach can be detected, through which the bowels come.

Treatment.—Rupture at the navel in colts should be let alone, as a majority of them will disappear themselves by the time the colt is one or two years old. If, at the age of two years, the rupture is still present, it will generally require some mode of treatment to cure it. Sometimes a good blister, applied to the swelling, causes the rupture to disappear by closing up the opening. Bandages are useful, if they can be kept in place. Another mode of treatment is to cast the animal on his back, and carefully return the bowels into the abdominal cavity. A clamp, similar to those used in the old method of castration, is put over the loose portion of skin and tied moderately tight, and let remain on until it sloughs off. The skin just above the clamp is held so closely together that it unites, and, when the clamp drops off, the cavity is generally healed over. Rupture of the scrotum may cause a stallion very severe colicy pains by the circulation being shut off, or by the food not being able to pass through the loop in the bowels which forms the rupture. In severe cases of colic in stallions, these parts should always be examined. This form of rupture in colts will generally get well of itself if let alone; but, of course, there are cases that need treatment. In castrating colts, this is one thing that should be looked for. If you wish to castrate a ruptured horse, it may be done by returning the bowels into the abdominal cavity and applying a clamp over the testicle, bag and all, and let the clamp remain on until it sloughs off both the bag and the testicle. In rupture from an injury, it may be relieved by an operation. Fast the animal for twelve or eighteen hours, then throw him, and return the bowels into the abdominal cavity. Then the skin may be cut over the enlargement, and the edges of the divided muscles brought together with catgut sutures, and the skin securely sewed with silk. Feed the animal lightly for a few days, and apply a bandage around the body to support the stitches.

CHAPTER VII.

THE URINARY ORGANS.

The urinary organs are, the kidneys, ureters (tubes leading from the kidneys to the bladder), bladder, and urethra (tube leading from the bladder through which the urine is expelled). Their functions are to secrete the urine from the blood, and expel it from the body. The urine is a watery fluid holding in solution a varying quantity of earthy salts, and a peculiar substance, urea, which, if not expelled from the body, acts as a blood poison. The kidneys are very important organs of the body, and have a very essential duty to perform; therefore, it is all-important that they be kept in proper working condition, and free from disease. Certain affections, with imperfect nutrition or destructive waste of the bony tissues, tend to charge the urine with phosphates of lime and magnesia, and induce the formation of stone and gravel. All general diseases of the system more or less affect the kidneys by giving them extra work to do — carrying off the waste products and poisons of the disease. The kidneys are located under the loins, one on each side of the backbone. The bladder is located in the pelvic cavity, and it serves as a reservoir for the urine. From the bladder leads the urethra, through which the urine escapes. Below will be found a brief description of the more important diseases of the urinary organs.

NEPHRITIS—INFLAMMATION OF THE KIDNEYS.

Inflammation of the kidneys is not so common among the lower animals as in man. It usually occurs in the chronic form, being rarely met with in the acute form. Only one kidney may

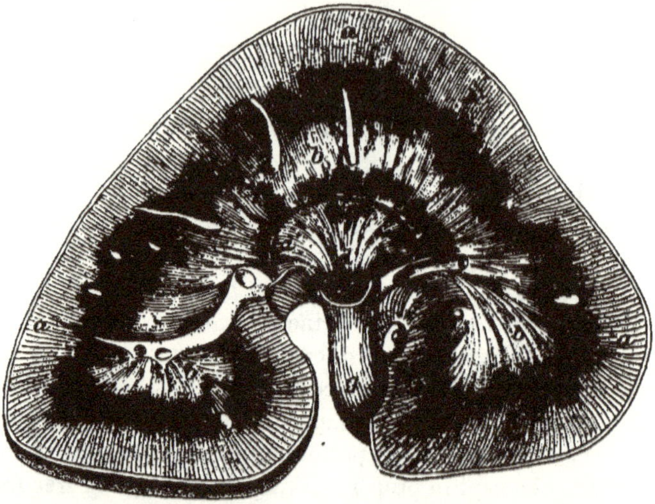

THE KIDNEY—LONGITUDINAL SECTION.

(*a*) Cortical or vascular portion; (*b*) medullary or tubular portion; (*c*) peripheral portion of the latter; (*d*) interior of the pelvis; (*d' d'*) arms of the latter; (*e*) border of the crest; (*f*) infundibulum; (*g*) ureter, the tube leading to the bladder.

be affected, while in other cases both are affected at the same time.

Causes.—Exposure to wet and cold weather, feeding on inferior food, as damaged corn, mouldy hay, etc., the administration of large and repeated doses of resin, saltpetre and other diuretics. A spanish-fly blister, as well as injuries, such as jumping, falling, carrying heavy weights, etc., may cause nephritis.

Symptoms.—The pulse ranges from 45 to 50; there is usually a high fever; the animal shows pain and uneasiness by lying down, and sometimes rolling (but not so violent as in colic), and turning his head toward the region of his kidneys; frequent attempts are made to urinate, but little is passed, and is usually mixed with blood. The flanks are sunken, the belly tucked up, and the animal may walk with a straddling gait. In the chronic form, the symptoms are not so well marked as in the acute. Swelling of the limbs may be noticed, the animal appears dull and languid, and stretches himself in the stall, stretching out his hind legs, and will stand, sometimes for hours, in that position. When brought out of the stall, the animal shows stiffness in the region of the loins, but this, upon exercise, soon disappears.

Treatment.—Every effort should be made to relieve the kidneys of their work, and keep them quiet. Give one quart of raw linseed oil to move the bowels. If this doesn't physic the animal well, repeat it in thirty hours. Give three tablespoonsful of our Colic Cure every four hours in one pint of cold water, as a drench. This will quiet the pain, and lower the fever. Make the animal sweat by blanketing the body heavily. Apply hot cloths over the region of the loins, and cover with dry blankets. Renew the hot cloths every half-hour. Our Liniment, well rubbed in over the loins two or three times per day, will be found of great benefit. Feed the animal on a good, nutritious diet, and use very easily for some time.

DIURESIS — DIABETES INSIPIDUS — PROFUSE STALING.

Diabetes consists in the passage of large quantities of a clear watery urine, accompanied by great loss of strength and spirit, great thirst, etc.

Causes.—This disease in most cases is due to faulty feeding, as damaged corn, moldy hay, etc. Food of any kind that is damaged in any way or inferior in quality, may cause the disease. Other common causes are the continued use of impure water, the reckless use of certain medicines which are commonly found in quack horse powders, as well as in certain plants and grasses, which set up irritation of the kidneys and produce the trouble.

Symptoms.—The horse appears to be always thirsty and drinks at every opportunity, and passes his urine every time you stop him, the discharge being clear and watery, and without any odor (smell.) The eye becomes dull, the spirits are depressed, the animal is weak and sluggish, sweats easily, and can endure but little. The flanks become tucked up, the animal gets poor, the skin becomes tight, the hair stands erect and has lost its gloss. The animal may live for months, or may die early, according to the severity of the attack.

Treatment.—The first thing to do is to look to the feed, and see that the animal is supplied with sound hay and grain. It is advisable to make a change in the feed any way, as well as the drinking water. A liberal supply of boiled flaxseed in the drinking water is very useful. Also feed on boiled oats, bran, etc. Pure water should be frequently given, and in small quantities. The following powders generally act like magic in curing this disease:

Iodine	3 drams.
Iodide of potassium	4 drams.
Sulphate of iron	1 ounce.
Powdered gentian	2 ounces.

Mix, and make six powders, and give one powder night and morning in damp feed.

DIABETES MELLITUS.

Diabetes Mellitus (sugar diabetes) is more a disease of the nervous system or liver, than that of the kidneys.

Causes.—Its causes are various, but most of them may be included under any disorders of the liver or of the brain.

Symptoms. — Great thirst, profuse passage of a pale urine, rapid loss of condition, scurvy, unthrifty skin, indigestion, etc., and the presence in the urine of a sweet principle—sugar. The best way to detect this is to touch the tip of the tongue with a drop.

Treatment.—This is a disease that has received a great deal of study and investigation, but as yet no reliable remedies have been discovered. Great attention should be paid to the diet of the animal. Give food that is as free of saccharine properties as possible. Some good may be obtained by giving our Condition Powders for two or three weeks in the feed.

BLOODY URINE—HAEMATURIA.

As seen in the horse, bloody urine is usually the direct result of some injury across the loins (small of the back) or irritation caused by stones (calculi) in the kidney, bladder, etc.

Treatment.—You must first find out the exact cause. If due to a stone in the bladder you must endeavor to remove it. Give slippery-elm and linseed tea to drink. If the discharge is abundant, apply cold water to the loins and keep the animal quiet. Give:

Sugar of lead	1 dram.
Water	1 pint.

Mix, and give as a drench.

Or give—

Tincture of iron	1 ounce.
Water	1 pint.

Mix, and give as a drench.

CYSTITIS—INFLAMMATION OF THE BLADDER.

Inflammation of the bladder may occur in all animals, but it is not very frequently seen.

Causes.—It may be caused by stone in the bladder, or from feeding the animal on strong, irritating medicine or food. Anything that will make the urine of an irritating character is liable to cause cystitis.

Symptoms.—The animal shows considerable pain and passes urine frequently, but only a small quantity. Pain, more or less, is shown after each effort to urinate, by strainging and groaning, and moving the tail and hind legs. On passing the hand into the rectum or vagina the bladder is found to be hot and tender. Pressure in the flanks may cause pain.

Treatment.—If in the mare or cow, inject into the bladder warm water 1 quart, laudanum 1 ounce, using a suitable syringe. Repeat the injection once daily. Apply blankets wrung out of hot water over the loins, and feed on bran mashes, linseed meal, grass, etc. If much fever is present, give 15 drops of tincture of aconite in one-half pint of cold water as a drench, and repeat every four hours. Give 1 pint of raw linseed oil as a drench. Use the animal carefully for some time.

These failing, injections of warm water containing 2 ounces of laudanum may be tried; also give the following:

Sweet nitre	2 ounces.
Laudanum or chloral hydrate..............	1 ounce.
Water	1 pint.

Mix, and give as a drench.

If in a horse, the catheter (Fig. 14), well oiled, may be gently passed up the penis and the urine drawn off. In a mare, all that is necessary to dilate it is to insert one finger into the neck of the bladder.

Fig. 14. Horse Catheter, for drawing the urine from the bladder of horses.

SPASM OF THE NECK OF THE BLADDER.

This condition consists in a tight closure of the outlet from the bladder by contraction of the small circular muscles that open and close it.

Causes.—Hard, continuous driving, without a chance to pass urine, draughts of cold air when warm and fatigued, extensive blisters of Spanish-fly over the loins, certain medicines, stone in the bladder, and exposure to cold rain storms.

Symptoms.—Frequent stretching and straining to pass water, without being able to do so. On resuming his natural position, the animal still continues uneasy, paws, shakes the tail, looks back to the flank, kicks at his belly with his hind feet, lies down and rises, and tries to urinate as before. With the oiled hand introduced into the rectum (last gut), the bladder full of urine may be felt.

Treatment.—As some mares refuse to make their water in harness, they should be unhitched at suitable times for such purposes. In all cases, take the animal out of the harness, spread clean hay or straw beneath the belly, or turn the patient out on the dung heap. Some accomplish the act by slow whistling, others by pouring water from one vessel into another with a dribbling noise.

PARALYSIS OF THE BLADDER.

Causes.—It is associated with diseases of the spinal cord, broken back, where there is palsy of the tail and of the hind limbs.

Symptoms.—When the neck of the bladder is affected, there is constant dribbling of urine, which runs down the inside of the thighs. When the neck is not affected, the urine is retained until the bladder is very full, when it may be forced out with a gush. This, however, does not entirely empty it, as it may still remain half-full.

Treatment.—Gentle pressure with the oiled hand, well inserted into the rectum, may force it out, but it is better to use the catheter (Fig. 14) to draw the urine off. Give the following:

Saltpetre	2 ounces.
Iodide of potassium	1½ ounces.
Powdered nux vomica	1½ ounces.

Mix into twelve powders, and give one morning and night in damp feed.

GRAVEL—STONE.

This is the formation of calculi (stones) in the kidneys and bladder. They may be few or many, and vary in size from the finest grain of sand to that of a man's fist. We have a specimen on hand now of a stone taken from a horse's bladder, after death, by Earnest Witte, of Shelby, Texas, that weighs over three pounds. Gravel is seen more frequently in districts where stock are compelled to drink water highly impregnated with lime.

Symptoms.—Stones may be present in the kidneys or bladder for a long time before they cause the animal any inconvenience. The urine may be passed with difficulty, and changed in color, becoming unnaturally white or milky in appearance. Gravel in the bladder often causes a great deal of irritation, and more or less inflammation of the same. The urine may be passed with pain being checked before the bladder is empty, and dribble away in a small stream, or be shut off entirely. Blood and mucus may be passed. If a close examination of the urine is made, gravel may be found. The pain may be so severe that the horse will have severe colicy pains by a stone blocking up the passage of urine. Stone in the kidney is often very severe, and causes the horse a great deal of pain and uneasiness. Urine will be passed often in small quantities, with pain with each effort. Pressure on the loins may cause a great deal of pain.

Treatment.—If due to drinking lime water, discontinue it, and give cistern water entirely. Also, give plenty of salt. If the animal is in much pain, he can be relieved by giving our Colic Cure in ordinary-sized doses. Repeat every hour until relieved. Give in the drinking water every morning 1 dram of carbonate of potash; also, give 1 teaspoonful of our Condition Powders morning and night in damp feed for two or three weeks. Where the gravel gets lodged in the canal leading from the bladder, it has to be removed by cutting upon it and removing by an operation. Stone may be removed from the bladder of a mare or cow by inserting a long pair of suitable forceps into the bladder through the urethra.

AZOTURIA—POISONING BY ALBUMENOIDS.

This is more a disease of the liver and blood than of the kidneys, as a great many suppose.

Causes.—Any horse that is kept up and well fed and has not regular exercise, is liable to this trouble, especially driving horses. For instance, a horse has regular work and receives a large supply of good food, when from some cause or other he is allowed to stand idle in the stable for several days and still receives the usual quantity of rich and stimulating food. Now, if the animal is taken out and given exercise, it is then the disease will show itself, especially if the drive be rapid.

Symptoms.—The horse, after having been well fed and rested for several days, comes out of the stable full of life and in high spirits. After traveling a short distance, he is noticed to become somewhat dull and sluggish, sweats freely, and then shows stiffness in the loins and goes rather lame behind. In traveling he drags the limbs along, may stagger slightly, manifests weakness in the hind quarters, and finally stops, being unable to proceed any further on his way. He may remain standing, but usually falls or lies down. When down he is unable to rise, and shows considerable pain. If allowed to stop at first, he would lie down and roll like a horse with the colic. The muscles of the hip soon become as hard as though composed of iron. In some cases the fore limbs become affected; in this form it is not so severe as when affecting the hind quarters. The pulse is usually quickened, the breathing increased, with a high fever, and the bowels are found to be loaded. The urine is thick and of a very dark color, and invariably has to be drawn with a catheter. (See Fig. 14.)

Treatment.—As soon as the horse is noticed to be getting stiff and lame he should be stopped at once and taken out of the harness. Give at once a good purgative, as follows:

Barbadoes aloes	9 drams.
Bromide of potassium	6 drams.
Ginger	4 drams.
Water	1 pint.

Mix, and give as a drench.

If no other physic can be had, give 1 quart of raw linseed oil. Keep the animal on his feet if possible. If he goes down it may be well to raise him up with slings. Apply to the hips and loins blankets wrung out of hot water and cover them with dry ones. Have the water just as hot as he can stand it, and change the blankets every twenty minutes. After removing the blankets bathe the affected muscles with some good stimulating liniment, and there is none as good as Dr. LeGear's Liniment. (See Appendix.) Use the liniment two or three times a day. Draw off the urine two or three times a day with the catheter (Fig. 14) if he can't pass it. After giving the physic follow it up with the following:

Bromide of potassium	3 ounces.
Nitrate of potassium	1½ ounces.

Mix, and make six powders, and give one powder morning, noon, and night, dissolved in one-half pint of water.

Give the animal all the pure water he will drink, and feed on bran, boiled oats, grass, fodder, etc. Keep the patient in a comfortable place and have him well cared for. This is a disease if taken in time and has the proper treatment that can in most cases be cured in from two to six days. After the horse has improved considerably, give him the following tonic powders:

Nitrate of potassium	1½	ounces.
Powdered gentian	3	ounces.
Powdered sulphate of iron	2	ounces.
Powdered nux vomica	1½	ounces.
Powdered anise seed	2	drams.

Mix, and make twelve powders, and give one powder morning and night in damp feed.

Or Dr. LeGear's Condition Powders (see Appendix) may be given, which are just as good and much cheaper.

CHAPTER VIII.

THE SKIN.

The skin of the domesticated animals performs several very important functions. Besides covering and protecting the body, it removes daily about one-sixty-seventh of the weight of the body. Experiments go to show that of eight parts of food taken into the healthy body, about three parts leave it by the bowels and kidneys, three by the lungs, and two by the skin. It is an important breathing apparatus, excreting carbonic acid and absorbing oxygen. On account of its constant and large secretion of fluid, the skin is an important factor in regulating animal temperature. So important are the purifying functions of the skin that if an animal be covered by a complete coat of varnish, which completely prevents sweating, the animal will die in a remarkably short time from suffocation and poisoning of the system.

The sweat glands are very numerous, there being in the skin of a horse from 2000 to 3000 on every square inch. The activity of these glands is regulated by the sweat centres located in the brain. The amount of natural perspiration depends mainly upon the dryness and temperature of the air. Unnatural sweating is brought on by exercise, the taking of food, drinking warm drinks, and by certain medicines that stimulate the nerve centres.

NON-SWEATING.

It will be seen by reading the above remarks on the skin how important it is for horses to sweat. It is quite a common occurrence among horses in this country, especially large horses that are shipped in here from the North, to have the sweat checked on them and they do not sweat no matter how hard or fast you drive them on a hot summer day.

Causes.—The causes of this trouble are generally by being cooled off too quickly, by being watered or stood in a draught when very hot from a hard drive. It is caused more readily in horses not acclimated, or when the animal is not well. Northern horses that are fed corn all summer, and worked hard in the hot sun, are very liable to suffer from this trouble.

Symptoms.—Perhaps the first thing noticed will be dullness of the animal, and no sweating. When driven, the animal will breathe very fast and almost suffocate, but does not sweat. The pores of the skin become blocked up and the nerve centres deranged, and the waste and poisonous material that should come out with the sweat remains in the system. The blood becomes impregnated with this effete material, and on going to the lungs to be purified it gives extra work to the lungs, thus the cause of the panting breathing and suffocation. An animal in this condition is very easily overcome by the heat and subject to sunstroke.

Treatment.—In the treatment of this trouble, the great object in view is to promote the secretions of the skin. If the animal is much exhausted, and breathing fast, give the following:

Sweet nitre	1 ounce.
Alcohol	3 ounces.
Water	1 pint.

Mix, and give as a drench, and repeat every hour until relieved.

Give a change of feed; feed oats and bran, but no corn; give the animal a good bath, and put three or four blankets on him and stand in a stall and let him remain covered up for one hour. Then remove the blankets and rub him dry. Repeat this bathing and blanketing every morning for one or two weeks. It may be well to give the above drench at each time of bathing. Clean the skin well once or twice a day with a curry-comb and brush. Give regular, but gentle, exercise. Give 1 teaspoonful of our Condition Powders morning and night for two weeks. After the animal is relieved to a considerable extent, a run at pasture will be beneficial.

ECZEMA.

This disease is a very common one, especially so during the hot months of summer, and is often mistaken for mange. Eczema is a non-contagious disease of the skin, characterized by the formation of a small pimple, which afterwards becomes a vesicle (blister), and finally a pustule (containing pus or matter).

Causes.—It is caused by a changed condition of the blood, produced, or at least aggravated, by a change from cold to hot weather, and by certain kinds of food, etc. It is commonly seen in horses on pasture, especially when grazing on over-ripe grass, etc. An animal once having the disease is more liable to another attack than he would be if he had never had it, especially when fed on a highly nutritious diet.

Symptoms.—Dryness of the hair is noticed, and itchiness of the skin, causing the animal to rub his head and neck with very great violence on being brought in from work. When running out at-pasture he will often rub the fence down in his frantic efforts to obtain relief. The head, neck, the region of the mane, root of the tail, etc., are the parts most affected. Eczema comes on suddenly, while mange comes on gradually, and it is quite as difficult to treat, if not more so, than mange.

Treatment. — This disease requires both local and constitutional treatment. Wash the animal every second day for at least ten days with castile soap and water, and apply the following wash every morning to all the affected parts with a swab or brush.:

Corrosive sublimate	2 drams.
Alcohol	4 ounces.
Water	4 ounces.

Mix.

On mornings of washing apply the wash directly after washing. After using the wash for about ten days or two weeks, discontinue it and grease all the affected parts every morning with carbolized salve, which will bring out the growth of hair. The internal treatment consists of tonics and alteratives to purify the blood and act on the skin. Give every morning in damp feed two tablespoonsful of Fowler's Solution of Arsenic. At night give one teaspoonful of Dr. LeGear's Condition Powders (see Appendix) in damp feed. Make a complete change of feed. Give bran mash freely, in which put the medicine. Give oats, but no corn, for some time. Give gentle but not severe exercise during treatment or for some time afterwards.

CRACKED HEELS—SCRATCHES.

Cracked heels, or more commonly called scratches, is a very common trouble among race horses, affecting both runners and trotters. The heavier breeds of horses are, however, the most liable to this trouble. The hind legs are usually the ones affected.

Causes.—Cracked heels may be caused in many ways, as washing the heels and not drying them properly, irregular exercise, standing in filthy, wet stables, etc. A common cause of the disease in horses of fast work is, that on sweating freely the perspiration runs down upon the heels, irritates and causes them to crack. Sometimes the animal gets his foot over a rope and rubs it, setting up an irritation which by improper treatment terminates in cracked heels. Scratches may also be caused by the injudicious use of blisters; in fact, any irritant substance whatever may cause it. Cracked heels is a condition seldom seen among horses that are properly cared for.

Symptoms.—A reddened appearance of the heel is usually the first thing noticed. This is soon followed by the appearance of cracks or fissures, which usually extend from side to side. If the trouble is in the fore limbs the animal will be very stiff in his action, until he becomes warmed up, or until the blood oozes out, when the stiffness will disappear. When in the hind limbs the stiffness is not so great. Sometimes there is a slight swelling of the affected limb, extending in some cases as high as the hock.

Treatment.—In the majority of cases the only treatment necessary is to apply to all the affected parts two or three times per day Dr. LeGear's Healing Lotion. (See Appendix.). Keep the parts as clean as possible, but don't wash very often. Keep the animal quiet for a few days and in a clean dry place. If the above treatment fails to cure, or greatly improve the case in a week's time, give the physic given in the treatment of Mallenders, and follow with Dr. LeGear's Condition Powders to purify the blood. Apply the Healing Lotion at least twice per day during the treatment, or until cured.

GREASE.

This disease shows itself in connection with the heels of a horse, especially the hind ones. It is known as "grease" on account of the oily or greasy character of the discharge which takes place form the affected parts. Heavy horses are far more subject to an attack than the lighter breeds. It is not contagious.

Causes.—Certain kinds of horses are subject to this trouble, as the heavier breeds, those possessing flat feet and having large quantities of hair on their limbs, etc. The most common cause of grease is scratches, and the various causes which operate in producing cracked heels also operate in producing grease, as washing the parts too frequently, or washing and not drying, the improper use of blisters, etc.

Symptoms.—There is more or less swelling of the parts, accompanied by redness, and soon followed by a slight discharge. Soon the discharge becomes oily in character, the hair comes out, and the skin is considerably inflamed. The odor of the discharge draws attention to the parts whenever one approaches the animal, and if not actively and properly treated the tense tender skin cracks open, leaving open sores from which vascular bleeding growths grow up, constituting the "grapes." This is known as the grapous stage. The heel may now appear as one mass of rounded, red, small, angry, tumor-like processes (similar to grapes), which bleed on handling and have a very offensive discharge. When grease extends to and involves the frog of the horse's foot it is known as canker. Neglected or improperly treated grease may terminate in big leg.

Treatment.—In bad cases of grease the first thing to be done is to give a good physic to clean out the bowels, and follow it up with Dr. LeGear's Condition Powders, given in the usual size doses morning and night in damp feed to purify the blood. The best physic in a case of this kind is as follows:

Powdered Barbadoes aloes ....1 ounce.
Powdered ginger ....2 drams.
Mix.

The above can be made into a bolus with vaseline and put back on the root of the tongue with the hand, or dissolved in 1 pint of warm water and given as a drench. Clip the hair closely from the parts and wash off all the scabs and matter with castile soap and water, and use a little carbolic acid (1 part to 40 of water) to destroy the bad smell. Apply to the affected parts twice per day Dr. LeGear's Healing Lotion, and dust well on to the parts after putting on the Healing Lotion, Dr. LeGear's Screw Worm Powder. If there is much fever and swelling in the parts, put on a linseed meal poultice and change it twice per day. Mix it up with warm water and tie it on with a soft cloth. Give easily digested food, as bran, oats, chops, grass, etc. In mild cases the Healing Lotion and Screw Worm Powder will generally effect a cure when applied according to directions. But in the grapous stage of the disease caustics, or the hot iron, must be used, the latter is the best. Caustic potash is the best caustic to use to remove the grapes, but blue stone, burnt alum, etc., may be used instead; or use the following:

White arsenic .... 2 drams.
Vaseline .... 1 ounce.

Mix, and apply occasionally to keep down the excessive granulations (grapes).

It may be well in some cases to remove the shoe, but in most cases of Grease, as well as that of Scratches, a high heeled shoe will be found very beneficial to remove the strain from the cracks.

If an ointment is preferred, use the following:

Oxide of zinc	2 drams.
Carbolic acid	20 drops.
Vaseline	1 ounce.

Mix, and apply to the affected parts twice a day.

NETTLE RASH—SURFEIT—URTICARIA.

Nettle-rash is a skin affection characterized by the sudden appearance of small elastic eminences, varying in size from a hazel nut to a hickory nut, and which may be observed over the whole body surface, but more particularly in the region of the neck, shoulders, flanks, etc. It it also known as "urticaria," "surfeit," etc., and is most commonly seen during the hot months of summer.

Causes.—Certain kinds of food may produce it, and take it all in all, derangement of the digestive organs is the most common cause. Allowing an animal to cool off suddenly, or giving him a drink of cold water, when hot and sweating freely, is a very frequent cause of the trouble.

Symptoms.—The attack is sudden. The eminences are elastic to the touch, and usually round in shape. They may disappear in a few hours, or may remain on the animal for eight or ten days. In some cases as quickly as one set of elevations disappear they are followed by a new lot. Usually there is an itching sensation of the skin, as shown by the animal rubbing himself, as well as slight constitutional disturbance; pulse and appetite slightly affected, etc.

Treatment.—This is a disease that generally yields to treatment very readily when taken in time. Give as a drench one pint of raw linseed oil, after which give one-half teaspoonful of saltpetre in the drinking water or on damp feed night and morning. Bathe all the affected parts twice per day with 1 pint of vinegar to 1 gallon of cold water. Reduce the quantity of feed given to about one-half. Give bran mashes, grass, etc., if they can be had.

MUD FEVER.

Mud fever consists of an inflammation of the skin in the region of the hock behind, and the knees in front.

Causes.—Mud fever may result from any of the causes which produce cracked heels, as washing and not drying, irregular exercise, standing in filthy, wet stables, driving through mud and slush, etc. It is most common during spring and autumn, when cold water is used to wash the legs.

Symptoms. — On examination the outside layer of the skin about the hocks or knees is found to be inflamed. The pain is often quite severe, the hair comes out to a certain extent, the irritation extends to the deeper structures of the skin, often giving rise to considerable swelling. In some cases constitutional symptoms are present, the appetite interfered with, and if the exciting cause be kept up the general system becomes very much affected.

Treatment.—The treatment for mud fever is the same as for Mallenders, which see.

MALLENDERS.

This is an eczematious (like eczema) condition of the skin, localizing itself on the front legs just back of the knees, causing a scurviness and dryness of the parts. It is commonly seen among heavy horses, and stallions suffer more frequently than mares or geldings.

Causes.—The causes are a sluggish circulation, improper feeding, irregular exercise, improper grooming, etc. It may also be due to the action of certain blistering preparations.

Smyptoms.—At first there is an irritation, followed by redness in some cases, and a watery discharge takes place from the affected part. The cracks which form often extend quite through the skin. The first symptoms may after a while disappear, and the case take on a chronic form. The animal may also fall off in condition to a certain extent.

Treatment.—This disease, though apparently not very serious, is some times very hard to cure on account of the location of the trouble. Give the following prescription as a drench at one dose:

Barbadoes aloes	4 drams.
Tincture ginger	1 ounce.
Raw linseed oil	1 pint.

Mix.

Follow the above up with Dr. LeGear's Condition Powders (see Appendix) according to direction. Keep the horse as quiet as possible for a few days. There is no medicine that will heal it quicker than Dr. LeGear's Healing Lotion applied twice per day.

SALLENDERS.

Sallenders is the same as Mallenders, only that it is situated on the hind legs about the hocks. Its causes, symptoms, and treatment are the same as Mallenders. Sallenders occurs probably with greater frequency than Mallenders.

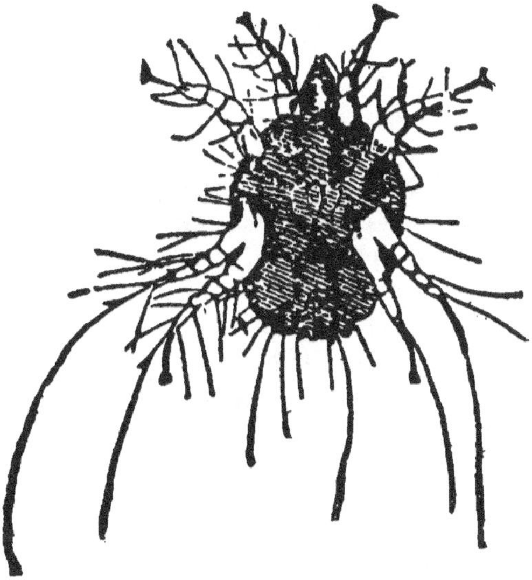

Fig. 15. The Mange Insect.

MANGE—ITCH.

Mange is an eruptive disease of the skin, characterized by more or less irritation of the same. It is due to the presence of a parasite belonging to the family called Sarcoptes—two Greek words meaning "flesh" and "to conceal." It is also called scab, or scabies, itch, etc. It is transmissible from animal to animal, and from one species to another. The parasites burrow down into the flesh, and are found in the horse, man, sheep, pigs, and cattle, and are also common to many other smaller animals. Besides the sarcoptes, there is another kind called "dermatodectes," signifying "the skin," and "to prick." The dermatodectes do not burrow beneath the skin, but simply hold on to and prick the skin. They are common to the ox, horse, and sheep. Another variety is known as "symbiotes." They neither burrow nor prick the skin, but cause considerable irritation, and are common to the horse and ox. Certain conditions appear favorable to the attack of the sarcoptic kind. A horse poorly cared for, badly groomed, and in an unthrifty state generally, is in a favorable condition for the reception of the disease. The attack of the sarcoptes is at first slow, but having once fairly secure a start, they spread with great rapidity, irritating the skin and sometimes destroying the animal. (Fig. 15.)

The dermatodectes are far less troublesome than the sarcoptes. The symbiotes are often found affecting the legs of horses, setting up considerable irritation or itching, and causing the animal to rub and scratch the parts. The parasites mentioned are those causing mange, although of the three families named, the sarcoptes is probably the one oftenest met with in mange, and most certainly is the one causing the worst form of the disease; either variety may be conveyed from one animal to another by means of the harness, saddle, clothing, etc. The dermatodectes can in some cases be easily detected by the naked eye, and either variety can of course be readily discovered by the glass, an ordinary magnifying glass in most cases being quite sufficient. During times of war mange is usually quite common. As a general thing the disease is not so very common on the American continent.

Mange in every instance is caused by coming into contact with affected animals, or infected clothing, harness, etc. At the same time it should be remembered that dirty, badly groomed and neglected animals are more prone to receive the parasites than well kept and properly cared for animals.

Symptoms.—The coat presents an unthrifty appearance, and on account of the irritation set up by the parasites in the skin, the animal rubs and scratches himself. Soon the hair falls out, leaving bare patches of skin on the neck, about the edge of the mane, and on the quarters near the root of the tail. The hair continues to fall out until the animal is almost devoid of hair. A sort of staw-colored fluid now may be seen coming out on the surface of the skin. After sometime the general health of the animal may be interfered with; he becomes, weak, feverish, and in some cases death takes place. Mange is accompanied by a far greater amount of irritation than eczema, which is a point well worth remembering.

Treatment.—In the treatment of mange the great object in view is to kill the parasites in the skin by using some good germicide, and to also destroy the parasites on the harness, saddle, saddle-blanket, stalls, etc. If the hair is anyways long, clip it all off closely and wash the body all over thoroughly with castile soap and water. Wash every third day, and apply either of the following lotions every morning to all affected parts:

Creolin . . . . 1 ounce.
Methylated spirits . . . . 1 ounce.
Distilled water . . . . 1 pint.

Mix.

Or—

Trikresol . . . . 6 drams.
Distilled water . . . . 1 pint.

Mix.

Solutions of carbolic acid or corrosive sublimate are beneficial in many cases, but must be used carefully. Sulphur and tar preparations are good in some cases, but are objectionable on account of their gummy nature. The harness and saddle must be thoroughly washed with soap and carbolic acid water. Blankets, pads, etc., may be boiled for one or two hours in water. The stalls, sheds, posts, etc., can be cleansed by painting them with boiling hot whitewash, to which may be added two ounces of carbolic acid to every gallon. If the animal is run down in flesh, give him two tablespoonsful of Fowler's Solution of Arsenic every morning, or one teaspoonful of Dr. LeGear's Condition Powders (see Appendix) night and morning in damp feed for two weeks.

LOUSINESS—LICE.

In this article two kinds of lice will be spoken of: first, the ordinary horse lice, invited by a filthy condition of the animal, improper grooming, debility, etc.; secondly, poultry lice, which are so common among horses kept standing near hen houses. Hen lice are smaller than the regular horse lice.

Symptoms.—Very easily detected. The animal manifests considerable irritation by scratching himself, a rough coat, an unthrifty appearance. The itching seems to be more severe about the root of the tail, mane, etc. On making a close examination, the lice may be detected swarming over the body of the animal. Chicken lice are common among horses kept near hen houses, and cause the animal a great deal of annoyance, causing the mane and tail to fall out.

Treatment.—It is well to clip the hair closely from the horse and apply freely to the body the following:

Stavesacre seed	1 ounce.
Veratrum album (white hellebore)	1 ounce.
Water	1 gallon.

Mix, and boil until the residue measures two quarts.

A strong solution of tobacco water is very good. A good but very old remedy for killing lice on cattle is one part of kerosene and four parts of lard, mixed well, and rubbed along the backbone, about the horns and ears, on the shoulders, etc. The harness, saddle blankets, stalls., etc., should have the same treatment as recommended for mange.

RINGWORM.

Ringworm is a skin affection also caused by a parasite, belonging to a class called cryptogama, being of vegetable origin. It is called ringworm on account of the manner in which it attacks the skin. All animals are attacked, and horses in good condition appear to be just as liable to take the disease as those in poor condition. The vitality of the parasite is very great, and in some cases it has been known to live upwards of six months. Ringworm is communicable from one animal to another, and from animals to man.

Symptoms.—Circular, scruffy patches appear on various parts of the body, usually about the head, neck, and loins, the hairs of the affected spot being erect, bristly, broken, or split up, and dropping out. The affection, unless checked, may spread over the whole surface of the body. There is a slight discharge of fluid from the affected parts. In the horse, the affection is usually circumscribed in character, that is attacking and remaining confined to one part only. It yields to treatment very easily in the horse.

Treatment.—Wash the affected parts well with castile soap and water and apply the following ointment every morning:

Iodide of potassium	1 dram.
Iodine	1 dram.
Vaseline	1 ounce.

Mix.

Carbolic acid lotions are always good and safe, except in the dog. The following lotion may be beneficial:

Nitrate of silver	20 grains.
Distilled water	1 ounce.

Mix, and apply every morning with a swab or brush.

The harness and blankets should be washed with a sloution of carbolic acid 1 part to 40 of water.

WARTS.

Warts may be defined to be unnatural growths, consisting of peculiar thickening or hardening of the true skin. They may appear upon any part of the body, but are of more frequent occurrence about the lips, eyelids, cheeks, ears, beneath the belly, and on the sheath, etc. They occur in every variety of shape, are very common amongst horses and cattle, in which animals they often occur in great numbers, and vary in size from a pea to that of a man's head. Sometimes the skin of an animal may be completely covered with them, while in others one or two of very large size may be present.

Causes.—It is no easy matter just to state what may cause warts to appear on animals; however, a very trivial irritation, as a chafe from the harness, etc., may stimulate the skin to such an extent as to produce them. A highly stimulating diet, producing a disordered state of the skin, may also cause warts, and there are probably other causes we know not of yet.

Treatment.—Where warts are due to high feeding, a run at grass is very beneficial. If a wart has a constricted neck it may be removed with the knife or the ecrasure, the latter instrument being useful to prevent bleeding. Small warts may be clipped off with a pair of scissors and the roots touched with caustic or the hot iron. Large flat warts can be removed by rubbing on them once a day for a week dry arsenious acid. After you have applied the arsenic for five or six days, the wart cracks open and you can generally remove it with the fingers.

Fig. 16.

OLD SORES ON JACKS.

These are very troublesome at times, as they are found so hard to heal. They are generally seen about the feet and legs and are caused in different ways. They may be due to bad blood, or come from an injury, as by the jack lying on the sore parts all the time.

Treatment.—There is no medicine that will heal up sores of this kind like our Healing Lotion. Wash the sores once or twice a day with castile soap and water, and apply the Healing Lotion after each washing. If you think the jack's blood is bad, this can be relieved by giving our Condition Powders. All jack owners will be more than pleased with this Healing Lotion when once tried.

OEDEMA—STOCKING—SWELLED LEGS.

This is quite frequently seen in the horse. It is caused by bad blood, debility, derangement of the kidneys, fast work upon hard roads, etc. It is often seen in connection with certain debilitating diseases, as distemper, influenza, indigestion, pnemonia, etc.

Symptoms.—It is oftenest seen in the hind legs at the ankles. The swelling may extend up above the hocks, but generally remains down about the ankles. After an animal has been driven one, two, or five miles the swelling may all disappear, but by letting the animal remain in the stable all night they will be swollen as bad as ever by morning. Stocking is more often due to bad blood and weak circulation. The blood is thin and watery, and a certain amount becomes lodged in the legs. In these cases the swelling will pit on pressure and is not fevered or sore. When due to any injury or from hard driving there is more or less fever and soreness, and it is quite firm and hard.

Treatment.—If caused by debility, bad blood, etc., give as a drench one pint raw linseed oil, and give full doses of our Condition Powders night and morning in damp feed for two or three weeks. Hand-rub and bandage the legs on coming in from a drive. The legs may be bathed with the following:

Sulphate of zinc	6 drams.
Sugar of lead	1 ounce.
Water	1 pint.

Mix, and apply well to the swelling two or three times per day.

Give soft, easily digested food to eat. A run at grass is very beneficial. It is undoubtedly the very best treatment if the grass is good. The animal needs regular exercise, good care, and good food. The weak circulation and watery condition of the blood can be entirely rectified by giving our Condition Powders. If due to hard driving, bandage the legs nicely with wet bandages every time on coming in from a drive. Let bandages remain on one or two hours.

LYMPHANGITIS—WEED—MONDAY MORNING DISEASE.

It is an inflammation of the lymphatic glands and vessels. The disease is also known as "weed," "water farcy," "Monday morning disease," "shot of grease," etc. It is usually confined to the hind limbs, and seldom affects more than one leg at a time. The heaviest breeds of horses are more liable to an attack of lymphangitis than the lighter breeds.

Causes.—A common cause is, after an animal has been used to hard work, allowing him to stand in the stable for a few days, and giving at the same time as much food as he had when working; consequently the lymphatic glands and vessels become overworked and clogged, inflammation follows, and lymphangitis becomes established. Other causes are: direct injuries, as punctured wounds and kicks, cracked heels, etc.

Symptoms.—The disease usually begins with a chill, rise in temperature, laboured breathing, and in a very short time followed by lameness in one leg and swelling on the inside of the thigh. The swelling gradually surrounds the whole limb, continues on downward until it reaches the foot, often causing the animal to hold the limb up from the ground. The leg is very tender to the touch, and the animal has great difficulty in moving it about. The limb is also found to be hot, the countenance bears a very anxious expression, and the animal usually stands. Constipation is usually present and the urine decreased in quantity and heightened in color. Lymphangitis is liable to terminate in "big leg" if not properly treated.

Treatment.—If the proper treatment is adopted at the beginning of the disease and properly carried out, it can be easily and successfully treated. The first thing to be done is to give a good purgative, as the following:

Powdered Barbadoes aloes	10 drams.
Powdered ginger	2 drams.
Powdered nux vomica	1 dram.
Nitrate of potash	3 drams.
Water	1 pint.

Mix, and shake well together, and give as a drench.

Give 15 drops of tincture of aconite in one-half pint of cold water every four hours as a drench until the fever is checked. Feed sparingly on light food, as bran, grass, fodder, etc. Don't give any grain for a few days. Give 2 drams of nitrate of potassium in feed or drinking water morning and night for a week. Begin bathing the affected leg at once with right warm water. Wrap a woolen cloth around the leg and keep it wet with warm water for two hours at a time, two or three times a day. Each time after bathing with warm water wipe dry and bathe the whole affected leg with our Liniment well rubbed in.

CHAPTER IX.

THE NERVOUS SYSTEM.

The nervous system is composed of the brain, spinal cord, and nerves. The brain is situated in the upper part of the skull, the spinal cord in the back-bone, and the nerves branch off, like the limbs of a tree, from the brain and spinal cord and extend to every part of the body. The brain generates the electricity, as it were, and the nerves convey the messages to and from the brain. When a nerve is cut, or divided, or if by any means the nervous force is shut off from any part of the body, local paralysis will take place. Without nervous force there is no motion, nutrition, vitality, or life. If the spinal cord in the region of the back or loins is severed or injured there is immediate paralysis of the whole hind parts; while if the injury takes place in the neck, as by broken neck, death will soon follow. By piercing the spinal cord a few inches behind the ears with any sharp instrument, as a pin or small knife blade, death will immediately follow. Below will be found a brief description of the more important diseases and injuries of the nervous system.

SUNSTROKE.

Sunstroke occurs during the hot months of summer. It is a greater or less congestion of the brain, causing either partial or complete loss of motion, and often of sensation.

Causes.—Causes which lay an animal liable to suffer from an attack are high feeding, irregular exercise, an insufficient supply of good water, badly ventilated stables, debility, etc. The direct cause is exposure to the sun during very hot weather, and more especially if the animal is doing heavy work, or is put to severe exertion of any kind. An animal in perfect health may suffer from an attack of sunstroke, but is not so liable to, as an animal debilitated from any cause whatever.

Symptoms.—Generally before the trouble becomes well marked, there is an unusual dullness on the part of the animal, and as a rule he does not sweat as he should when put to exertion. The immediate attack is manifested suddenly. The animal stops, drops his head, begins to stagger, and soon falls to the ground unconscious. The pulse is very slow and irregular, cold sweats break out on different parts of the body, the breathing is laboured and snoring, and the animal often dies without recovering consciousness.

Treatment.—The treatment, to be successful, must be prompt and energetic. If the animal is out in the sun, put a shade over him and give a good stimulant, as:

Sweet spirits of nitre	1 ounce.
Whisky	6 ounces.
Water	1 pint.

Mix, and give as a drench, and repeat in one hour if necessary.

Apply cold to the head in the form of pounded ice or cold water in cloths, and blanket the body and hand-rub and bandage the legs. If the animal can't swallow, stimulants as given above may be injected into the rectum where absorption will take place to a certain extent. Prop up the horse so he will rest on his breast bone. If he begins to improve, give him one dram of nux vomica in damp feed for several days, night and morning. The animal must be used very carefully the remainder of the summer after an attack of sunstroke.

HEATSTROKE.

Heatstroke also occurs during the hot months of summer. It is quite similar to sunstroke, only that it is not produced by the direct rays of the sun.

Causes.—Exhaustion produced by long continued heat is often the cause, and may properly be called heat exhaustion. Race horses on the track undergoing continued and severe work in hot weather often succumb to this trouble.

Symptoms.—For sometime previous to an attack, the animal usually requires urging, usually ceases to sweat and then becomes weak in his gait, the breathing hurried and panting, eyes watery and bloodshot, nostrils dilated, the pulse is rapid and weak, the heart bounding, followed by unconsciousness and usually death. If death should not take place, recovery usually extends over a long period of time, during which paralysis of the muscular system may persist.

Treatment.—The treatment of this affection is about the same as that of sunstroke, with the exception that instead of applying cold to the head, heat in the form of cloths wrung out of hot water is found to be of benefit. In both troubles, after recovery begins a good tonic is needed, as our Condition Powders, given in the usual size doses for several days. Use the animal with care and feed carefully for sometime after an attack.

HEAD STAGGERS.

Causes.—As a rule it is due to some lesion of the brain, caused by temporary congestion, cerebral tumors, tight-reigning, stomach derangements, etc. A lack of blood to the brain may also cause it.

Symptoms.—While being driven, the animal suddenly stops, elevates his head, staggers about from one side of the road to the other, becomes unmanageable, and falls to the ground. After lying down awhile, he gets up, stares about in a vacant manner, shakes himself, and apparently is all right. It is liable to come on a horse that is subject to it at any time.

Treatment.—Give a good physic, and apply cold water to the head. Also give 4 drams of bromide of potash to quiet the nervous system. Some animals have but one attack, while others are subject to it.

STRINGHALT.

Stringhalt is a violent spasmodic jerking, or an irregular movement of one or both hind limbs, while the animal is in motion. Very rarely it may be found to affect one of the fore limbs.

Causes.—It is caused by some lesion or derangement of the nervous system. What this derangement may be is no easy matter to determine. It is no doubt due to irregular distribution of nervous influence to the muscles that bend and extend the limb affected. This may be brought about by pressure on some part of the nervous system, as from tumors, blood clots, etc.

Symptoms.—It is manifested by a sudden jerking up of one or both hind legs when the animal is in motion. This symptom may be very slight in some horses, but has a tendency to get worse with the age of the animal. In some the jerking up of the leg is very violent, the foot in some cases even striking the belly, and when it is lowered to the ground the motion is equally sudden and forcible. It is a difficult disease to understand, and the affection constitutes an unsoundness. Most cases develop gradually, but a case may develop in a very short time.

Treatment.—This is an incurable disease, therefore we can't recommend any treatment. There is an operation sometimes performed that occasionally gives relief, but we can't recommend it, therefore we will not describe it.

PARALYSIS—PALSY.

Paralysis is the loss of the power of motion, either with or without the loss of sensation. It usually comes on suddenly, hence has been described as a "stroke," but occasionally it comes on slowly. Paralytic affections are of two kinds: the "perfect" and the "imperfect." The former includes those in which both motion and sensation are lost, causing death very quickly; the latter those in which only one or the other is lost or diminished. It may again be described as "general" and "partial." The latter being divided into "hemiplegia," paralysis of one side of the body, and "paraplegia," paralysis of the hind quarters of the body. The latter form is the kind usually seen in animals. When only a small portion of the body is affected, as the face, a limb, the tail, etc., it is known as local paralysis.

Causes.—The causes are many. Most of the affections of the brain and spinal cord may lead to paralysis, such as injuries, tumors, disease of the blood vessels of the brain, etc. Pressure upon, or cutting in two of, a nerve causes paralysis of the parts to which the nerve is distributed.

Symptoms.—In general paralysis the power of motion and sensation is lost and death soon follows. Hemiplegia is paralysis of one lateral half of the body. In severe cases the animal will go down and be unable to rise, death taking place in a short time; or he may live for several days and then die or he may recover. In mild cases he will not go down, but will drag the front and hind foot on the side paralyzed. In paraplegia the hind parts only are affected. In severe cases the animal can not rise at all, while in mild cases he may rise but will drag his hind feet more or less in walking. There may be local paralysis of the face, of the lips, of the tail, and other parts of the body.

Treatment.—If treatment is thought advisable, give a good physic, such as reccommended for inflammation of the brain. If the animal is much excited give him 4 drams of bromide of potassium every four hours in the drinking water, or as a drench. If the animal is inclined to improve, give him 1 dram of powdered nux vomica night and morning in damp feed. Give bran, grass, fodder, hay, boiled oats, etc., to eat and plenty of cool water. In paraplegia rub our Liniment (see Appendix) well on his hips and loins three times a day, also apply blankets wrung out of hot water. In local paralysis rub the affected parts well two or three times a day with our Liniment. In cases that recover it may takes months to do so.

CONCUSSION OF THE BRAIN.

Concussion of the brain may take place in any animal, and occurs in a variety of ways.

Causes.—It is usually caused, in the horse, by the animal running away and striking his head against some hard object in a violent manner, rearing up and falling backwards, passing through a low doorway, blows, etc. Sometimes the bones of the skull are fractured and death soon follows.

Symptoms.—If the animal has run away and fallen, he will be insensible to pain and unable to rise and walk. The pupil of the eye will be enlarged, the temperature of the body is considerably lower than in health, the breathing is snoring, etc. In an hour or so the patient may show signs of returning consciousness, and usually makes an effort to rise exactly like a cow, hind legs first. If the pulse is strong, pretty good hopes of recovery may be expected in a few hours or even a few minutes.

Treatment.—Apply cold applications to the head, as ice or cold water, blanket and hand-rub the body, and bandage the legs. Give stimulants, as 1 ounce sweet nitre, 2 ounces alcohol, and water one-half pint. Mild cases generally recover in a short time, while in severe cases there may be fracture of the skull and death in a short time. Keep the patient as comfortable as possible and sometimes recoveries take place where all loooked hopeless.

ENCEPHALITIS—INFLAMMATION OF THE BRAIN.

This is an inflammation of the whole of the brain. It is also known as "phrenitis."

Causes.—Among the causes to be mentioned are exposure to extreme heat or cold, long continued brain excitement, direct injury to the brain, such as concussion, or fracture of the bones of the skull, from blows, etc. The character of the food, such as over-ripe grasses, decomposing roots, certain poisonous weeds or plants, etc., will produce it; in fact, mouldy or bad food of any kind. Tumors or abscesses forming in the brain also operate as causes of encephalitis.

Symptoms.—The symptoms vary in different cases. In most cases the animal assumes a dull, listless attitude, but is easily excited by a little noise, after which he soon relapses into his former dull, sleepy mood. When standing quietly in a box stall, he usually rests his head against the wall or the manger. In other cases the breathing becomes stertorous (snoring), the pulse becomes quickened, the eyes bloodshot, and the poor animal, in a state of frenzy (crazy), will knock himself about in the most violent manner. Sometimes the animal will lie on his side and keep pawing for hours. At other times he will try to place his fore leg over his head, or may stand until his nose comes in contact with the ground. Again he will raise his head, rear up, and make frantic efforts to climb up the wall or manger. In other cases he will continue to walk in a circle for hours at a time, and it is next to impossible to make him go in any other direction; in fact, it seems impossible for the animal to walk in a straight line. The frenzy is well marked, and when present he bites and tears at any object in his reach.

Pigs fed on refuse from kitchen, and cows fed on slops, also suffer from encephalitis. Over-ripe grasses, or too rich food, will also cause it in cattle.

Treatment.—In a great may cases of this disease the animal is so wild or "crazy-like" that it is almost impossible to give any medicine, and unless you can get the bowels moving freely with a good physic there is not much hopes for the animal ever recovering. Try and give the following:

Powdered Barbadoes aloes	1 ounce.
Powdered ginger	2 drams.
Calomel	2 drams.
Bromide of potash	6 drams.
Water	1 pint.

Mix, and shake well, and give as a drench.

The above ingredients, except the water, may be made into a bolus with vaseline and put down over the root of the tongue. Keep the animal in as quiet a place as possible and where he can't injure himself. Keep a bucket of cool water before him all the time, into which put 6 drams of bromide of potash to quiet nervous excitability. A bag of ice or cold cloths applied to the head is soothing to the brain. If the animal should happen to get better, give him 1 dram of powdered nux vomica in damp feed for two weeks, morning and night.

HYSTERIA.

Hysteria is a disease of the nervous system, characterized by a highly nervous and excitable condition. It is usually observed in mares and bitches.

Causes.—The cause is supposed to be a change of some kind taking place in connection with the generative system.

Symptoms.—Excitement is a well marked symptom. One peculiar symptom is continual neighing, with a sort of hiccough, in some cases, caused by spasm. In some cases there is a whitish or reddish discharge from the vulva. Hysteria usually occurs about the time of the animal coming into heat, but has been noticed in pregnant mares. These symptoms usually last for one or two days, and disappear without anything having been done. The appetite, in some cases, is interfered with; the animal often urinates, etc.

Treatment.—Give the following:

Calomel	2 drams.
Bromide of potassium	4 drams.
Raw linseed oil	1 pint.

Mix, and give as a drench.

Give 4 drams of bromide of potassium morning, noon, and night until relieved. Keep the animal quiet, and give a light, laxative diet. One ounce of laudanum or one-half ounce of fluid extract of belladonna may be given to quiet the animal.

EPILEPSY—FALLING FITS.

Epilepsy is occasionally observed in the horse, but is more frequently seen among dogs, when it is generally called fits. The attacks may be quite frequent, or may occur only once or twice a year.

Causes.—Softening of the brain may cause it. In dogs, the cause is some irritation or derangement of the bowels, as worms, etc.

Symptoms.—The attack is indicated by a well-marked convulsive fit. The animal suddenly staggers, falls to the ground, froths at the mouth, etc., the attack lasting for three or four minutes, after which he gets up, walks about in a dull manner, and in a short time is apparently all right.

Treatment.—About the same treatment as that indicated for Hysteria.

APOPLEXY.

Apoplexy is not a very common trouble in the horse, but quite often seen among pigs. It is more commonly seen in fat animals not getting much exercise.

Causes.—It is due to an arrest of the circulation of the blood in the brain, caused by a rupture of some of the blood vessels, or the formation of a small blood-clot, etc.

Symptoms.—It is suddenly developed with loss of sensation and motion, profound stupor, difficult breathing, etc. Sometimes partial paralysis is present.

Treatment.—Give a good physic and follow it up with bromide of potash in 4-dram doses. Apply cold water to the head, and keep the patient in a comfortable, quiet place.

BLIND STAGGERS.

Blind staggers of horses is a disease occurring with greater frequency in the Southern States of our country than in the North. It usually attacks but few horses at a time, but in certain years prevails to such an extent as to attack numbers of animals at the same time and place.

Causes.—Blind staggers is not contagious, as some suppose, but is a disease intimately connected with the character of the food. No doubt the most common cause of this disease is corn that is damaged in some way; such as mouldy, rusty, or smutty corn; or corn that is worm-eaten, rotten, or blasted, etc. Damaged grain or fodder of any kind, such as the result of very wet seasons, is quite sure to produce "Staggers." Some have noticed it in horses that have not had any grain. The mould, or fungus, which produces the disease is very common during wet seasons. It is not believed that any one species of fungus growth is entirely responsible for the disease, as several species of moulds, rusts, and smuts possess such poisonous properties. The green pencil mould is the fungus which is much the most abundant in our cornfields and cribs, and is no doubt the chief cause of Staggers resulting from feeding unsound corn. In those cases of the disease in horses not fed on grain, the same or other fungus growths may be found in the hay, pasture grasses, ensilage, etc.

Symptoms.—About the first thing noticed by the owner is weakness in the hind quarters, and a staggering gait when walking. Colicy pains may precede this symptom. Walking in a circle, reeling, drowsiness or stupor, blindness, leaning or pushing the head against some object, and occasionally more or less frenzy, are all symptoms which may be seen in this disease.

Other cases are entirely different, the horse showing no "brain symptoms" until a short time before death. Paralysis usually begins in the hind quarters and extends forward. In some cases the animal can not swallow, and the bowels are usually constipated. Few cases recover and death usually takes place in from one to three days. But in some cases a slow and imperfect recovery takes place.

Prevention and Treatment.—As the cause of the disease is in feeding musty or mouldy corn, oats, hay, etc., the prevention must be to do away with all inferior or damaged feed. Moulded or smutty ears of corn should never be fed to horses. As there is little that can be done after a horse takes blind staggers, it is all important to try and prevent it by being careful with the feed. In mild cases a good purgative may be given, such as is prescribed for constipation. Also give 1 dram of iodide of potassium, and 1 dram of powdered nux vomica night and morning. In bad cases there isn't much that can be done.

CEREBRO-SPINAL MENINGETIS.

This disease is quite similar to blind staggers and is considered by some to be one and the same disease. It is an inflammation of the spinal cord, brain and coverings.

Causes.—It is said to be caused by the influence of the air, bad ventilation, etc. Among the exciting causes are food and water containing vegetable and animal matter in a decayed or putrid state, which have a poisonous effect on the system and produces the disease. Other causes which might be mentioned are: decomposing roots, brewers' grains, oats, hay, etc.

Symptoms.—The symptoms of this disease vary considerably, according to the part or parts most affected. It is so similar to "Staggers," spoken of before, that it requires an expert to distinguish the one from the other. There may be loss of power, spasm, and twitching of the muscles, either of the hind quarters or those of the head and neck. In very severe cases, the animal reels about, falls, and is unable to rise; the bowels are constipated and urine scanty, etc. In some cases well-marked brain trouble is present, the animal is dull and drowsy, and becomes quiet; this may soon be followed by convulsions and death.

Treatment.—The treatment of this disease is not satisfactory, most of the cases dying. Where there is complete loss of power, they always die. The preventative treatment consists in changing the food and water. If thought advisable to treat this disease, you may use about the same treatment as that given for Blind Staggers.

If the animal has any difficulty in swallowing, one-fourth-grain doses of sulphate of atropine may be injected under the skin every four, six, or eight hours, as the case may demand. The application of blisters to the spine, neck, throat, etc., may be found very beneficial. After giving a physic, and the animal is very excitable, 1 to 2 drams of the solid extract of belladonna may be alternated every four hours with 4 drams of bromide of potash. In cases of unconsciousness allow the animal to inhale ammonia water from a sponge. Allow all the cool water the animal will drink, and, if necessary, support them in slings.

SPINITIS—SPINAL MENINGITIS.

This is inflammation of the substance of the spinal cord, and if the coverings of the cord are also affected it is known as spinal meningitis.

Causes.—Anything affecting the brain may also affect the cord. It may be induced by irritant properties of blood poisons, exhaustion, spinal concussion, exposure, all forms of injury to the spine, tumors, rheumatism, etc.

Symptoms.—In the worst form of the disease the animal shows very great nervous irritation, sweating very freely, which would almost lead one to suspect that it was bowel trouble. He may fall to the ground, unable to rise without assistance. When upon his feet, he looks at his side—again suggesting a bowel trouble. When lying down he struggles violently to get up, and when up he makes the most frantic efforts to retain the standing position, but can not. Sometimes a bone is broken in the attempt to remain standing. The animal may die in twenty-four or forty-eight hours from the first appearance of the attack. In the milder forms these symptoms are not so prominent.

Treatment.—This is a disease that is not very successfully treated only in mild cases. When due to an injury and the back is broken, have the animal killed. A purgative may be given where there is any hope of recovery, and 1 dram of nitrate of potassium and 4 drams of bromide of potassium may be given three times a day. After the acute symptoms have passed, give 1 dram of nux vomica morning and night for several days. Hot cloths should be applied to the spine and our Liniment well rubbed in three times a day over the whole length of the spinal cord. Good care is very necessary. Not many cases of this disease will get well.

LOCKJAW—TETANUS.

This disease is commonly known as lockjaw, but Tetanus is a better name, as in many cases the jaws are not set. It is a very fatal disease of the horse, as very few severe cases ever recover.

Causes.—It was until recently supposed to be caused by some injury or lesion of the nervous system, but now it is known to be caused by a specific microbe (bacillus of Nicholaier), which must gain access to the animal's body before the disease can be produced. This microbe, or bacillus, is found in many soils, barnyard manure, filth, dirt, on rusty nails, partly-masticated food, etc. When this microbe once gets into the system it produces a toxine (poison), which acts like strychnine on the spinal cord, producing the tonic muscular spasms which are always seen in lockjaw. The disease is more often seen following a nail in the foot or any sore or wound in the foot, through which the microbe gains access to the system. It may follow any wound or operation in any part of the body, or may come on without any wound or sore being present.

Symptoms.—The disease may set in twenty-four hours after the microbes get into the animal's body, or it may be from eight to fourteen days. After once seen, the disease is generally easily detected. At first there is more or less stiffness, slight elevation of the tail and poking out of the nose. When you excite the animal, these tonic muscular spasms are plainly seen, as well as the haw flashing over the eye. The jaws may or may not be set, but as a general thing they are set. The haw flashing over the eye, due to nervous spasms, is a never failing symptom of tetanus.

We have seen cases where the owner said his horse had the hooks, but it was a mild case of the tetanus.

If by going in front of an animal and frightening him or raising his head quickly the haw flashes over the eye and the animal gets somewhat excited, it is an unmistakable sign that he has or is getting the lockjaw. When the jaws are firmly set the animal can not eat at all—only suck a little water or liquid food between his teeth. They are generally great sufferers, as a look at their expression and action shows signs of severe agony.

Treatment.—Almost every medicine in the pharmacopoeia has been tried in the treatment of tetanus (lockjaw), and the only one we can recommend as of any use is hyposulphite of soda. It must be remembered that perfect quietude in a darkened stall is very necessary. Have it perfectly quiet about the stall, as the least noise will excite the animal and aggravate the disease. Have no one go about the stall but one man who is caring for the horse. Put 4 drams of hyposulphite of soda in a bucket of drinking water three times a day and have the bucket of water before the horse all the time so he can drink when he wants to. As the jaws are genearlly locked, the only nourishment the animal can take is water and sloppy food. Keep such sloppy food as bran, boiled oats, linseed tea, etc., before him, very wet and sloppy, all the time. If the animal is very excitable, give him dissolved in the drinking water 2 drams of bromide of potassium with the hyposulphite of soda three times per day. Don't try to drench the horse, as that excites him too much. Keep up the hyposulphite of soda until the animal is well. Of course we don't claim this remedy will cure every case nor a majority of cases, but we do claim it will cure where all other remedies fail. It is inexpensive and easily given. It will after a few days regulate the bowels and kidneys, so don't feel uneasy if they are not moving at first. The legs may swell and the hair come out all over the body, but don't feel uneasy about that, as that will all come right if the animal lives. It may take two or four weeks to cure an animal with lockjaw, but don't despair, as there is hope as long as there is life. If the disease is due to an injury or nail in the foot, it should be cleaned out and washed clean and dressed daily with

Iodine	1 part.
Iodide of potassium	2 parts.
Distilled water	100 parts.

Mix, and apply to the sore once or twice a day.

If at the very beginning of an attack, and before there is much excitement, the following treatment has proved quite successful in many cases: A good physic containing 2 drams of the solid extract of belladonna may be given in the form of a ball or as a drench; or dissolve the physic in a small quantity of oil and throw it back on the back part of the animal's tongue with a syringe. In no case force medicine down the horse's throat if there is difficulty in swallowing. In such cases give the following every four, six, or eight hours, according to the excitement of the animal:

Sulphate of atropine	¼ grain.
Sulphate of morphine	5 grains.
Distilled water	1 dram.

Mix, and inject under the skin.

Also, injections per rectum of the following may be given every four or six hours:

Fluid extract of belladonna	1 dram.
Indian hemp	1 dram.
Milk or gruel	1 quart.

Mix.

Sprinkle the stall or room the horse is in once a day with carbolic acid 1 ounce, water 1 gallon. There is a preparation called Tetanus Antitoxin, that is of rather recent discovery, that is proving to be a very valuable agent in the treatment of this disease in the hands of the veterinary profession. It is a serum preparation and is injected under the skin to destroy the toxin (poison) caused by the germs of the disease. This antitoxin is but little used as yet in the South, and is rather expensive to use on the common class of horses in Texas.

CHAPTER X.

DISEASES OF THE EYE.

We can scarcely overestimate the value of sound eyes in the horse, and hence all diseases and injuries of the eye, if they prove permanent, will greatly depreciate the usefulness and value of the horse. A blind horse is always dangerous in the saddle or in single harness. Again, a horse with partial sight or impaired vision that sees things imperfectly, or imagines he sees things that are not present, is still more dangerous than a totally blind horse.

SIMPLE, OR EXTERNAL OPTHALMIA.

This is a disease nearly always caused by an injury and is an inflammation of the lining membrane (conjunctiva) of the eye, and if neglected will in many instances cause great trouble.

Causes.—It may be caused by blows with whips, clubs, or twigs, the presence of foreign bodies like hay-seeds, grassburrs, chaff, dust, lime, sand, etc. Foul air from badly kept stables or keeping a horse in a dark, damp stable and sudden exposure to the bright sunlight may cause the trouble.

Symptoms.—The eye is partially or completely closed, watering of the eye, swollen lids, redness of the mucus membrane, etc. After a short time the whole cornea may turn a bluish or whitish color, and a thick, yellow deposit may take place in the lower part of the eye. If due to a direct injury to the cornea a white spot can be plainly seen on the cornea. This bluish or whitish film or scum that forms is not on the outside of the eye, but is between the layers of the cornea.

Treatment.—In treating simple ophthalmia it is very essential to find the cause and remove it if possible. If any foreign body, like a grassburr, hayseed, splinter, chaff, etc., is in the eye, remove it. To examine a horse's eye apply a twitch to the nose and gently part the eyelids with the thumb and forefinger pressed on the middle of the respective lids, or use Eye Speculum

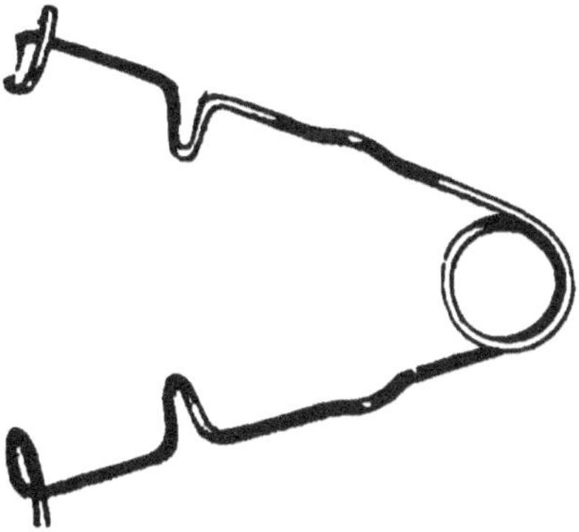

Fig 17. Eye Speculum, used to open the eye for examining and operating on the eye.

(Fig. 17). After removing any foreign substance, if there is much fever bathe the eye freely with warm water in winter, and cold water in summer, and apply as directed some of our Eye Water (see Appendix) morning and evening. If taken in time, this treatment will remove all inflammation and all white spots and whitish films from the cornea.

THE HAW—MEMBRANE NICTITANS.

The haw is an appendage of the eye placed there by nature for the express purpose of removing any foreign substance, as dust, cinders, sand, or anything that may get on the eyeball and cause pain. The haw, sometimes called "washer of the eye," is supplied by nature to the eyes of all animals and birds, except man and the monkey tribe, which use their hands or paws for that purpose. In the normal restful state of the eye only the thin anterior edge of the haw can be seen at the inner angle of the eye, but when by some cause the eyeball is pushed back into its socket or drawn back by muscular contraction it can be plainly seen projecting over and partially or completely covering the eyeball. When foreign bodies, such as sand, dust, chaff, etc., get into the eye it is projected to push them out, their expulsion being favored by a free flow of tears. In lockjaw, the haw is plainly seen projecting over the eye by the muscular contraction in each spasm, and it is also seen in a lesser extent in all painful inflammations of the eye. The projection of the haw, no matter from what cause, is universally known, by people not familiar with the anatomy and diseases of the horse, as the "hooks."

HOOKS.

Hooks, like bots, and hollow horn, is not recognized by the Veterinary Profession as a disease. It is no disease, but is simply a symptom of some disease. What is universally known as hooks by most of the horsemen in this country is the projection of the haw (read the article on the haw) partially or completely over the eyeball as the result of some disease. It is a symptom of lockjaw, inflammation, or a foreign substannce in the eye. If due to a foreign substance, such as sand, chaff, cinders, dust, etc., remove it and bathe with hot water. If due to inflammation, bathe with hot water and apply morning and night some of Dr. Le Gear's Eye Water (see Appendix), which will cure it in a few days. The cruel practice of cutting out the "hooks," as a supposed cure by some men, is brutal in the least, and should not be tolerated. What they cut out is the haw, or part of it, and when removed the eye's greatest protection is gone, therefore the value of the horse is depreciated to a considerable extent. Only in very rare and extreme cases is it ever necessary to remove the haw or a portion of it, and that is when it is greatly ulcerated or diseased by a tumor. If removed at all, it should be done by a qualified veterinary surgeon. We would advise all horse owners to use no other treatment than warm water and Dr. LeGear's Eye Water, as that will cure nine out of every ten cases of the would-be disease "hooks."

PERIODIC OPHTHALMIA.

This disease causes more blind horses in Texas than any other disease, and is characterized by the suddenness of the attack and the reappearing of the disease in a few weeks, a few months, or perhaps not before several years. By some it is called "moon-blidness," or "moon eyes," as the changes of the moon was formerly thought to be the cause of the recurring attacks.

Causes.—The causes of this disease are sometimes pretty hard to account for. There exists within the system, a predisposition to the disease; in other words, the disease must exist within the system in a latent form, which must take some exciting cause to bring it out, as overheating by driving or working, extremes of heat and cold, improperly ventilated and badly lighted stables, poor food, debilitating diseases, etc. This is one of the hereditary diseases, as a sire or dam affected with the disease nearly always transmits it to their offspring. We would strongly urge all breeders of fine horses never to use a mare or stallion for breeding purposes that has weak eyes or blindness. Lexington, one of the greatest race horses and sires America ever produced, went blind from over work, and a large number of his colts became blind from Periodic Ophthalmia. A horse may have several attacks of the disease and still the eye not be much changed, while again two or three severe attacks may cause total blindness.

Symptoms.—The disease is very sudden in its attacks. Your horse may be all right at night, but in the morning he may have one or both eyes swollen, and sore and discharging great quantities of tears. As a rule, one eye is generally affected at a time, and it may have half a dozen attacks or more and go blind; then the other eye is liable to become affected in the same way. After each attack the eyeball becomes smaller and the eyelid more shrunken, and the cornea gradually becomes of a bluish white color. The attacks vary greatly in severity in different cases, but all cases finally terminate in cataract and blindness.

Treatment.—The treatment of the disease is not satisfactory, as there is no known remedy that is a sure cure for the disease, and the animal is very liable, sooner or later, to go blind. The object of treatment, therefore, is to lessen the severity of the attacks, and try to ward off the occurrence of the same. The treatment consists of local applications to the eye and medicine given internally for the blood and nerves. Give as a drench 1 pint of raw linseed oil, and follow up with one-half dram of powdered colchicum every morning and 1 dram of iodide of potassium every night in damp feed. Give the colchicum and iodide of potassium for four or five days, and then give regular for ten days one teaspoonful morning and night of Dr. LeGear's Condition Powders. (See Appendix.) In the beginning of an attack bathe the eye with warm water and apply a few drops with a soft feather of Dr. LeGear's Eye Water (see Appendix) night and morning. Put the animal in a dark stall, or bind a piece of soft cloth over the eye to keep out the bright light. If this treatment is carried out at each attack, a horse can, in most of cases, be kept from going blind for a long time.

CATARACT.

As there is no successful treatment for Cataract, it will be of no benefit to the reader of this book for us to give a long description of the disease, so we will make it very brief. Occasionally it is caused by a direct injury to the eye, but is invariably the result of Periodic Ophthalmia. Cataract is an opacity of the crystalline lens, or its capsule, and can be recognized by a white spot in the pupil, which spot may be large or small.

Treatment is useless, as it is incurable in the horse.

WHITE SPOTS AND BLUISH WHITE SCUM ON THE CORNEA.

The white spots on the eyes of so many horses are generally due to a lick in the eye with a whip or the like, and the white scum that covers the eye is generally the result of Simple Ophthalmia. If these spots and scums are not too thick and of too long standing they can be removed by using Dr. LeGear's Eye Water twice per day for one or two weeks.

After giving the Eye Water a fair trial and it fails to remove them, try the following lotion:

Nitrate of silver	8 grains.
Sulphate of morphine	5 grains.
Distilled water	1 ounce.

Mix, and apply a few drops into the eye with a camel's hair brush or a feather, morning and night.

ULCERS OF THE CORNEA.

Ulceration of the cornea is generally due to direct injuries, and may be cured by applying Dr. LeGear's Eye Water morning and evening for a few days.

In very bad cases get a stick of solid nitrate of silver, scrape it to a point, and touch the growth on the cornea with it; in a few minutes wash the eye thoroughly with warm sweet milk. Repeat every three days if necessary. Be careful not to touch any other part with the caustic than the growth. Spread the eyelids with the thumb and finger, or use the eye speculum (Fig. 17.)

Or the following lotion may be used:

Sulphate of zinc	5 grains.
Nitrate of silver	12 grains.
Cocaine hydrochlorate	15 grains.
Distilled water	1 ounce.

Mix, and apply a few drops into the eye morning and night.

TUMORS OF THE EYEBALL.

This is rather a rare affection, but is occasionally met with. The tumor may be of a cancerous nature, or only a simple fatty tumor. The only treatment is to have it dissected out as soon as possible, or removed by the use of caustics.

PALSY OF THE NERVE OF SIGHT—AMAUROSIS.

This is a partial or complete blindness as a result of paralysis of the optic nerve (nerve of the eye) without there being much change in the looks of the eye. The eye may look clear and all right and the horse be perfectly blind.

Causes.—It may be caused by tumors or other diseases of the brain; blows on the head that injure the optic nerve. Severe bleeding may cause this trouble, and it is sometimes seen in mares heavy with foal.

Symptoms.—The eyes are clear and sound looking, with the exception that the pupil is generally dilated and round, and the horse can see only partially or not at all. Both eyes are generally affected, except where it is due to an injury of one eye.

Treatment.—The treatment of this disease is not generally successful. Unless taken when first affected, treatment is useless. Give one dram of powdered nux vomica once a day in damp feed and apply a blister behind the ear.

CHAPTER XI.

DISEASES OF THE HEART.

The heart is a hollow, muscular organ, situated in the cavity of the chest, and divided into four compartments, known as the auricles and the ventricles. In form, it resembles a blunt cone, and has an average weight in the horse of six and one-half pounds. The heart is the centre of the circulation of the blood, and like a force pump, it forces the blood to all parts of the body through certain tubes or vessels called arteries; the blood returns to the heart through another set of vessels called veins. The arteries carry the pure blood, which contains nutritive principles, to nourish and build up every living tissue; while the veins in turn carry the blood which is impregnated with impurities of the body back to the heart, thence it goes to the lungs to be purified again by coming in contact with the oxygen of the air.

The heart is a vital organ and has an important work to perform, but the diseases of the same are rather difficult to recognize. Not many of the diseases of the heart can be influenced by treatment, so we will confine ouselves to but a very few of the principal ones.

THE PULSE.

What is the pulse, and where can it be found? It is the beating of the arteries (tubes carrying blood from the heart), which follow each contraction of the heart. The pulse tells you how fast the heart is beating. The artery usually selected in the horse for taking the pulse, is the one (submaxillary) that winds around the lower jawbone. It can be readily felt with the fin-

Fig. 18. The manner of taking the pulse.

gers by gently pressing the artery against the inner side of the jaw, as seen in Figure 18.

In the healthy horse the pulse will beat on an average about 35 a minute; yet in some horses it may only be 30 or even 40 and the animal be in perfect health. The breed and temperament of an animal has a great deal to do with the number of pulse beats. In a thoroughbred the number of beats is generally greater than in a coarse-bred horse. The pulse is less frequent in a dull, plethoric animal than in an excitable one. The pulse rate, then, should always be taken when the animal is quiet and at rest. Work, exercise, etc., increases the number of pulsations. A horse's pulse taken when he is standing quietly in the stable will be found less frequent than when he is at pasture. The number of pulsations in a given time differs considerably in different animals. In cattle the pulse varies in adults from 40 to 50. But in cows it varies considerably from a great many different causes. In the dog the pulse beats from 70 to 80 times per minute.

TEMPERATURE.

It is important in disease to know what the temperature of the body is, and also how to take it. The average temperature of a healthy horse is about (nearly) 100 deg. F. Still it may range

Fig. 19. Clinical or Fever Thermometer.

from 99 deg. to 101 deg. F. The temperature of the body is subject to changes by certain influences. The animal temperature is increased by heat, while cold decreases it. Exercise, work, etc., also increases it. Drinking cold water lowers the animal temperature. It is higher in young animals than in old ones. Mares have a higher temperature than males. During the process of digestion the temperature increases.

The proper and most accurate method of taking the temperature is by means of a registered clinical thermometer (Fig. 19) inserted into the rectum. Before inserting it you should see that the mercury is below the minimum (say 90 degrees). The end containing the mercury should be pushed in gently, leaving only sufficient of the other end outside to take hold of when you desire to withdraw it. The thermometer should be left in the rectum (last gut) from three to four minutes.

The method of taking the temperature by placing the finger in the mouth requires considerable practice and delicacy of touch to become expert, but, when a thermometer is not at hand, a little practice will enable most any person of ordinary intelligence to detect the presence or absence of fever.

The temperature, like the pulse, varies considerably in different animals. The average normal temperature of cattle in confinement is about 101 deg. F.; in cattle at liberty, or oxen at work, it runs up about 102 deg. F. In calves it runs up a little higher, while in very old animals it is lower than the average normal temperature.

PERICARDITIS.

This is an inflammation of the pericardium (sack surrounding the heart), and occurs in all animals, especially cattle.

Causes.—It may be induced by cold and damp stabling, exposure and fatigue, from wounds caused by broken ribs, etc. Pericarditis is often associated with rheumatism, influenza, pleurisy, and other debilitating diseases.

Symptoms.—Usually the disease abruptly manifests itself with pain in moving, a short, painful cough, rapid and short breathing, and high temperature, with a rapid and hard pulse. By placing the ear against the left side of the chest behind the elbow a rasping sound (known as the to-and-fro friction) may be heard. In three or four days this sound may disappear, due to a distention of the pericardium with a watery fluid. When dropsy takes place, death is quite sure to follow.

Treatment.—In the acute form, mix equal parts of tincture of digitalis and tincture of aconite, and give 20 to 30 drops as a drench every hour until the temperature becomes reduced. The body should be clothed in blankets and the legs well bandaged. If considerable pain is present give 2 ounces of tincture of opium once or twice a day as a drench. Put nitrate or bicarbonate of potassa, half an ounce, in drinking water every six hours; after three or four days, iodide of potassa, in 2 dram doses, should be substituted. Besides this, a good mustard plaster may be applied well up the sides of the chest with benefit. Feed on light but highly nutritious food, such as will be easily digested.

CARDITIS.

This is an inflammation of the heart itself, but is usually accompanied by other diseases of the heart. Death is usually the result where the whole or a large part of the heart substance is inflamed. If the inflammation is situated in a small part, recovery may take place.

Treatment.—The treatment is about the same as laid down for pericarditis, which see.

There are many other diseases of the heart, such as endocarditis, hypertrophy, dilatation of, rupture of, valvular disease of, venous regurgitation, foreign bodies in, etc. As it is rather a difficult matter to detect these troubles, and but few of them yield to the best of treatment, we will not give a separate description of them. If treatment is adopted, treat about the same as for pericarditis.

CHAPTER XII.

BONES.

The bones of a vertebrate animal form the skeleton (Plate I.), or frame-work upon which the body is built. There are about 216 separate bones; or including the teeth, 256 pieces in the skeleton of a horse. These bones come together by means of joints, and are held in place by ligaments, tendons, and muscles. Bones are divided into long, flat, and irregular bones, for convenience of description. Long bones are found principally in the legs, and are composed of a very hard, compact tissue, in the centre of which is a hollow, called the bone cavity, and filled with a substance called the marrow. In the marrow will be found nerves, blood vessels, lymphatics, and fatty tissue. The bones in the legs of a thoroughbred horse are smaller but stronger than those of the heavy draft, coarse-boned animal.

Bone is composed of earthy matter and animal matter. To the earthy matter it owes its hardness, and to the animal matter its toughness. The relative proportions of earthy and animal matter vary according to age. In the young animal they are about equal, but as age advances the earthy matter becomes more abundant, and in old animals the bones become very brittle and easily broken. In the trouble known as rickets, the earthy salts are wanting, and, as the animal matter predominates, the bones are soft and bend easily. Bones are surrounded by a fine, fibrous enveloping membrane (the periosteum), which is closely adherent to the external surface of the bone, and is, in fact, the secreting membrane of the bony structure. Below will be found a brief description of the various diseases and injuries to which the bones of the body are liable.

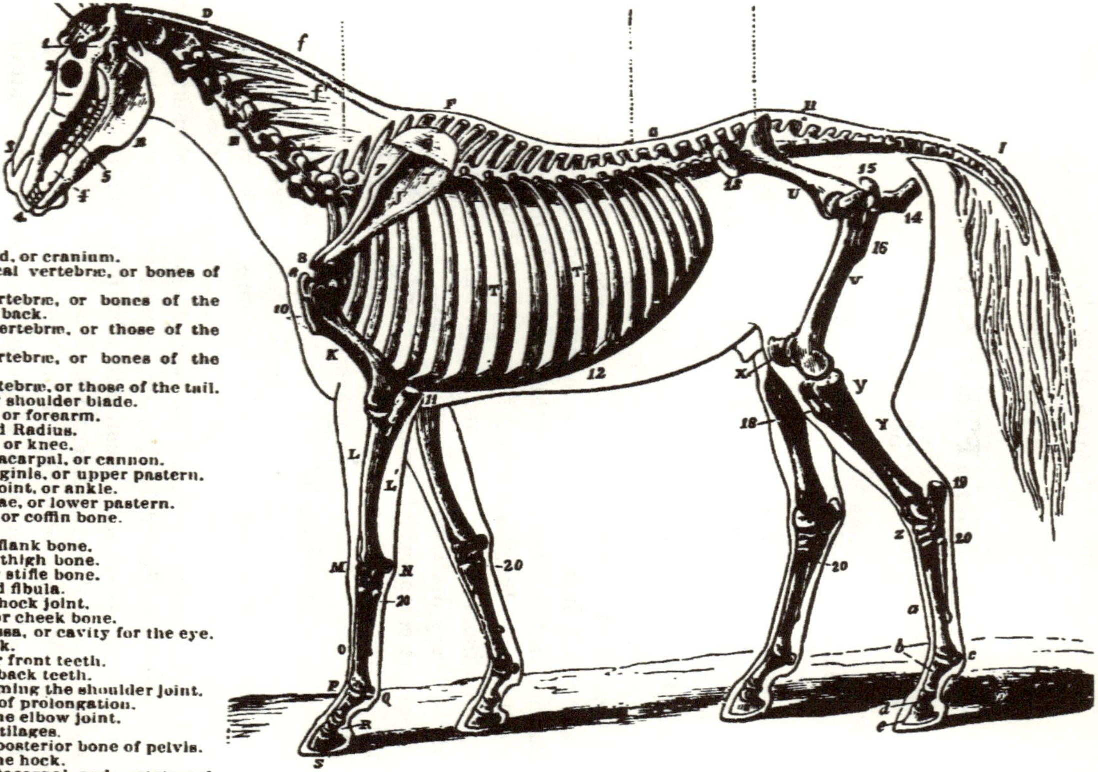

(A B) The head, or cranium.
(C D E) Cervical vertebræ, or bones of the neck.
(F) Dorsal vertebræ, or bones of the withers and back.
(G) Lumbar vertebræ, or those of the loins, etc.
(H) Sacral vertebræ, or bones of the rump.
(I) Caudal vertebræ, or those of the tail.
(J) Scapula, or shoulder blade.
(K) Humerus, or forearm.
(L L) Ulna and Radius.
(M N) Carpus, or knee.
(O) Large Metacarpal, or cannon.
(P b) Os suffraginis, or upper pastern.
(Q c) Fetlock joint, or ankle.
(R d) Os coronae, or lower pastern.
(S e) Os pedis, or coffin bone.
(T T) Ribs.
(U) Ilium, or flank bone.
(V) Femur, or thigh bone.
(X) Patella, or stifle bone.
(Y y) Tibia and fibula.
(Z) Tarsus, or hock joint.
(1) Zygoma, or cheek bone.
(2) Orbital fossa, or cavity for the eye.
(3) Nasal peak.
(4) Incisor, or front teeth.
(5) Molar, or back teeth.
(6, 8) Bones forming the shoulder joint.
(9) Cartilage of prolongation.
(11) Point of the elbow joint.
(12) Costal cartilages.
(14) Ischium, posterior bone of pelvis.
(19) Point of the hock.
(20) Small matacarpal and metatarsal, or splint bones.

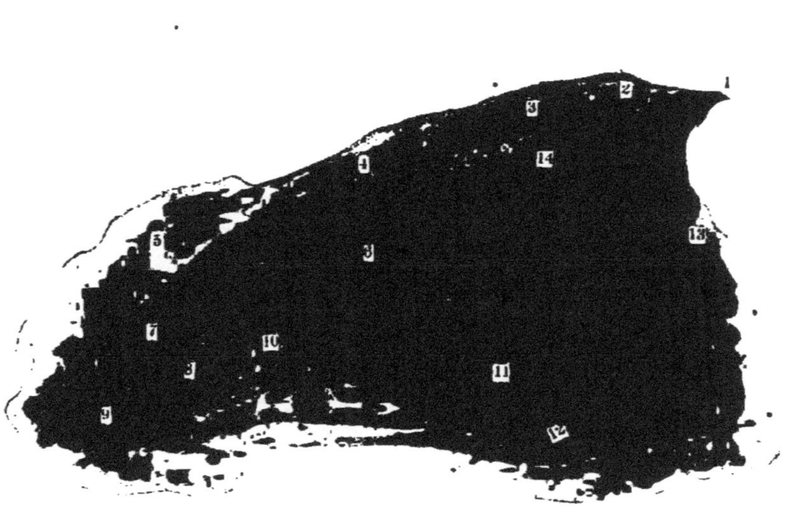

A. CRANIUM OR SKULL OF THE HORSE.

(1) Crest of the occipital bone.
(2) Temporal fossa (cavity).
(3) Frontal bone.
(4) Nasal (nose) bone.
(5) Nasal peak.
(6) Superior maxilla (upper jaw).
(7) Pre-maxilla.
(8) Canine teeth (tusks).
(9) Incisor teeth.
(10) Molar teeth (grinders).
(11) Inferior maxilla (lower jaw).
(12) Angle of lower jaw.
(13) Styloid process.
(14) Orbital fossa (cavity for the eye).

B. BONES OF THE FOOT.

(1) Splint.
(2) Large Cannon.
(3) Sessamoids.
(4) Small Cannon.
(5) Coronary.
(6) Navicular.
(7) Coffin.

PLATE II. SKELETONS OF THE HEAD AND FOOT OF THE HORSE. [p. 151]

FRACTURES.

Fractures are more or less common among the lower animals, but probably occur with greater frequency amongst dogs. They rank among the most serious troubles to which an animal can be subjected. There are several kinds of fractures, which are as follows:

Simple fracture is that form in which the bone is broken in a clean manner, and straight or nearly straight across.

Compound fracture is where the broken ends of the bone separate, pierce the soft tissues, injure the skin, etc.

Comminuted fracture is where the bone is broken in several places or shattered.

Compound comminuted fracture is a combination of the two forms of fracture described above. In this form of fracture the shattered bone also enters the soft tissues, lacerating them to a greater or less extent. Besides the above kinds of fracture, we may have the "complicated," when important blood vessels, nerves, or a joint are involved; an "oblique fracture" is so called on account of the break extending obliquely (slantingly) across the bone. It frequently happens that there is fracture without displacement, being held in place by the periosterim (bone covering) for days or weeks, until complete reunion takes place.

Fractures may occur in a great many ways, and sometimes in a very simple manner; slipping in some cases being sufficient to break a bone. Muscular contraction, during the struggles of an animal when thrown and tied for an operation, is not an uncommon cause of fracture; rearing up and falling backwards is a common cause of fracture of the bones of the neck or back part of the head. External injuries, such as blows, kicks, etc., also cause fractures.

Symptoms.—As a general thing, fractures are easily recognized, but in cases of much swelling it becomes a matter of difficulty to state positively whether a fracture has taken place. Sometimes the fractured ends of the bone may pass each other, when it is easily recognized, as it can be felt with the fingers, or even detected with the eye. On examining a fracture, the broken ends of the bone come into contact, and passing over each other give rise to a grating sound. In some cases this sound is very plain, but in cases of swelling, or where the bone is deeply situated, this grating sound might not be heard.

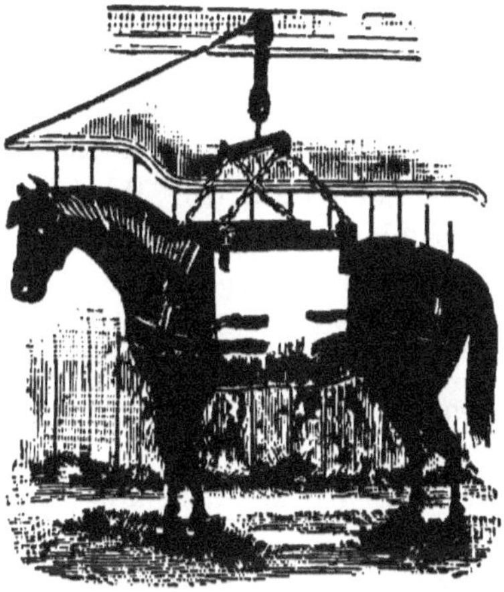

Fig. 20. The Sling.

Treatment.—There is good reason to believe that a fractured bone in the lower animals can be repaired in much less time than would be occupied in the union of a similar fracture occurring in man; but treatment of fracture in the lower animals is rendered a matter of great difficulty on account of the trouble in applying and retaining splints and other appliances; also on account of the difficulty in keeping the patient quiet. Generally speaking, if the animal be of little value it will be well to have it killed and put out of its misery. On the other hand, if the animal be a valuable one and the fracture not too extensive, it may be well to try treatment. The fractured ends of the bone should be brought as nearly together as possible and kept in place by bandages, splints, or other appliances, according to the location and extent of the fracture. If the fracture be in one of the limbs, the animal should be placed in slings (Fig. 20) to keep him quiet and keep the weight off the injured limb. Plaster of paris bandages may be applied by spreading the plaster of paris on a domestic bandage about four inches wide and as long as necessary. Then roll the bandage up and wet it, and apply it snugly to the leg above and below and right over the fracture. When the bandage dries it will get very hard and stiff and make a good support to the broken bone. Bandages wet in starch may be used in place of the above, which work well in some cases.

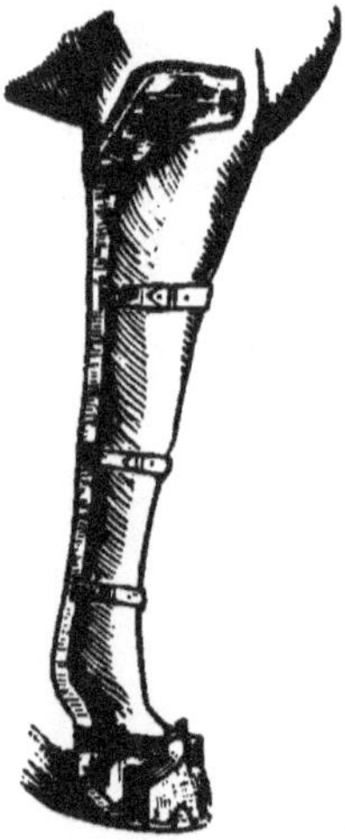

Fig. 21.
Fracture Splint.

Splints may be bound on with bandages of plaster of paris, which in some cases are a great help in keeping the bones in place. Cooling applications should be applied above and below the bandages if any swelling takes place, such as cold water. Also bathe the parts well with our Liniment (see Appendix) two or three times per day. Keep a bucket of cool water before the animal all the time, into which may be dissolved 1 dram of saltpetre twice per day. Keep the bowels moving freely by giving raw linseed oil as a drench. Give bran mashes, chops, boiled oats, green grass, fodder, etc., to eat. Give regularly in the feed morning and night one teaspoonful of our Condition Powders (see Appendix) to purify the blood and aid reunion of the broken bones. Broken legs in dogs can generally be successfully treated by applying a plaster of paris bandage nicely to the parts and keeping the animal quiet for two or three weeks. It generally takes from one to three months for a fracture to unite in a horse, so don't be in too big a hurry to put the animal to work after you think a fracture is healed. A horse may be kicked on the inside of the hind leg just above the hock, and although the bone is cracked or broken it may not separate for one or two weeks, and then the bone gives way and the leg breaks clear off. Why it remains in place so long is because the periosteum (covering of the bone) is so thick in this location. If a horse gets kicked in this place he should be kept perfectly quiet for two or three weeks to give the bones a chance to unite if they are broken. If any of the bones of the leg become broken clear off and the bones come through the skin, it is advisable to kill the animal at once, as a recovery is hopeless.

RICKETS—RACHITIS.

Rickets, or rachitis, occurs in young animals of all kinds, but is more common in puppies than the young of other animals. It is due to a lack of lime salts, or an excess of animal matter, in the bones.

Causes.—It has a tendency to occur among the offspring of stallions or dogs that have been overdone in stud service, and is more likely to appear in weakly or unhealthy animals. Weaning the animal at too early a period, and forcing him to eat food that is only fit for an old animal to eat, or milk deficient in certain elements received from the mother, may also be mentioned as causes of rickets.

Symptoms.—The bones of the limbs are seen to bend unnaturally; the fore-legs may bend outward and the hind ones bend inward; and in the horse there is a tendency to curb, bog-spavin, etc., and the joints usually become enlarged. There is also weakness and debility, and in a well marked case affecting the horse the fetlock may descend nearly to the ground on the outside, with stiffness and difficulty in progression.

Treatment.—The treatment of this trouble must be both local and constitutional. If the mother's milk is the cause by not being rich enough, increase her feed, and let it be of the very best quality: wheat bran, ground oats, good hay, fodder, grass, etc. Give the mother the following:

Powdered sulphate of iron	1 ounce.
Powdered gentian	2 ounces.
Quinine	4 drams.
Anise seed	2 drams.

Mix, and make eight powders, and give one in her feed night and morning.

She will impart strength to the colt from the medicine through her milk. Support the weakened legs with nice soft bandages. Keep the colt in a comfortable place and nature will do a great deal in forming a cure. Give the puppy bones to gnaw on; lime water and cod liver oil will be found beneficial.

CARIES.

This is decay or death of bone in small particles. The bones of the spine (backbone) are often affected, as in poll-evil and fistula. The bones oftenest affected in the extremities are the bones of the hock, the pastern, and navicular bones. A dried specimen of decayed bone presents a dry, worm-eaten appearance. In the hock-joint caries is associated with spavin, and in the navicular bone with navicular disease. Caries is sometimes accompanied by a discharge of a very offensive odor.

Treatment.—If it is in connection with fistula or poll-evil, cut down upon the parts and remove all diseased portions of bone with a bone spoon or pair of bone forceps, and cleanse the ends of the bones with peroxide of hydrogen applied full strength twice a day. If the decay of bone is in a joint, a good stimulating, penetrating blister should be applied, and there is nothing equal to our Spavin Cure (see Appendix) in these cases.

NECROSIS.

This simply means death of bone. It is not very common in the lower animals, and when it does take place it is generally due to some injury. After a bone dies it looks real white, and it seems to be harder than natural, and finally, becoming exposed to the air, it crumbles, separates, and comes away. Necrosis is seen in connection with the lower jaw, caused by the action of the bit. When a portion of bone dies it must be got rid of in some way; if nature fails to remove it, surgical means must be employed.

Symptoms.—After necrosis takes place a kind of material is thrown out which covers the dead portion to a certain extent. After a while a discharge from the affected parts takes place and an abscess is formed, at which time the dead bone is separated from the living, etc. The discharge from decayed bone is very offensive.

Treatment.—Enlarge the opening with a sharp lance and with a pair of forceps or tweezers remove any dead portions of bone that are present. Thoroughly syringe out the cavity with clean water and carbolic acid, 1 to 40. Then wash out the cavity every morning with clean water and inject peroxide of hydrogen, which will cleanse and heal the bone.

SPLINTS.

A splint is a bony enlargement, usually situated on the inside of the leg between the knee or the hock and the fetlock (ankle) joint. Occasionally splints are seen on the outside of a horse's leg. There is what is called the high splint and the low splint, the former being the most serious. Splints are more often seen in young horses.

Causes.—Some colts are more subject to splint than others, owing to their build and action when traveling. External injuries of various kinds, as kicks, blows, cuts, etc., are quite common causes of the trouble. The most productive cause of splint, however, is concussion, due to riding or driving on hard roads. Country horses coming to the city usually develop splint very quickly, and it is very common among city horses. Improper shoeing and allowing the feet to grow out of shape, are conditions which are apt to cause splint, especially if the animal is driven on hard roads.

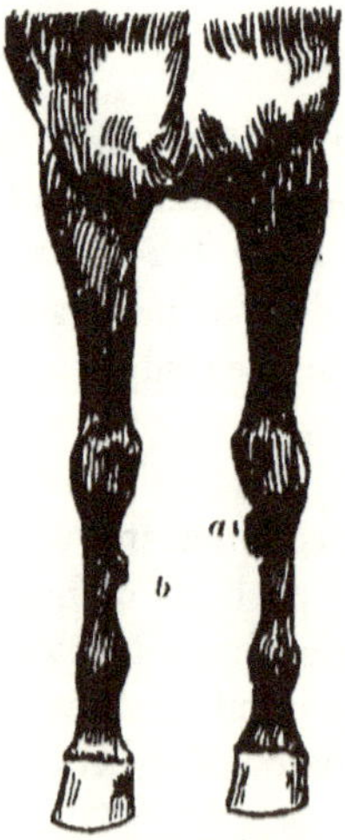

Fig. 22. Splints. (a) High. (b) Low.

Symptoms. — In most cases the animal shows lameness; he walks almost or quite sound, and when trotted he drops on the sound leg, especially if driven on hard ground. The hand should be passed down the sides of the cannon bone of the leg affected, to discover, if possible, any enlargement. This may be of some difficulty, as the enlargement may not be as large as a pea. The presence of heat in the part may be of some use as a guide to discover the trouble. When found, press upon the enlargement with the fingers and observe whether the animal shows or manifests pain; tap upon it and the animal will flinch, and on being trotted out immediately afterwards the lameness is increased. An animal may have very large splints for years and never be lame from them.

Treatment.—Unless a horse is lame from a splint, it is advisable to let it alone. After a horse has had a splint for several months, it becomes solid bone, and there is no medicine that will take it off without seriously injuring the leg. If the splint is taken in time, before it turns to solid bone, it can be removed by using our Spavin Cure (see Appendix) as directed. If taken in time a splint may be rubbed off by thoroughly rubbing it two or three times a day for several weeks. If the animal is lame nothing more is required to cure him than our Spavin Cure well rubbed in according to directions. If the animal is much lame he should have two or three weeks rest during treatment or a run at pasture.

RING-BONE.

A ring-bone is a bony enlargement extending around the leg just above the foot. They are divided into high and low ring-bones. A low ring-bone is one where the bony enlargement comes down under the hoof and affects the coffin-joint, while a high ring-bone affects the pastern joint, and may even affect the ankle joint. It is a false ring-bone when the bony growth does not come on any of the joints. Ring-bone may come on the front or hind legs, but is oftener seen on the hind legs.

Causes.—The most common cause of this trouble is hard and fast work, especially on rough ground or on hard roads. Improper shoeing, blows, kicks, etc., all are causes of ring-bone.

It is a hereditary disease, and will be transmitted to the colts from the sire or dam if they are affected.

Symptoms. — Occasionally a well developed ring-bone will come on a horse without making him lame, but it generally makes him lame from the start and all the time during its growth. In the early stages a ring-bone is sometimes very difficult to detect, but after they are well formed they are very easily seen.

Treatment.—The treatment is similar to that of spavin. Give the animal complete rest for one or two months, and repeatedly blister with our Spavin Cure. If after you have blistered thoroughly for three or four times and the animal is still lame, the only remedy is the operation of firing (see Fig. 26), which should not be undertaken except by a qualified veterinary surgeon. Occasionally after an animal has been repeatedly blistered or fired he still remains lame; but on putting him to work the lameness gradually disappears.

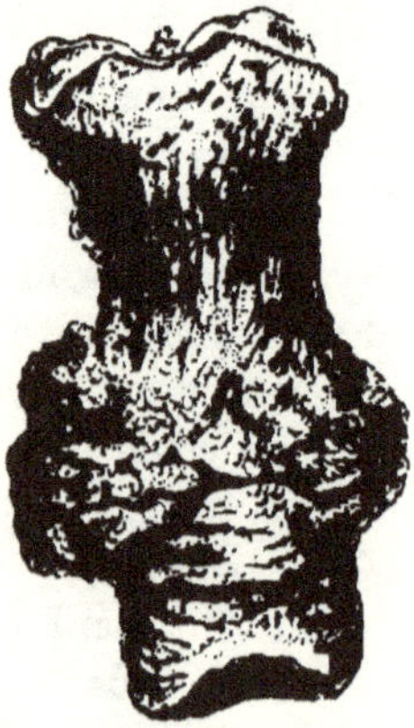

Fig. 23. A Ring-bone.

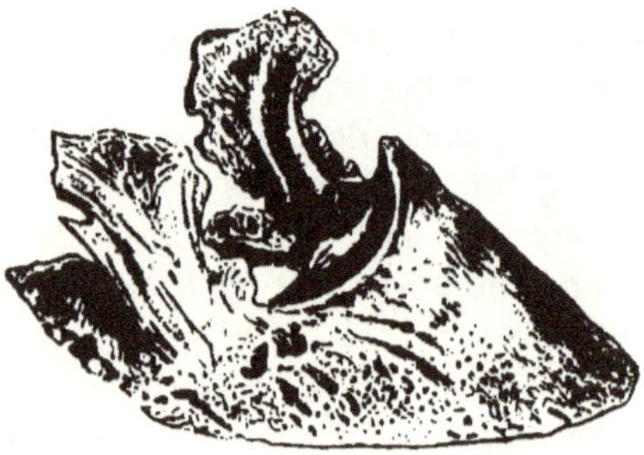

Fig. 24. Side-bones.

SIDE-BONES.

A side-bone is a bony tumor situated on one or both sides of a horse's foot just above the hoof. It is due to ossification (turning to bone) of the lateral cartileges. The lateral cartileges are pads of cartilege (gristle) one on each side of the foot partially inside the hoof, which are so situated that in their natural state they form a spring to the heel while the horse is traveling. In the healthy foot these cartileges are pliable and will spring on being pressed with the fingers. But when, from some cause, they are turned to bone, they are then called side-bones and are enlarged, hardened, and unpliable.

Causes.—Side-bones are caused by hard and fast work upon hard roads. A horse traveling rapidly upon a hard road strikes the road very hard with his feet, which is apt to bruise the foot, set up inflammation in the lateral cartileges which is very likely to turn them to bone. Side-bones are also caused by punctures, bruises, and injuries, as by one horse stepping on the side of his mate's foot, injuring the lateral cartilege and resulting in side-bone.

Symptoms.—Side-bones very seldom come in the hind feet, but are nearly always seen in the front feet. They are more common in heavy draft horses, but are not nearly so serious as when affecting light horses used for driving or riding. In some cases the cartilege turns to bone and remains the natural size, while in others it becomes very much enlarged, making an ugly appearance on the side of the foot. While traveling, the toe of the foot is first brought to the ground, and there is—in case both front feet are affected—a peculiar stilty action and stiffness of gait.

Treatment.—If there is much fever and soreness in the foot, remove it by frequent bathing and poulticing. Give the animal a good long rest. After the inflammation has been relieved, blister the enlargement well with Dr. LeGear's Celebrated Spavin Cure. (See Appendix.) In most cases this will effect a cure. There are some cases that baffle all treatment, and the only relief is to perform the operation of neurotomy. This is an operation which should be undertaken only by a qualified veterinary surgeon.

SPAVIN.

There are two kinds of spavin recognized by the veterinary profession—bone spavin and bog spavin. We will first consider bone spavin, and later on consider bog spavin.

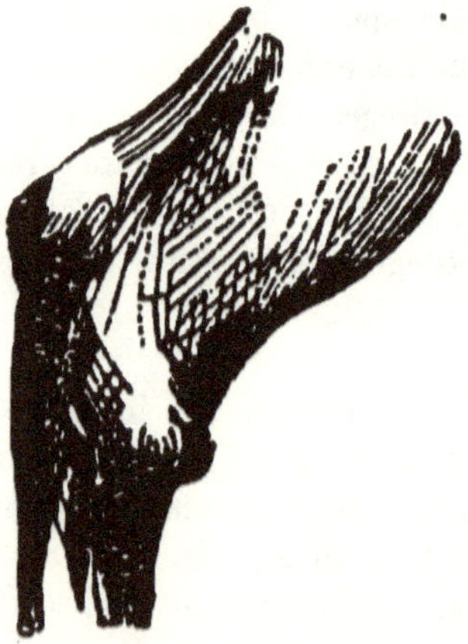

Fig. 25. Bone Spavin.

Bone spavin is a bony growth affecting the hock (gamble) joint. The general location of the enlargement is on the front of the inside of the joint, but the disease may affect the whole joint. It is called high spavin when the enlargement comes on the upper part of the joint; and low spavin when it comes on the lower part of the joint. High spavin is by far the worst disease and much harder to cure. Spavin never comes on the front legs, and only on the hock joints of the hind legs. A horse may be spavined and not show a lump at all on the joint. Such a spavin is called an ocult spavin (not visible), and is a very bad disease, as it affects the true articulations of of the joint.

Causes.—There are various causes of spavin, the most common of which are hard and fast work, straining by slipping in the mud, injuries to the joint, etc. In the case of an injury to one of the hind legs, causing the animal to stand upon the sound leg, the latter becomes liable to spavin in consequence of the extra weight thrown upon it. Spavin is one of the hereditary diseases, and it is a mistake to breed a mare or breed from a stallion affected with the disease, as the colt invariably will be born with weak joints and predisposed to spavin, and will in most cases take the disease after being put to work.

Symptoms.—Spavin is a disease that nearly always comes on very slowly, and when once started it will continue to grow worse unless checked by treatment. The first sign of spavin is slight stiffness or lameness in the affected leg, which will disappear on exercise, but will show again after standing for a few minutes. In some cases the horse will be lame all day, or in fact get worse the farther he goes, but in most cases they will warm out of the lameness after being driven a short distance. On causing the animal to move over in his stall, to move about from side to side, etc., it is noticed that he drops on the affected limb; but on being made to walk or trot it is noticed that he drops on the sound leg. Sometimes the enlargement is seen first, but generally the animal is lame one, two, or three months, or even longer, before the lump can be plainly seen. The lump keeps on growing as long as there is fever, soreness, and lameness present, and sometimes becomes larger than a man's fist. In long standing cases the hip will be perished, making it look as though the disease was in the hip.

If you have a horse lame in one of his hind legs and you can notice nothing wrong in any other part of the leg, it is well to look for spavin, as the hock joint is more liable to disease than any other part of the hind leg. In most cases the horse will knuckle at the ankle in starting off, which may lead you to think the trouble is in the ankle and not in the hock.

Treatment.—There is no medicine better than Dr. LeGear's Spavin Cure in the treatment of spavin. If it used soon enough, before the disease gets too old, and used according to directions, it will cure every time. Rest is very necessary in treating spavin. The animal should be kept quiet and not worked for four or six weeks, as every step the animal takes works the joint, irritates the disease, and prevents the medicine making a cure. What we mean by a cure in spavin is to stop the lameness and put the animal in a condition so he can do his usual work. After the lump has been on the horse for several months there is no medicine that will remove it. In old chronic cases there is no medicine that will cure them, and the treatment we would recommend is the operation of firing. (See Fig. 26.) This is an operation which requires practice and skill to perform, and when properly done is the most successful treatment in old chronic cases of spavin. After this operation it is very necessary that a good penetrating blister be applied, and there is none better than Dr. LeGear's Spavin Cure.

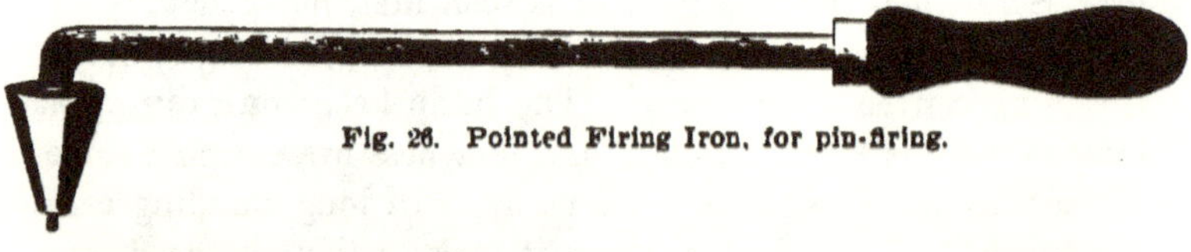

Fig. 26. Pointed Firing Iron, for pin-firing.

Fig. 27. Firing Iron, for feather-firing.

BIG-HEAD.

This disease is properly termed "Osteo-porosis," as it is a porous condition of the bones. It is commonly known as big-head, as the disease is more noticeable about the head by the bones of the face and lower jaw becoming enlarged. The bones become enlarged, but are lighter, more porous, and more easily broken than in health. Not only the bones of the head are affected, but every bone in the body becomes more or less changed. It is a disease of young horses, as it is never seen in an old horse. Big-head is rather rare in Texas, but we have seen a few cases in our practice during the last three years. We are often called upon to examine and prescribe for horses said to have the big-head, when it is nothing but an enlargement on the face caused by a bad jaw tooth.

Causes.—The causes of big-head are rather obscure. Some authors claim it is due to a deficiency of lime, while others claim it is due to eating certain grasses and foods, and drinking certain kinds of water.

Symptoms.—Perhaps the first symptom noticed is the enlarging of the face. One or both sides may enlarge, and usually both sides of the face and each side of the lower jaw bulge out. The animal may appear somewhat stiff and dull in its movements. In many cases when the animal lays down it is difficult for it to get up. Also as the bones are so very porous and brittle, fracture may take place very easily.

Treatment.—Treatment is almost useless. A complete change of food, water, and climate is about all that can be done. A change of climate has been known to cure big-head, but as a general thing, when a horse becomes affected with the disease it is a hopeless case.

CHAPTER XIII.

WOUNDS.

Wounds may occur in any part of the body, and are classified as *incised, punctured, lacerated, contused, gun-shot,* and *poisoned.*

Incised Wounds, or cuts, are made with some sharp body. The edges of the wound are smooth, as though cut with a knife. These wounds are the simplest we are called upon to treat. If they occur in fleshy parts, where no important structures are injured, they soon recover, and often without very much treatment.

Punctured Wounds are made by either sharp or blunt pointed substances, as sticks, thorns, nails, etc. The depth of these wounds is always greater than their width. In veterinary practice, punctured wounds are very common, and more dangerous than the other kinds, and require special care and treatment.

Lacerated Wounds are those in which the soft tissues (skin, muscles, etc.) are more or less torn. Lacerated wounds are usually caused by coming into contact with some blunt object, as where a horse runs against fences, the corners of buildings, through barb wire fences, or by a kick from another animal. The edges of such wounds are ragged and uneven. As a rule these wounds are not attended with any serious results when early given proper attention.

Contused Wounds are commonly called bruises, and are those wounds in which the skin is not injured to any great extent, and in some cases is not even broken; but the deeper structures are more or less affected. A good example of contused wound is "speedy cut" (interfering). A black eye, quite common among certain classes of men, is a good example of a contused wound.

Gun-Shot Wounds are seldom seen except in times of war, when they are quite common. Such wounds should be thoroughly probed to be sure that the bullet is not lodged somewhere in the body. If the ball should strike a bone it is usually shattered and splintered to such an extent as to warrant us in having the animal destroyed.

Poisoned Wounds most frequently result from the bite of some venomous reptile, as the rattlesnake, copperhead, viper, etc., in America, and the cobra, etc., in India. This kind of wound may also be caused by the careless and improper use of certain poisonous medicines, as arsenic, etc., getting into a sore or cut and poisoning it.

Treatment.—The treatment of wounds varies considerably, and is governed by the nature, variety, situation, and extent of the wound under consideration. When bleeding to any considerable extent follows a wound of any kind, we must first of all stop the flow of blood before attempting to close the wound itself or apply any other treatment. This object is effected in different ways, according to whether the bleeding is from an artery or a vein. If from an artery, the blood will be bright red or scarlet in color, and flows in spurts, spouting out with every beat of the heart. If from a vein, the blood is darker in color and flows in a regular stream. Bleeding from large vessels may be stopped by either compress bandages, torsion, hot iron, or ligatures.

By Bandages.—If the blood is from an artery, the pressure should be applied between the wound and the center of circulation, that is, towards the body; if from a vein, toward the extremities.

Fig 28. Artery Forceps.

Torsion (twisting).—This is done by grasping the divided vessel with the artery forceps (Fig. 28) and twisting it the proper number of times, or until the bleeding ceases.

The *hot iron* may also be used to sear the end of a blood vessel, and thus stop the bleeding.

The *ligature* is, however, the best means to stop the flow of blood from a large vessel. The cut end of the bleeding vessel is to be caught up with a pair of artery forceps and firmly tied about one-half inch from its division.

In case of profuse bleeding from the incision of a great number of small vessels, it is best stopped by compresses of cotton, tow, cobwebs, etc., moistened with the tincture of the chloride of iron, ice water, etc. Our Healing Lotion is a good application for such purposes.

After bleeding has ceased we should endeavor to remove all foreign bodies, if any be present. Very often splinters of wood or other foreign substances are thus lodged, and unless removed prevent the wound from healing. All deep wounds should be thoroughly examined or probed to the very bottom to see if any foreign body be present. After a thorough exploration, and all foreign substances have been removed, the wound should be carefully and thoroughly cleansed with cold or warm water, according to the season of the year, after which bathe the parts nicely with Dr. LeGear's Healing Lotion. Now, if the character of the wound admits of it, the edges are to be brought together and secured, which is usually done by means of sutures (stitches); the interrupted suture being the best.

Fig. 29. Surgery Needles—full curve.

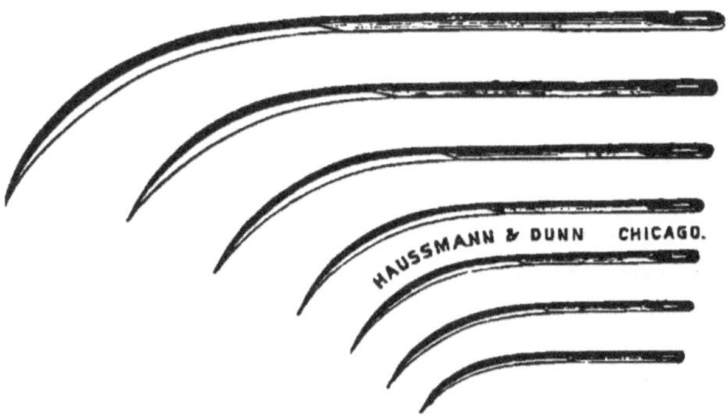

Fig. 30. Surgery Needles—half curve.

Sutures may consist of wire, either of tin, silver, or some soft metal coated with silver, and are known as metallic sutures. There are also sutures of silk, catgut, etc., which may or may not be carbolized. For ordinary wounds silk thread will do as well as any of the other kinds. A medium sized suture needle will be found the most convenient and best to use. (Figs. 29 and 30.) Sutures are further described as twisted, quilled, interrupted, etc.

The *twisted suture* is the one usually employed to close the wound made by the fleam in bleeding from the jugular vein—the large vein in the neck. The edges of the wound are to be brought together and secured in place by means of a pin, which in turn is to be held in position by hair or silk, which is wound around the pin after the manner of a figure eight (8).

The *quilled suture* consists of two pieces of whalebone, wood, or some other material, one on each side of the wound, and connected by a silk thread, wire, etc. This form of suture is very useful in large wounds where the lips have a tendency to gape, and considerable force is required to prevent the wound opening, the ordinary suture in such cases being liable to tear out.

The *interrupted suture* is formed by passing the silk or wire through the edges of the wound, drawing them together and tying the ends of the suture. By this method each stitch is separate from and independent of all the others; so that if one or more stitches break, sufficient may still be left to hold the edges of the wound in position. This is the best of all forms of sutures.

In sewing up a wound, you should have the animal well secured, to prevent any injury to himself. Take a good firm hold of the lips of the wound with the fingers, as the animal will offer less resistance than if the parts are handled in a gingerly manner. Be sure to bring the edges of the wound into perfect apposition, and you should have your mind made up as to where the first stitch should be made. If the wound is not properly stitched and the parts brought into perfect apposition, an ugly pounch or gap may be left to constitute an eye-sore and ever after be a source of aggravation. Always leave a sufficient opening at the lowest part of a wound to allow of proper drainage, the free escape of puss, etc. Other ways of securing wounds are by straps, bandages, etc.

Strapping is done by causing a number of pieces of domestic, or other material, of proper size, shape, etc., to adhere to the parts by means of an application of pitch, or some similar adhesive. Where it is feared that sutures may give way, strapping is frequently of great assistance in affording support to sutures, especially in large wounds.

Bandaging consists of binding or securing a part by means of a roll or sheet of some material, usually cloth or rubber. Certain kinds of incised wounds are readily secured and the edges kept in place by a properly adjusted bandage; and a bandage, as a rule, leaves less blemish than the sutures. Bandages also serve a useful purpose in keeping out dirt, flies, etc., and in many cases afford a useful support to sutures.

Dressing of Wounds.—Most unprofessional people have an idea that there is a specific for each variety of wound. Such is not the case. Still, there is a great difference of opinion among surgeons as to the best way of dressing wounds. Some believe that the air should be entirely excluded in the treatment of wounds; others do not believe in this theory, consequently do not make any attempt to exclude the air and scarcely dress wounds at all, merely having the wound kept clean. In veterinary practice wounds do very well in many cases when exposed, but of course may receive some poisonous germs through the medium of the air; but the probabilities are that in a large majority of cases the air not only does no harm, but, on the contrary, often exerts a beneficial influence. Wounds in a healthy animal heal faster than in an unhealthy animal. So don't expect to heal up wounds in animals with unhealthy constitutions as fast as you would if the system is healthy. After the wound has been thoroughly cleansed with warm water and stitched up, the treatment must be governed altogether by circumstances. If inflammation be present, a free use of hot or cold applications to the parts will be beneficial; where there is not much pain cold water will be found very good. Inflammation may often be prevented, and, when present, may be reduced by a dose of physic and giving the patient a laxative diet. As a cooling application, and at the same time exerting great healing powers, there is nothing better than our Celebrated Healing Lotion. (See Appendix.) This wonderful antiseptic and astringent preparation should be applied according to the directions on each bottle. In all external sores and wounds, and where flies are liable to bother a sore, there is nothing equal to our Screw Worm Powder. It has wonderful antiseptic, healing powers, and is a sure prevention against the much dreaded "screw worm."

ABSCESSES AND TUMORS.

These enlargements are quite often seen in connection with horses' shoulders, as the result of some injury. Badly fitting collars sometimes cause them, and they are often caused by sudden jars from the plow striking a stone or the wagon hitting a stump. They may also be caused by a kick, or by an animal running against some hard object.

Symptoms. — The swelling will be seen, which is generally hard, and may be hot and tender. Sometimes fluid can be detected in an abscess, but generally they have to be lanced before it is certain that fluid or puss is present. At first the fluid is thin and watery, called serum, but later on it turns to white pus. A tumor has no matter or fluid in it, but consists of a solid mass of callous tissue.

Treatment.—If a serous abscess, it should be opened up freely with a clean sharp knife or lance, to let the matter out. Make a good big opening, as success will depend upon keeping the hole open until the cavity heals inside. Syringe out the cavity well with water 1 pint and carbolic acid 1 dram. Sometimes the secreting cells in the sack will have to be destroyed by using a caustic. This can be done by packing the cavity full of cotton soaked in a very strong solution of bluestone. Let it remain in twelve hours, then remove and dress the sore with our Healing Lotion. If it is a tumor, cut it out, and then heal up the wound as an ordinary sore.

BURNS AND SCALDS.

These may be slight or may be so severe as to cause death from pain and exhaustion. In the former case, where only a reddened condition of the skin is produced, the pain and irritation soon subside. Some burns are more serious, depending on the character of the burn inflicted. Some burns cause only slight blisters to form, while others destroy the skin and cause it to undergo complete destruction. The worst form of burn is that in which the skin, and the tissue beneath the skin, is destroyed. This form of burn, when extensive, usually causes death.

Treatment.—As soon as possible after a burn is produced the air should be excluded. One of the best preparations is the following:

Raw linseed oil	Equal parts.
Lime water	

Mix, and apply freely to all the burned or scalded surface.

A good remedy to use at once to draw out the pain is to cover all the burned surface with a thick layer of baking soda. An ointment as follows is good:

Oxide of zinc .... 4 drams.
Vaseline . ... 3 ounces.

Mix, and apply freely to all affected parts.

SNAKE BITES.

This is a very common and serious trouble to stock owners in various parts of the country. Rattlesnakes, copperheads, etc., are very poisonous, and sometimes cause death to horses and cattle by biting them. The parts bitten generally swell up extensively, and after a time sloughing of the skin and flesh takes place, leaving a very ugly looking sore.

Treatment.—If bitten on the leg, and the animal is seen immediately afterwards, a string or rope should be wound tightly around the leg above the bite, so as to keep the poison from being absorbed into the system until some of it can be destroyed by applying hot irons, caustic, or bleeding freely at the point of injury. Large doses of alcohol, whisky, or brandy should be given often to counteract the effects of the poison. After the swelling forms it should be bathed well with warm water two or three times a day and our Liniment (see Appendix) well rubbed in. If sloughing takes place, it should be treated according to treatment for wounds.

PHLEBITIS.

Inflammation of a vein is called phlebitis. It was at one time quite common in the horse, the juglar vein (the large vein of the neck) being the one most commonly affected, as it is the vein usually selected for blood-letting. At one time the poor horse used to be bled for nearly every disease horseflesh is heir to. The age of bleeding horses is a thing of the past, except among some of the old-time "horse doctors," who still cling to their old-time customs.

Causes.—Blood-letting from the large vein in the neck is probably the most common cause of the trouble and is the most dangerous kind. Other causes are injuries, abscesses, tumors, etc.

Symptoms.—In most cases the vein is swollen, thickened, and hardened considerably. The swelling, with great tenderness, may extend along the affected vessel, and the animal show general disturbance and fever.

Treatment.—Tie the horse's head up high and bathe the swelling with warm water for one or two hours at a time. After bathing with warm water, dry off the parts and rub them well with our Liniment (see Appendix). Give one pint of raw linseed oil as a drench, and give one teaspoonful of saltpetre in the drinking water twice a day. Use the animal carefully, and give a laxative diet. The large vein usually becomes destroyed, after which a horse is considered unsound.

OPEN JOINT.

What is meant by open joint is where a joint in the body is laid open by an injury and the joint-water (synovia) is allowed to leak out. It is one of the most serious injuries to which the horse is liable. Every joint is surrounded by a thin membrane, called the synovial membrane, which has the power of secreting or making the joint-water. When the joint is not in motion, very little, if any, is secreted, but while the joint is working there is sufficient oil (joint-water) secreted to keep the joint oiled so it will work easily. The joints are like all machinery—they need plenty of oil to keep them in good working order. It is a mistaken idea, if a joint is opened and the joint-water runs out, that it will not be formed again. Stiff-joint is caused by the inflammation forming a bony deposit about the joint, which forms anchylosis (stiff joint). The joints most liable to this injury are the stifle, ankle, hock, and knee. There are little bursae (membranes) that secrete synovia to lubricate the tendons (leaders) where they ply over joints and prominent places. Sometimes these are opened and by the synovia (oil) running out of a wound might lead a person to suspect open joint. This is not open joint nor nowhere near as bad an injury.

Causes.—The causes of this trouble are generally some kind of an injury, as kicks, blows of any kind, falls, punctures, etc. It is often caused by unprofessional parties trying to perform some surgical operation in the region of a joint—by cutting into the joint and allowing the synovia to escape. Any person not thoroughly familiar with the anatomy of the joints should never cut into one under any consideration. The worst form of open joint is where it is caused by a kick, or by an animal falling on his knees and cutting them wide open. This form of injury not only opens the joint, but bruises and lacerates the tissues, causing very severe inflammation and extensive sloughing of the parts.

Symptoms.—In a case caused by a sharp instrument, as a knife, pitchfork, etc., penetrating the joint there may not be any severe symptoms for one or two days. The synovia (joint oil) runs out, air gets into the joint, irritation and severe inflammation follow, accompanied by great swelling, and the suffering of the animal becomes most agonizing, and, unless speedily checked, death is certain. Joint oil is a clear fluid, of a watery, oily nature, and will coagulate (thicken) on the edges of the wound on becoming exposed to the air. At first the discharge is clear joint-water, but later on it becomes mixed with pus, and in some cases streaked with blood. When pus and blood escape in any great quantity, there is very liable to be stiff-joint. The animal has a very high fever and may not eat at all on account of the excruciating pain he has to suffer. We have known several cases to die within one week, from the severe pain of open joint.

Treatment.—In the treatment of open joint our great aim should be to check the flow of joint-water as soon as possible. It is a very serious disease, and the treatment is very difficult and not very successful. Keep the animal as quiet as possible, as the working of the joint irritates the disease and prevents recovery. A stream of cold water should be let run on to the parts for hours at a time. This may be done where the waterworks are convenient by fastening the hose to the ceiling over the horse and let the end come down and fasten it to the affected part by bandages. Then turn on a small stream of water and let it run for hours at a time. This is to take out the fever and swelling. Wash the sore as little as possible to keep it clean. Apply some astringent healing wash as our Healing Lotion once or twice a day. A poultice of equal parts of wheat flour and oatmeal, to be applied warm two or three times a day, is an excellent remedy, as it has a tendency to coagulate the joint-oil and close up the wound; or equal parts of tannic acid, dried alum, and gum arabic, well applied to the parts, and held in place by pledgets of tow or cotton, will be found an excellent application to arrest the flow of synovia. With close attention and proper treatment a few cases will recover, but the majority of cases terminate in stiff-joint or death. If the joint is enlarged after the wound heals, blister it well with our Spavin Cure, which will remove a great deal of the enlargement and perhaps limber up the joint.

CURB.

A curb is a small enlargement on the back part of the hind leg, about five inches below the point of the hock. It is caused from a strain of the calcaneo-cuboid ligament, which is a strong ligament passing from the point of the hock down to a short distance below the location of the curb. (See Fig. 31.)

Causes.—It may be caused from slipping and straining the leg while drawing heavy loads in the mud or up hill. In some cases it is hereditary, as certain breeds of horses have curby hocks (bowed behind), and are liable to throw out a curb on being driven fast or worked to a heavy load.

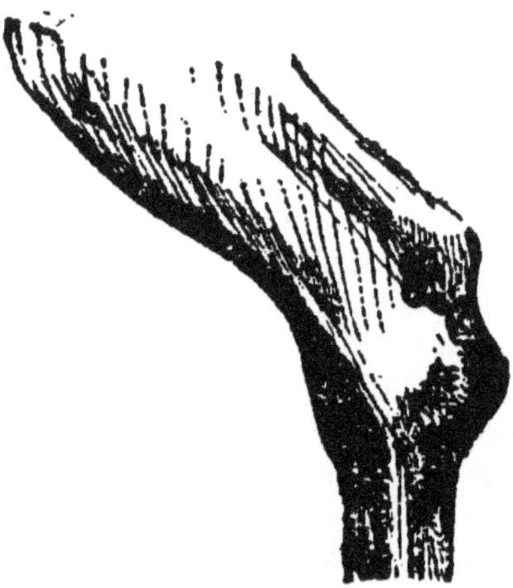

Fig. 31. Curb.

Symptoms.—After a hard day's work pulling a heavy load, the animal may be noticed lame, and on examining the leg you will notice a firm, hot swelling on the back part of the hind leg about five inches below the hock. On pressing it the animal shows pain. After the soreness and inflammation passes away it forms into a hard knot, and unless properly treated will always remain there.

Treatment.—Lay the horse off work, and don't use him at all for at least one week. In the early stages when fever and soreness are present, bathe it with cold water and afterwards rub it well with Dr. LeGear's Liniment (see Appendix). A great deal will depend on rubbing it well. Rub the Liniment in thoroughly twice a day with a corn-cob or a smooth piece of bone. If you fail to remove the lameness and the lump by this treatment, kept up for one week, then there is nothing better to cure it than our

Spavin Cure (see Appendix), which, if properly used, will remove the lameness and take off the enlargement.

WIND PUFFS.

Wind puffs are soft, puffy tumors at the back of the fetlock (ankle) joint. They were formerly supposed to contain air, but are now known to contain the same kind of fluid as bog spavin and thorough-pin. They seldom ever cause lameness. They are seen more frequently on horses with straight pasterns and those that are driven fast on hard rocky roads.

Causes.—Wind puffs are generally brought on by hard and fast work on hard roads, drawing heavy loads, jumping, or any work that is liable to strain or weaken the legs. In most cases they are just soft, flabby, cold swellings, which appear to do the animal no harm at all, but occasionally they are hot and firm and cause lameness.

Treatment.—Old chronic cases of wind puffs are generally very hard to cure. Any fever or soreness in connection with them should be removed by using Dr. LeGear's Liniment and bandaging with cold, wet bandages. Thorough hand-rubbing two or three times a day may do good. All else failing, there is nothing equal to our Spavin Cure (see Appendix) well rubbed in and repeated when necessary.

THOROUGH-PIN.

Thorough-pin is a soft, puffy swelling in the hollow on each side just in front of the point of the hock. It is very often seen in connection with bog spavin, and when seen alone seldom causes lameness. It is the same kind of an enlargement as bog spavin, only is in a different place on the joint.

Treatment.—A thorough-pin truss (Fig. 32) is very beneficial in some cases, but there is no treatment better than Dr. LeGear's Spavin Cure when used according to directions.

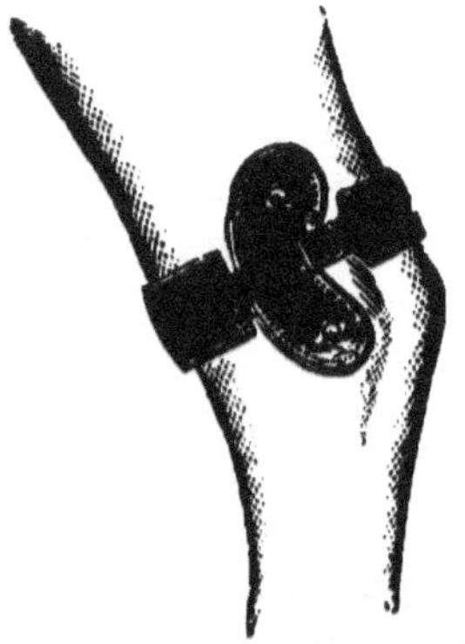

Fig. 32. Thoroughpin Truss.

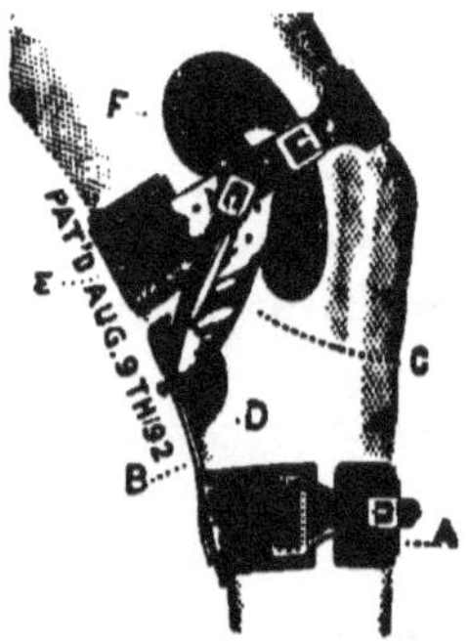

Fig. 33. Bog-Spavin and Thorough-pin Truss.

BOG SPAVIN.

A bog spavin is a soft, puffy swelling on the inside of the front of the hock joint, in about the same location as high bone spavin. It is an accumulation of synovia (joint-water) in a distension of the capsular ligament. Large heavy draft horses are very liable to bog spavin, and it very seldom injures such horses. But in light horses, or those used for fast work, the presence of bog spavin or any unnatural fullness in the region of the hock should always be viewed with great suspicion. Where bog spavin is present thorough-pin is nearly always found.

Causes.—Bog spavin is usually caused by hard and fast work, irregular or too little exercise, high feeding, etc. It is sometimes produced very easily, especially in young horses.

Symptoms.—Bog spavin can generally be detected quite easily, as the swelling can be easily seen. In large horses the swelling is generally flabby and cool, and does no harm. In light driving horses it is very liable to cause lameness, and if much fevered is very liable to turn to a fibrous or bony lump.

Treatment.—Give rest and blister thoroughly with our Spavin Cure. In heavy horses and those that are not lame, it is best to let the spavin alone, as it will seldom do harm. Hand-rubbing is very useful, and what is still better is a bog spavin truss (Fig. 33), which gives pressure. Careful firing is sometimes very beneficial, but there is no remedy better than Dr. LeGear's Spavin Cure. (See Appendix.)

CAPPED HOCK.

Capped hock is an enlargement on the point of the hock. It is generally quite small, but may become very large. (See Fig. 34.)

Causes.—Capped hock is generally caused by blows, kicks, etc., or by the horse lying with the points of the hocks on the hard ground. It is sometimes due to a dropsical condition of the legs. If a horse has capped hock it is well to suspect him as a kicker.

Treatment.—The best treatment in the early stages of the disease, when it is due to an injury, is to bathe it thoroughly two or three times a day with Dr. LeGear's Liniment. (See Appendix.) If it does not go away in the course of a week, apply some of our Spavin Cure (see Appendix), and repeat in two weeks if necessary. Always remove the cause. If the horse is a kicker, try and keep everything away from his hocks. If he lays on them, put a large pad on his hocks and give him a good soft bed to lie on.

Fig. 34. Capped Hock.

Fig. 35. Capped Elbow.

CAPPED ELBOW, OR SHOE BOIL.

This is commonly called Shoe Boil, and consists of an enlargement at the point of the elbow, due to an injury. Capped elbow is a very common condition, and varies considerably in character, size, etc. (See Fig. 35.)

Causes.—The most common cause of this condition is the elbow coming into contact with the shoe when the animal is lying down. It may also be caused by the elbow coming in contact with the hoof, the ground, or the belly band, etc.

Symptoms.—At first there is only a slight irritation of the part, producing more or less enlargement. In some cases there is considerable inflammation, which terminates in a collection of fluid. In aggravated cases this fluid solidifies and forms a hard tumor on the point of the elbow, and in some cases an abscess may form.

Treatment.—If taken when the swelling first comes on, bathe it well with hot water three times a day and apply our Liniment after each time of bathing. Remove the shoe and keep the pressure off the parts, and the swelling will soon disappear. It may be well to not let the horse lay down for several nights during treatment. Sometimes a quantity of fluid forms in the swelling, which will have to be let out by lancing the place. After lancing, syringe out the cavity every day with a weak solution of carbolic acid until healed. The swelling sometimes will develop into a fibrous tumor, and may get to be very large. In such cases the only treatment is to dissect the tumor out, and let the place heal up as an ordinary sore. Before the tumor gets too large it may be removed by blistering well with our Spavin Cure. A seaton put through the tumor may drain it out. A circular padded leather boot can be buckled around the horse's foot just below the ankle to keep the shoe pressing on the elbow while the animal is lying down. This boot will prevent the tumor from forming again.

KNUCKLING, OR COCKED ANKLES.

Knuckling is an unnatural position of the fetlock joint, which is more or less bent, causing a prominent enlargement on the front part of the joint. While knuckling is not always an unsoundness, it nevertheless predisposes to stumbling and to fracture of the pastern.

Causes.—It is a condition often seen in young foals, due, no doubt, to a bent condition of the limbs before birth, and as a general thing soon disappears. Horses with straight pasterns are very apt to knuckle as they grow old, especially in the hind legs. All kinds of heavy work, especially in hilly districts, severe pulling, and fast work on race tracks are exciting causes of knuckling. It may occur as a result of irregular exercise, sprain of the ligaments, disease of the suspensory ligament, or of the flexor tendons, whereby they are shortened. Allowing the feet to grow out of shape, poor shoeing, etc., no doubt have a great deal to do with it.

Treatment.—In young foals, treatment is not necessary, as all that need be done is to keep the feet in proper shape and the legs will straighten up in a few weeks' time. In adult animals it may be relieved by shoeing when due to contracted tendons. Shorten the toe of the foot as much as possible, leaving the heels high; or thin the shoe at the toe with thick heels or high calks. On the hind feet put long-heeled shoes with calks. An operation in some cases is indicated, that of dividing (or cutting) the back tendons, between the fetlock and knee, for the purpose of securing relief. Firing and blistering in some instances may effect a cure.

KNEE-SPRUNG.

This is a bending forward of the knees, in consequence of contraction of the back tendons. (See Fig. 36.)

Causes.—The causes which may be mentioned are hard and fast work, irregular exercise, as keeping the animal up and feeding well for several days, then taking out and driving freely. It is often the result of a hores standing in a stall with a floor sloping from before backwards, especially so when there is a weak conformation of the parts. Overgrowth of hoof, poor shoeing, etc., must be included among the causes.

Treatment.—If it is due to standing on a sloping floor, place the animal on a level surface, or in a stall lower in front than behind. It is considered incurable in old horses, and is liable to return even in young animals. Special atten- should be paid to the shoeing. Be sure that the feet are balanced from side to side. If he drops on his toe while traveling and wears his shoe at the toe most, the toe is too high or too long, and it must be lowered. If the toe can not be lowered sufficiently, attach heel corks to the shoe. If he lands on the heels first while at speed, and wears his shoe at the heels most, his heels are too high, and must be lowered to overcome the trouble. A stimulating liniment, as Dr. LeGear's (see Appendix), or even a good blister, as Dr. LeGear's Spavin Cure, or the firing iron, may be found very beneficial in cases of knee sprung. This is to be applied to the back tendons as directed for use on other parts. Great benefit will also be found by giving the animal a run at pasture for two or three months.

Fig. 36.
Knee-Sprung.

CALF-KNEES.—This is exactly an opposite condition to that of sprung knees. Such a limb is very weak, and liable to sprains, etc.

Treatment.—We know of nothing that can be done for it.

SPRAIN OF THE FETLOCK.

This is most common in the forelegs, and usually affects one at a time. Horses doing fast work and those that interfere are particularly liable to this injury.

Causes.—It is generally produced by a misstep, stumbling, slipping, etc., or where the foot is caught in a rut, hole in a bridge, or in a car track.

Symptoms.—There is more or less lameness, accompanied by heat, pain, and considerable swelling. While at rest the affected leg is flexed at the joint affected, but this is not to be considered an infallible sign, as the animal may have picked up a nail, in which case he will also knuckle at the fetlock.

Treatment.—If the injury is slight, cold water bandages and a few days' rest is all that is necessary. In severe cases the leg should be placed under a stream of cold water for hours at a time, and after drying, apply some good, stimulating liniment and put on a cold water bandage. There is no better than our Liniment for such purposes. Keep up the applications of water, liniment, and cold water bandages for several days, or until the fever and swelling are reduced. When the inflammation has subsided a good blister, such as our Spavin Cure, should be applied, well rubbed into the part.

SPRAIN OF THE SUSPENSORY LIGAMENT.

The suspensory ligament is a strong band of fibrous tissue extending from the knee down the leg between the bone and the back tendons (leaders), and divides just above the ankle joint; the divided portions passing over the ankle joint and becoming attached just below. This ligament is the stay to the ankle, as when it becomes ruptured (torn in two) the ankle joint will come clear to the ground, constituting what is known as break-down. The suspensory ligament is liable to sprain from various causes, as from stepping on a stone, slipping, jumping, etc.

Symptoms.—The animal will be more or less lame, and will especially show it when turning around short. It is invariably seen in the front leg. There is seldom any swelling takes place, which makes it such a hard lameness to locate by inexperienced parties. If you squeeze the ligament with the thumb and finger the animal will show considerable pain.

PLATE III. SHOWING THE MUSCLES OF THE HORSE.

Treatment.—This lameness needs complete rest, as by working the animal before the sprain is cured the ligament is liable to rupture, and break down. If in summer apply a bandage wet in cold water two or three times a day. Let the bandage envelop the leg from the knee to the foot. Also rub the parts well two or three times a day with our Liniment. Keep the animal quiet for perhaps one or two months. When the fever is pretty well gone from the parts, apply our Spavin Cure and give the animal a run at grass.

BREAK-DOWN.

Break-down is rupture of the suspensory ligament. It generally ruptures just above the ankle joint. It may be caused by an animal being worked or ridden while suffering from sprain of the suspensory ligament. By the ligament being sprained it is naturally weakened and very liable to tear or rupture if too much weight is put upon it. It is seen more frequently in race horses.

Symptoms.—The animal goes suddenly lame, and the fetlock (ankle joint) comes clear down to the ground, or nearly so. If only one portion of the ligament is broken the ankle will come only part way down, but will lean to one side. If partial break-down is suspected, don't put the animal to work again for several months, or until the parts are entirely well and strong again.

Treatment.—In break-down there may be a great deal of fever and swelling take place, which must be removed by bathing with warm water and a good stimulating liniment, none being better than our Liniment. Keep the animal perfectly quiet and apply a bandage snugly to the ankle, which will serve as a support. After the fever is reduced apply a good stimulating blister, as our Spavin Cure, applied as directed. The animal may be given a run at pasture for two or three months. It is surprising how this injury will in some cases recover and the animal be useful for slow work for years.

SWEENY.

This, properly speaking, is Shoulder-slip, but in this article we have used the name in common use. It is atrophy (wasting away) of the muscles of the shoulder.

Causes.—Sweeny is a condition frequently met with, as it may be caused in a variety of ways. It is more commonly seen in young horses that are put to heavy work when the muscles are soft. Plowing is a common cause, where the animal walks with one foot in the furrow and one foot out. Sudden jerks, such as might be caused by a plow striking a root or a rock, or suddenly starting a heavy load, a badly fitting collar, jolts or jars, bruises, or any injury to the shoulder, etc., all tend to produce the condition known as sweeny. Long standing cases of lameness cause sweeny by the disuse of the muscles of the limb and shoulder.

Symptoms.—About the first thing noticed by the owner is wasting away of the muscles of the shoulder, and the animal may be somewhat stiff, or even lame, for a few days previous. There is also an unnatural bulging of the shoulder joint. In some cases atrophy occurs to such an extent that one might think the muscles had disappeared entirely.

Treatment.—There are a great many forms of treatment used in curing sweeny, and some of them are very cruel and useless. The only treatment we use, and we never find it to fail, is our Spavin Cure. (See Appendix.) This is a stimulating, penetrating, sweating blister that stimulates the growth of the muscle and reproduces the shoulder in a remarkably short time. It seldom if ever requires over two or three applications to make a cure. Use according to directions. A good, but very simple, remedy is as follows:

Oil of turpentine	2 drams.
Sweet oil	4 drams.

Mix, and inject under the skin in several places at the upper part of the wasted muscles.

A swelling may follow the above injection, extending as far down as the knee and lasting for forty-eight hours, when it gradually disappears. Give the horse a run at pasture, or gentle exercise by riding, or driving with a breast collar.

SHOULDER-JOINT LAMENESS.

The shoulder joint is liable to injuries in various ways, although not so often affected as some people commonly suppose. Among a certain class of "horse doctors," who, when they can not locate a case of lameness, always refer it to the shoulder joint at once, and blister and seton the same, putting the poor animal to an endless amount of torture, when in all probability the trouble is in the feet.

Causes.—A common cause is direct injury, as by an animal running away, falling down, slipping, etc., and in young horses is often produced by turning and circling them violently when breaking them to work. It is a common trouble among cavalry horses.

Symptoms.—Where the lameness is well marked, the animal has considerable difficulty in extending the limb; and in traveling the limb is kept as straight as possible, and is brought forward with difficulty—swinging it outward instead of carrying it forward in a natural manner. When the animal stands at rest the affected limb will be slightly bent, with the toe resting upon the ground. In some cases there will be swelling, heat, etc., in the region of the shoulder joint. On pulling the limb forward the animal will rear up, showing considerable pain. On allowing the animal to stand all night after being driven and warmed

Fig. 37. Shoulder-Joint Lameness.

up, he is found in the morning to be very stiff and lame; warm him up and the lameness decreases. He usually strikes the toe and stumbles when traveling, and on being made to step over some object, he either refuses, or does so with the utmost difficulty; in which case he drags his limb over, or strikes his toe against it. In some cases it is rather difficult to distinguish between shoulder-joint and foot lameness, especially where the lameness is slight and not well marked. In causing an animal to back, if he drags the foot it is a good indication of shoulder lameness. (See Fig. 37.)

Treatment.—The animal should be given a rest, and hot water applied to the affected parts for an hour at a time two or three times a day. Bathe the parts with our Liniment (see Appendix), well rubbed in two or three times a day. This is undoubtedly the best liniment made for sprains and bruises and all muscular soreness. After the inflammation and swelling has gone down and the horse is still lame, the parts should be slightly blistered by rubbing in our Spavin Cure (see Appendix) lightly, according to directions, and give the horse a run at pasture.

ENLARGED JOINTS.

Enlarged joints are very frequently seen on horses that have had rough usage and hard work. They may be due to an injury, as from being snagged, kicked, or from a thorn. They are often due to sprains and hard work, that inflame the joint and cause an inflammatory swelling which may remain until removed by treatment.

Treatment.—If the enlargement is of a bony formation it can not be removed. If the horse is lame, the lameness may be removed, but the enlargement will remain. If the enlargement is of a fleshy nature it may be removed by applying some good absorbing, sweating blister, as our Spavin Cure. If our Spavin Cure will not remove an enlargement of this kind, no medicine will, for it is the best absorbing, penetrating, and sweating blister made. Use according to direction on each bottle.

STIFLED.

Stifled is the general name for "dislocation of the patella"—meaning that the patella, or little bone covering the stifle, has slipped out of place. The patella in the horse is a little bone covering the stifle, the same as the knee-cap covers the knee in man. This is rather a rare trouble in the horse, but still we see it quite often.

Causes.—Stifle may be caused by a horse slipping, falling, stepping on a stone that rolls or gives way, especially if the animal is in a weakened condition or suffering from some debilitating disease. Partial stifle is where the litte stifle bone slips partially out and in, making a clucking noise at every step, which is often seen in colts, especially those running on hilly pastures.

Symptoms.—Stifled is an affection which when once seen can be easily told. The little bone (patella) slips to the outside, causing an enlargement on the outside of the stifle joint. But the most noticeable symptom is the position and action of the leg. The foot is extended backward and the animal can't bring it forward. The stifle bone (patella) serves as a pully to the hind leg, and when once out of place the leg can't be brought forward until the stifle bone is put back or flies back in its place. In "partial stifle" there is a peculiar stiffness of the hind leg, and a clucking noise is noticed at every step, which is produced by the stifle bone slipping in and out of its socket.

Treatment.—The treatment is not difficult, and as a rule is successful, if properly carried out. The first thing to do is to put the stifle bone back in place, which is done by tying a rope around the foot of the affected leg and letting one man stand in front of the animal and gently pull on the rope, while you press in on the stifle bone or enlargement on the outside of the stifle, when the bone will slip back in place with a clicking sound. In some cases, by exciting the animal, as by whipping, causing him to move suddenly, etc., the bone may fly back into place and the animal have free use of the leg until it slips out again. When once in position keep it there by tying the foot so it can't extend backwards, and bathe the stifle thoroughly with warm water, and use Dr. LeGear's Liniment (see Appendix) twice per day, well rubbed in. Give the animal complete rest for some time. After about ten days the whole stifle should be well blistered to strengthen the ligaments that have been stretched and torn. There is no blister better than Dr. LeGear's Spavin Cure. In some cases a stifle shoe is very beneficial. In "partial stifle," where the bone slips in and out at every step, the animal should be kept quiet for a week or two and a good blister applied as recommended above.

HIP-JOINT DISEASE.

The hip-joint, one of the strongest joints in the body, is sometimes the seat of disease, but not so often as is commonly supposed. Why this should be is plain to any one understanding the structure and situation of the joint, it being formed of some of the heaviest bones in the body, secured in place by extremely powerful ligaments, etc.

Causes.—Any exercise of a violent character, as jumping, sudden turns while running, slipping, falling, etc., may all operate in causing hip-joint lameness. When inflammation occurs in this joint, a series of pathological changes take place in exactly the same manner as in other joints.

Symptoms.—The animal persists in standing; the foot is elevated from the ground and not allowed to descend, unless the animal is forced to move. Wasting away of the muscles of the part takes place, and in many cases the animal becomes unable to lie down, or does so with the greatest difficulty. In milder cases the animal may be able to place the foot upon the ground, and even travel. The animal travels with a kind of hop, and has considerable difficulty in bringing forward the limb. The limb may also be brought forward in a circular manner, with the toe dragging upon the ground.

Treatment.—Give absolute rest, and apply fomentations of hot or cold water, according to the season of the year. After fomenting for several days, and the heat and soreness is considerably removed, thoroughly blister the parts with our Spavin Cure, or use the firing iron, according to the directions for spavin.

COLLAR GALLS.

Collar galls are very common among working horses, and may be the means of considerable trouble and render the animal less liable to do his work. They are found in the region of the neck and shoulder, and are caused by a badly fitting or rough-seated collar, which sets up an irritation, resulting in a kind of tumor, etc., which being pressed upon by the collar causes considerable pain.

Treatment.—If the sore is on the top of the neck, clip the hair closely and have the sore washed every morning thoroughly with castile soap and water and apply Dr. LeGear's Healing Lotion (see Appendix) two or three times per day. This is without doubt the finest preparation ever used for collar galls and saddle galls. It will heal the sore and let the horse work every day. Apply the Healing Lotion every morning after washing the sore, and on coming in at noon or night bathe the sore with a little cold water and apply the Healing Lotion. Keep the collar scraped perfectly clean. If the collar is too small or too large, change it and put on one that fits well.

SADDLE GALLS.

Saddle galls are similar to collar galls, only they have a different situation and are caused by badly fitted saddles, etc., and are more common in hot weather.

Treatment.—The treatment of saddle galls is precisely the same as that given for collar galls, which see.

SITFASTS.

Sitfasts are horn-like sloughs of limited portions of the skin, the result of pressure by badly fitting saddles, collars, harness, etc. They are most common under the saddle, but may be found under collar or breeching, as well. The sitfast is a piece of dead tissue which would be thrown off but for its firm connection with the healthy tissue beneath.

Treatment.—By laying a horse off work for a few weeks a sitfast will generally heal up quite smoothly, but when put to work again it breaks out as bad, if not worse, than it was at first. There is a callous piece of dead skin that must be removed, and the only way to do that successfully is to thoroughly dissect it out. Split the skin and dissect out all the diseased tissue from under the healthy skin, and put in two or three stitches if necessary. Then have it well washed every day with soap and water to remove all matter and scabs, and apply a little of our Healing Lotion (see Appendix) twice a day. The Healing Lotion will heal it rapidly and toughen the skin, and thus prevent it from breaking out again when the animal is put to work. A long rest of two or three months should be given after a sitfast is cut out before a horse is rode again.

KIDNEY-SORES.

Kidney-sores are of the same nature as sitfasts, but are located back on the loins over the kidneys. They are caused by badly fitting saddles and require exactly the same treatment as sitfasts, which see.

POLL EVIL.

Poll evil is similar to fistula, only in a different location—on the poll just back of the ears. It is an inflammation of the parts named, and pus may burrow down between the muscles until it reaches and causes disease of the bones.

Causes.—The cause is an injury of some kind, as blows, the horse striking his head while passing through a low doorway, and the wearing of badly fitting halters and bridles. It is also said to be caused by too tight reining.

Symptoms.—The heat, pain, and swelling of the parts soon follow the injury, whatever kind it may be. Swelling continues, an abscess forms, and pus is discharged, at which time the swelling goes down. Pipes are formed, which may extend in all directions, and the poll soon becomes one mass of disease. The animal protrudes his head, and on handling the inflamed parts pain is manifested. In some cases the swelling is so slight as to be overlooked, especially in those cases where the mane hides the diseased parts.

Treatment. — As poll evil is the same kind of a disease as fistula, only situated in a different place, it requires the same kind of treatment as recommended for fistula, which see.

FISTULA.

A fistula really means a pipe or duct which leads from a cavity to the surface of the body, through which a discharge is constantly taking place. A fistula may then exist at any part, but it is commonly understood to mean a diseased condition of the withers. In this article it means disease of the withers.

Causes.—Fistulous withers are seen mostly in those horses that have thick necks and in those that are high in the withers; or among saddle horses that are very low on the withers, the saddle moving forward and bruising the parts. It is often caused by badly fitted collars or saddles, by direct injury from blows, and the horse rolling upon rough or sharp stones. At first there may be only a simple abscess, or an ulcer of the skin, which if not properly treated may become fistula. In such cases the pus burrows and finds lodgment deep down among the muscles, which makes it very difficult for the matter to escape.

Symptoms.—About the first thing noticed is a swelling on one or both sides of the withers, which is hot and painful and rapidly enlarging. If the matter which has formed in this cavity does not get out by natural or other means, it dries up and becomes hard and forms a kind of tumor which gradually develops into a fibrous nature.

Treatment.—This is a very common disease of the horse in Texas, and is in most cases very hard to cure. If taken when first coming on it may be driven away by applying some good penetrating blister, as Dr. LeGear's Spavin Cure (see Appendix) well rubbed in. After some standing the only treatment to pursue successfully is to thoroughly open up the enlargement and cut out what diseased flesh you can, and give free drainage to the pus by opening the sore low down. If the bone is diseased it should be scraped and all diseased portions removed. The cavities should be injected with turpentine every three or four days to destroy any unhealthy tissue that is left. Grease the horse's shoulders under the sore well with lard just before putting in the turpentine, so as to keep the turpentine from burning him. If the holes you have made have a tendency to close, you can keep them open by inserting a seton of domestic or linen cloth. The wound should be washed well every morning with soap and water and one of the following lotions injected well into the sore every morning except when the turpentine is used:

Corrosive sublimate	10 grains.
Alcohol	1 ounce.
Water	7 ounces.

Mix.

Or—

Creolin	1 dram.
Water	8 ounces.

Mix.

Or use Dr. LeGear's Healing Lotion. If in the summer time, you can keep the flies away by using Dr. LeGear's Screw Worm Powder. (See Appendix.)

CROOKED TAIL.

Horses are occasionally seen that carry their tails to one side when traveling, but when standing the tail generally hangs straight. They are either born that way or do it from habit. It is very annoying to the owner of the horse if he uses it for single driving. It is not objectionable as a general rule in a farm horse, but looks bad in a driving horse.

Treatment.—As a general rule the tail can be straightened by cutting in two one of the muscles at the side to which the tail crooks. The muscle on that side is shorter than the one on the opposite side. The place of operation is a few inches from the root of the tail. An incision is made through the skin and the muscle cut in two. The tail is then fastened around to the other side to allow a division to grow in between the divided ends of the muscle. The tail is kept tied around to the side for eight or ten days. The wound should be washed and dressed every day and a bandage applied. Use our Healing Lotion as a dressing to heal the sore. If the muscle that is too short is fully developed, the tail can as a general thing be straightened; but if the muscle is not developed fully, a cure is hopeless.

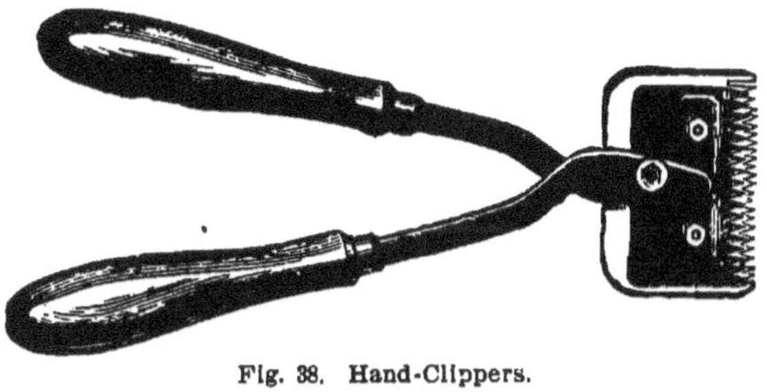

Fig. 38. Hand-Clippers.

CLIPPING HORSES.

This is practiced to a considerable extent in some parts of this country during the winter and spring, when horses' hair is heavy, thick and long. The points in favor of clipping are that a horse will drive easier and freer and is not so liable to take cold as when they have such a heavy coat of hair. When a horse with very long, heavy hair becomes warmed up and sweaty, it takes him a long time to dry off; while a horse with short hair will dry off in a few minutes. To make a universal practice of clipping horses, we would condemn it, but in certain cases it is all right. Nature grows the thick, long coat of hair on a horse as a protection against the cold; therefore if we remove it, we must provide an artificial protection during the cold weather while the horse is not driving. A blanket should be carried to put over the horse while standing in the street if the air is cold or chilly; and one is to be worn in the stable during the cold weather if the stable is not extra warm. To clip a horse and let him stand out in the cold without any protection, is a cruel practice. Some horses, generally those that are well bred, have naturally short, fine hair and never need clipping. As a general thing, if a horse has a warm stable for winter and is well groomed once or twice a day, the coat will not grow so long that it will need clipping. In some of the large stables in the cities they have clipping machines run by motor power, which can clip a horse in a few minutes, but it is generally done by the use of the hand clipper. (Fig. 38.)

CHAPTER XIV.

PARTURITION, OR FOALING.

The period of gestation in the mare is usually about eleven months, although it may vary from ten to thirteen months. As a general thing, horse colts are carried a few days longer than fillies, and as a rule an old mare will carry her foal longer than a young mare. The period of pregnancy with the cow is about nine months; the sheep and goat about five months; the sow four months; the bitch two months; and the cat on an average of eight weeks.

SIGNS OF PREGNANCY.

As a rule, when a mare conceives, heat or the desire for the male is no longer observed, and when brought in the presence of a stallion she is generally unusually vicious. She becomes of a more quiet disposition, especially noticeable in nervous, vicious mares. An increase of fat, with softness and flabbiness of muscle, a loss of energy, indisposition for active work, and manifestations of laziness are pretty good signs of pregnancy. The belly gradually enlarges and the udder increases in size as gestation advances. The vulva becomes swollen and the muscles on the hips sag down and the flanks get hollow. Milk forms in the udder, and a good sign of foaling time is the formation of a wax-like substance on the ends of the teats two or four days before. The foal can generally be made to kick by giving the mare a drink of cold water. It may also be felt or seen kicking while the mare is eating as well as drinking. There may also be a flow of mucus from the vulva for a day or two before parturition. The animal may show slight uneasiness and abdominal pain for a day or two before foaling.

NATURAL PRESENTATIONS.

As a rule, foaling is easily and quickly done in the mare, it requiring usually not more than ten or twenty minutes. If labor is continued any length of time the colt usually dies; while with the cow it may last one or two days and the calf live. When the time comes she becomes uneasy, getting up and down frequently. Presently true labor pains begin, the womb contracts on its contents, assisted by the diaphram and abdominal muscles; and the whole body becomes convulsed with the effort. The mouth of the womb becomes dilated, and the water bag appears and bursts, and a few efforts forces it out. If the head of the unborn is covered with membranes, they should be removd at once, and if the cord is large and strong it should be tied with a string about three inches from the navel and then cut off an inch below that. If the cord breaks off close and there is a leakage from the navel it should be sewed up as soon as possible.

The natural presentation is for the front feet to come first, with the head on top of or between the knees, as seen in Figure 1, Plate. IV., or the hind feet may come first, as in Figure 2, Plate IV. In some cases the mouth of the womb is rigid and doesn't open sufficiently to allow the passage of the foal. In such cases it may be dilated by the hand or by smearing the parts with extract of belladonna.

UNNATURAL PRESENTATIONS.

There are a great many unnatural presentations, and it will take too much space to describe them all here; therefore we will try and make plain a few of the more common ones. Considering the immense number of mares in a breeding district that will

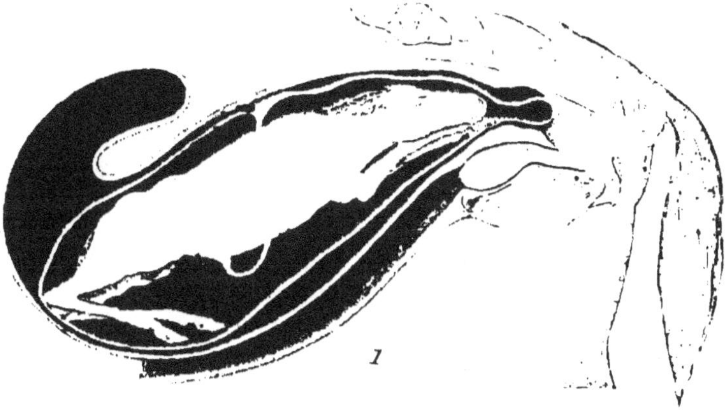

1

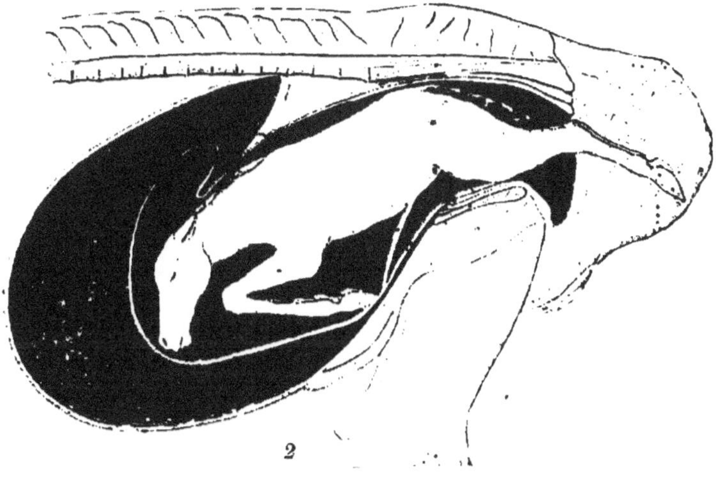

2

PLATE IV. NATURAL PRESENTATIONS IN THE MARE.

give birth to a foal every year, this trouble is very rare, but is more frequent in cows. A common presentation is that in which the head of the foetus is presented in a proper manner with the fore limbs turned backward. (Figs. 1 and 2, Plate X., as seen in unnatural presentations in the cow.) In all cases, before making an examination, the operator should prepare himself by taking off his coat and vest, shirt and undershirt, so as to have free use of the bare arms. Get your hand and arm warm and clean by washing well in warm water and soap, and lubricate them well with sweet oil. If after examination you should find the trouble to be as just mentioned above, the head should be pushed back to allow the hand to pass into the womb and grasp the ankles of the front feet, which may be brought forward, and as a rule delivery is then easily done. In some cases it may be necessary to pass a small cotton rope around the ankles to help pull them into position. After once in proper position, gentle pulling can be done to aid the mare in delivering the foal. It is best to pull when labor pains are on.

Presentation of the front legs with the head turned back is a very bad one, and often requires a great deal of work to get the foal in the proper position. (Figs. 4 and 5, Plate X.) Push back on the feet and try and grasp the underjaw with your hand, when the head may be brought into the proper position and delivery made easy. It may be well to fasten a cotton rope around each foot and then try and loop another rope around the lower jaw. When you have the rope fastened to the lower jaw, push back on the feet and pull gently on the jaw, and in this way you may succeed in bringing the head into the natural presentation.

Sometimes the foal is found lying on its back, and only the ears and back of its head can be felt. (Fig. 6, Plate X.) In a case of this kind every effort should be made to turn the foal on its belly, and by securing the front feet delivery may be made.

Breech presentation, or presentation of the hind quarters, is

14

one in which delivery is very frequently rendered impossible, or can be made only with the greatest difficulty. We have had cases of this kind in large mares, where we have worked six hours or more before delivering the foal, and in some cases delivery is impossible without cutting up the foal and taking it away in pieces. You must try and push the colt forward, and either try to turn it around or get hold of the hind feet, and get them in the passage, and then delivery may be effected quite easily. After the mare has been trying to foal for two or three hours, the colt will as a general thing be dead; so now every effort should be made to save the mare by getting the colt away as best you can. A pair of partu-

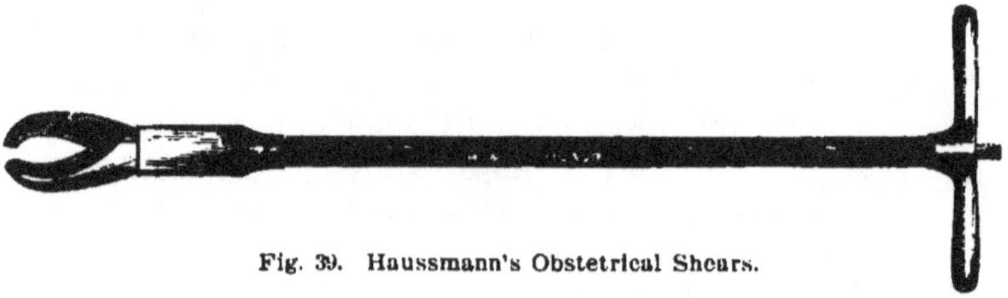

Fig. 39. Haussmann's Obstetrical Shears.

rition shears (Fig. 39) are very useful in cases of this kind. By pushing the foal forward you can then loop a rope around the hind legs above the hocks and straighten them back into a horizontal position. Then insert your parturition shears and cut off the legs above the hocks as far up as possible; then the foal may be delivered. The jaws of these shears can be opened and closed by turning the lever at the end of the handle.

Occasionally there may be one fore-limb and one hind-limb presented. In such cases great care should be taken not to pull on these two limbs, as it would be impossible to deliver the foal in this way. After making an examination and you decide to bring the colt away backwards, push the front leg back into the womb and secure the other hind leg, and then the foal may be delivered; or vice versa.

Back presentation is one of the most difficult of all unnatural presentations to deliver. Every effort should be made to turn the foal into its proper position.

In twins, one foal should come with the front feet and head first, while the other should come backwards.

Fig. 40. Embryotomy Knife.

Occasionally a case is met with in which there is a large accumulation of water on the brain, making it impossible for the head to come through the channel. In such a case the skull may be cut into with a knife, as in Fig. 40, and the water allowed to escape, when, as a general thing, delivery may be effected. There may be a large accumulation of water in the abdominal cavity (belly.) This can be punctured, and then delivery effected.

Monstrosities are sometimes found. A monstrosity is a deformed foetus (young animal), and it is sometimes of such a shape and size as to make delivery impossible without dissecting and removing it in pieces.

AFTER-TREATMENT OF THE MARE.

In all severe cases of delivery the mare should have special care for some time afterwards. If she is weak, and there is danger of inflammation setting in, give a drench of the following:

Laudanum	1½ ounces.
Sweet nitre	2 ounces.
Whisky	4 ounces.
Water	½ pint.

Mix, and give as a drench, and repeat every four hours until you have given three doses; then leave off the laudanum and repeat the sweet nitre until the animal is stronger.

Inject into the womb with a large syringe or injection pump (Fig. 13, p. 70) one or two gallons of warm water, into which put 1 teaspoon of carbolic acid to each gallon of water. If necessary, repeat the injections every morning for three or four days. Give her all the fresh water she will drink, and soft, easily digested food to eat.

RETENTION OF THE PLACENTA (AFTERBIRTH).

This is of rare occurrence in the mare, but is very common among cows. It is never advisable to remove the afterbirth immediately after delivery, as serious results are liable to follow. If it is allowed to remain twenty-four hours it may come away of itself. In the cow the placenta is attached to the womb by means of sixty or seventy small round fleshy bodies called *cotyledons;* while in the mare the attachment is by small *villi.* If the afterbirth remains in longer than twenty-four hours it should be removed, as decay will set in, and the animal is very liable to take blood poisoning from it. We advise its removal with the hand, where there is any one who understands how to remove it. Great care should be taken not to injure the womb and cause bleeding. The bare hand and arm should be oiled and gently inserted; and in the cow the afterbirth should be carefully unbuttoned, as it were, from each cotyledon, great care being taken not to pull off the cotyledons themselves. In the mare it can be gently separated from all its attached portions and removed. After removing the afterbirth wash out the womb well with water and carbolic acid as recommended above. If the afterbirth has started to decay and smells bad, the operator should oil his arm well with sweet oil 4 ounces and carbolic acid 2 drams, to prevent taking blood poison. The hand should never be inserted in cases of this kind if it has any sores on it. Sometimes the afterbirth may be brought away by giving the cow 1 ounce of ergot as a drench every four hours, until two or three doses have been given.

HEMORRHAGE AFTER DELIVERY.

Very profuse bleeding sometimes takes place after delivery in both the mare and the cow, due to rupture of some blood vessel in the womb. This may be checked by applying cold water and ice to the loins and cleaning out the blood clots and injecting into the womb a strong solution of tincture of iron. The womb may be packed full of cloths wrung out of cold water. Also may give 1 ounce of ergot of rye.

INVERSION OF THE WOMB.

This is a turning inside-out of the womb, generally due to difficult delivery, and of violent straining by the animal due to after-pains. It is more common among cows, and may take place immediately after calving or not until twenty-four hours or more. The womb protrudes from the vulva sometimes as large as a water bucket, and the animal in lying down gets the parts all dirty and filthy.

Treatment.—The animal should be made to rise and stand in a position so that the hind quarters are 8 or 12 inches higher than the front parts. The womb, if dirty, should be nicely washed with warm water and a little carbolic acid and gently returned to its place, which in some cases is found very difficult. If the animal has a tendency to strain after the womb is returned, it may be quieted by giving 1 ounce of laudanum in 1 pint of water as a drench every two hours. In some cases it is found very hard to keep the animal from forcing the womb out again. Keep the animal standing or lying with her head down hill, and a truss may be applied to keep the womb from coming out. The most convenient truss for a cow we have used is made from a piece of small cotton rope about twenty feet long. Tie a loop in the center of the rope large enough to go over her head and back on the neck. Pass the ends of the rope between the fore legs, and bring one up on each side and make a single tie over the loins; then pass it back and make another single tie right under the tail, and another over the vulva; then pass the ends of the rope between the hind legs, one on each side of the bag. Then bring them up on each side of the body and tie them to the ropes that pass along her sides. Keep this moderately tight for a day or two. If the womb has been out for two or three days and is partly decayed, it will have to be removed. This is not successful in the mare, but is quite so with the cow. It can be removed with the ecrasure, which is the best and safest means of cutting it off. It may be cut off with a knife, and the arteries tied to stop the bleeding.

INFLAMMATION OF THE WOMB.

This is a very serious condition, and when the womb is inflamed to any great extent, is invariably fatal. It is caused by difficult delivery, injuries to the womb, exposure to cold and wet, and from the irritant action of putrid products within the womb.

Symptoms.—There is a stiff, slow gait, an arched back, dullness, uneasiness with lifting of the hind feet, indicating pain, a discharge from the vulva of a watery nature at first, then becomes reddish or yellowish, and foetid in character. By pressing the animal's sides there is pain shown.

Treatment.—Great pains should be taken that the womb be thoroughly washed out with warm water and carbolic acid or warm water and corrosive sublimate; 1 part to 200 may be used with benefit. Syringe the womb out thoroughly every day. Give internally the following:

Laudanum	1½ ounces.
Tr. aconite	20 drops.
Alcohol	3 ounces
Water	½ pint.

Mix, and give as a drench every four hours until three or four doses are given.

Keep the animal in a comfortable place and give what water and food she will take. If a cow, you may give half a pound of Epsom salts, and repeat in twelve hours. If a mare, give half a pint of raw linseed oil. This is a very serious disease, and most cases will die.

LEUCORRHOEA, OR WHITES.

This is a white, glutinous, chronic discharge from the womb. It is generally due to a continued sub-acute inflammation of the mucus membrane of the womb.

Treatment.—Wash out the womb with warm water, and then inject the following:

Sulphate of zinc	6 drams.
Acetate of lead	1 ounce.
Water	1 quart.

Repeat this twice a day for several days. Or a solution as follows may be injected:

Permanganate of potash	2 ounces.
Water	1 gallon.

Give the following:

Sulphate of iron	2	ounces.
Powdered nux vomica	1½	ounces.
Gentian	3	ounces.

Mix into twelve powders, and give one powder night and morning in damp feed.

ABORTION.

Abortion is the expulsion of the young animal at any period from the date of impregnation until the animal can live out of the womb. Abortion is quite a common occurrence among mares, but still more prevalent among cows. There is one form of abortion that is contagious, and it causes immense losses to breeders in certain sections of the country.

Causes.—Abortion may be caused by rapid driving or riding, blows on the abdomen, drinking a quantity of cold water, excitement, or fright, etc. Slipping, falling, bleeding an animal, or inflammation of any of the internal organs, as the lungs, kidneys, liver, bowels, etc., may tend to cause miscarriage. Giving strong doses of physic, or for the animals to eat certain kinds of irritant foods and grasses, such as ergot of rye, etc., will have a tendency to cause the trouble. In the contagious form it is caused by a certain germ gaining access to the animal's system, and exciting the womb to contractions and abortion.

Symptoms.—The symptoms vary greatly according to whether the abortion takes place early or late in pregnancy. If it takes place during the first two or three months there are generally very little symptoms to be observed, and frequently an animal will abort and be in heat before the owner is aware that anything has happened. Later in pregnancy it may be very dangerous to the animal for miscarriage to take place. The animal will often become very sick, with severe straining and much uneasiness.

There is often swelling of the vulva with a mucus or bloody discharge. There will be all the symptoms of parturition, and unless the young is in a natural presentation, it will have to be rectified before delivery can be affected. Abortion may also be followed by retention of the afterbirth, bleeding, etc., as in parturition.

Treatment and Prevention.—Both in the pregnant mare and cow all treatment and usage that is liable to cause abortion should be abandoned; for if an animal is caused to abort, from whatever cause, it is very liable to abort again the next season. If the symptoms of abortion are noticed coming on, the animal should be removed from all other pregnant animals: and if there is much pain it should be quieted by giving one or two ounces of laudanum as a drench. Black-haw in 1-ounce doses may prevent the impending abortion. Keep the animal perfectly quiet and give the very best of care. If miscarriage takes place, the animal, especially if it be a cow, should be at once removed from all pregnant cows, and every trace of the calf, afterbirth, etc., removed and burned or buried deeply. Wash out the womb with warm water containing half an ounce of carbolic acid to the gallon. Keep her away from the other pregnant animals until all discharges from the vulva cease, which will be from eight to twelve days. If a cow that has aborted is let remain with the other cows, they are very liable to abort also. If the afterbirth does not come away with the foetus, it should be removed and destroyed. Cases are on record where contagious abortion has caused nearly all the pregnant animals on a farm or ranch to abort.

STERILITY, OR BARRENNESS.

This is a condition that may be found in all animals, both male and female. A very common cause in cattle is breeding too young and inbreeding too closely, which naturally weakens the constitution and causes barrenness. Jerseys have especially been injured in this way. Sterility in the stallion is often due to one or both testicles failing to come down into the scrotum (bag). The testicles that haven't come down are seldom developed sufficiently to secrete the semen. Therefore it is quite safe to say that ridglings are barren as a general thing. Inflammation of the testicles, resulting in a hardened condition of the same, may be a cause of barrenness; or fatty degeneration of the testicles. Any disease that weakens the system or makes it painful for the stallion or bull to mount, may be a cause of sterility. Occasionally there is a local paralysis or weakness in connection with the penis which makes it impossible for the animal to protrude his penis far enough for service. Cows and mares may be too fat to breed; also the opposite condition may be present. There may be an imperfect development of the ovaries, cysts or other tumors of the ovary. A chronic inflammation of the vagina and womb, as whites, etc., may cause barrenness. Another very common cause of this trouble in the mare is the closure of the neck of the womb. This can be remedied by introducing the hand and gradually dilating the parts with the fingers. Cows and mares used for breeding purposes shouldn't be overfed nor underfed, but fed moderately and well cared for. They should be free from all diseases and blemishes, and of strong mature age—not too old nor too young.

EXCESS OF VENERAL DESIRE.

This is seen both in mares and cows, and is very troublesome to the animal and very annoying to the owner. It is seen more frequently in cows, and they are called "perpetual bullers." It may be caused by certain strong, stimulating kinds of food, but it is more frequently caused by irritation in some portion of the generative organs. Disease of the ovaries is the most common cause, as it excites the sexual desire and causes the animal to seek the male continually. It may be due to tumors in the vagina or womb, and if they do become pregnant they generally abort. The animal is generally so irritable and restless that it falls off in flesh and is a source of annoyance to the whole herd.

Treatment.—If it is due to disease of the ovaries, remove them by spaying the animal, and the trouble will cease. If due to an inflamed or irritated womb or vagina, that may be relieved by injections of water containing a little carbolic acid. As it is incurable in a great many cases, it may be well to get rid of the animal, as they are not desirable property to have about.

CHAPTER XV.

CASTRATION OF STALLIONS.

The proper age usually for castrating colts is about one year old, but it may be perfomed at a few months old, or several years old. Taking everything into consideration, we believe at one year old is the best time for castration, provided the colt is in good health and his testicles are down. About the best time for castration is during March and April and October and November. It is not advisable to castrate during the summer, as the flies are too bad and the weather too hot. Any time during the winter does very well, if a norther doesn't blow up in a day or two after the operation; but if a warm stable is to be had, there is no danger from the cold. As far as the "signs" of the moon are concerned, that is all bosh. It is an old grandmother idea, and very hard to get out of some men's heads. Have your colts in good condition and the weather right, and that is all the "signs" you need; and then if the operation is properly performed your colts will do all right. Castrating old stallions is more dangerous than young colts, but if they are in good health, with clean surroundings, and the operation properly performed, there is no danger whatever to be feared.

There are several methods by which the operation can be performed, such as the clamps, searing, ligaturing, torsion, ecrasure (Fig. 41), and emasculator (Fig. 42). The last two ways are the only proper methods to be used. The first four methods named are old-styled and away out of date, and are not used at all at the present time by the veterinary profession. To operate by either of the two last methods the animal is either thrown or operated on standing; we prefer to throw (Fig. 43) the animal. When the animal is tied, make an examination of the parts, and

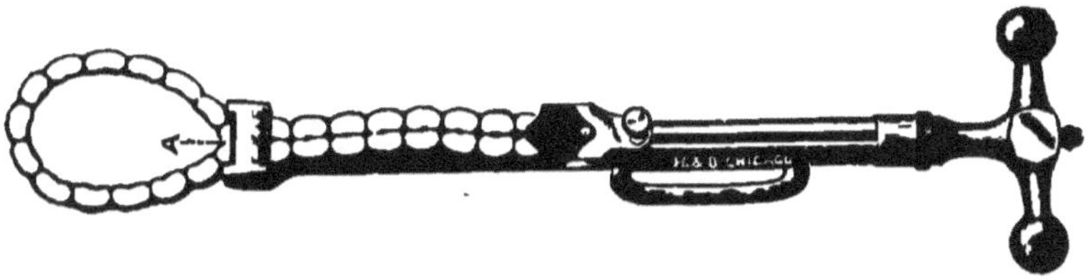

Fig. 41. Miles' Ecrasure.

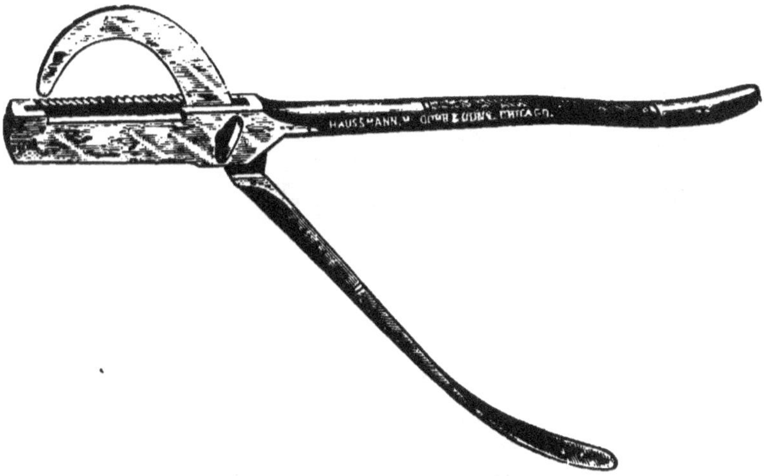

Fig. 42. Haussmann's Emasculator.

if no hernia (rupture) is present, take a firm hold on one of the testicles, and with a sharp knife (Figs. 44 and 45) make a free incision from before backwards about three-fourths of an inch to one side of the centre division (raphe). Be sure you have your hands and instruments perfectly clean before operating, so as not to poison the wound. Cut deep enough to let the testicle out of the scrotum (bag). Then grasp the other one and let it out by cutting on the other side about the same distance from the center. Put the chain of the ecrasure on the cord, or grasp it with the emasculator, and cut it in two with whichever instru-

a.

(*a*) The horse ready to be thrown.

b.

(*b*) The horse thrown and tied.

Fig. 43. THROWING THE HORSE.

ment you use. These, by their structure and method of cutting, stop all bleeding from the cord. Before letting the horse up, see that you have a good, big hole, so that all the matter will drain that forms in the wound for several days. The after-treatment consists in giving the animal good, nutritious food, plenty of exercise, and don't let him get wet in a cold rain for at least ten days. As there are certain normal and abnormal results that follow castration, we will give a few of them below:

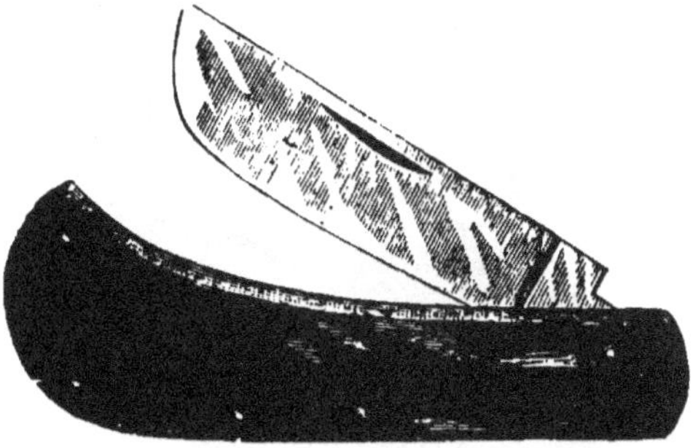

Fig. 44. Castrating Knife—single blade.

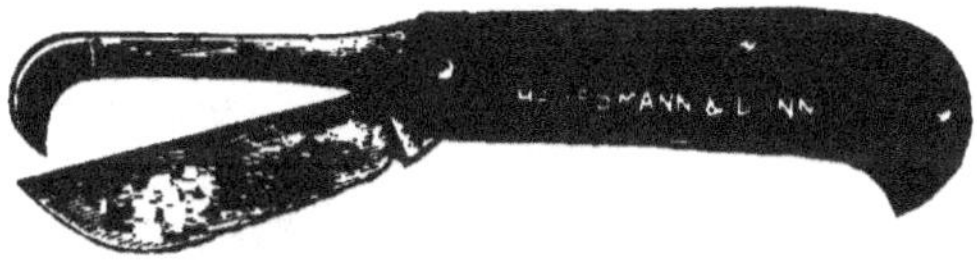

Fig. 45. Castrating Knife—double blade.

SWELLING.—This is a normal condition, as it takes place more or less after every castration. As long as the animal has its appetite and shows no signs of high fever, there need be no alarm over the swelling. If the swelling becomes considerable, bathe the parts frequently with warm water and insert your clean fingers up into the holes to keep them open. Give plenty of gentle exercise, and turn out to pasture if one can be had.

PAIN.—Pain, called "after pains," sometimes takes place after castration, and many occur in connection with the cord, or as a result of colic, etc. This may be relieved by walking exercise, but if it still persists, it can be relieved by giving Dr. LeGear's Colic Cure. (See Appendix.)

Fig. 46. Operating Hood, to protect the eyes and quiet the animal while being thrown for an operation.

BLEEDING.—Bleeding from the wound in the scrotum (bag) may be quite free, especially in warm weather, but need not cause any alarm, as it will invariably stop of itself. If bleeding takes place to any alarming extent from the large artery in the cord, it should be checked before the animal bleeds too much. This can gnerally be done by plugging up the wound with cloths wet in cold water. If this fails to check the blood, the animal should be thrown and the artery secured and tied with a silk string.

PERITONITIS.—Peritonitis (inflammation of the lining of the bowel cavity) may take place after the operation has been performed in a bungling manner, or by exposing the animal to wet and cold. This result is known by severe swelling, loss of appetite, high fever, severe internal pain, but the animal does not roll. When peritonitis sets in, the animal will die, as a general thing. Bathe the swollen parts freely with warm water and give internally Dr. LeGear's Colic Cure. (See Appendix.) Keep the animal comfortable, in a dry, warm place, etc.

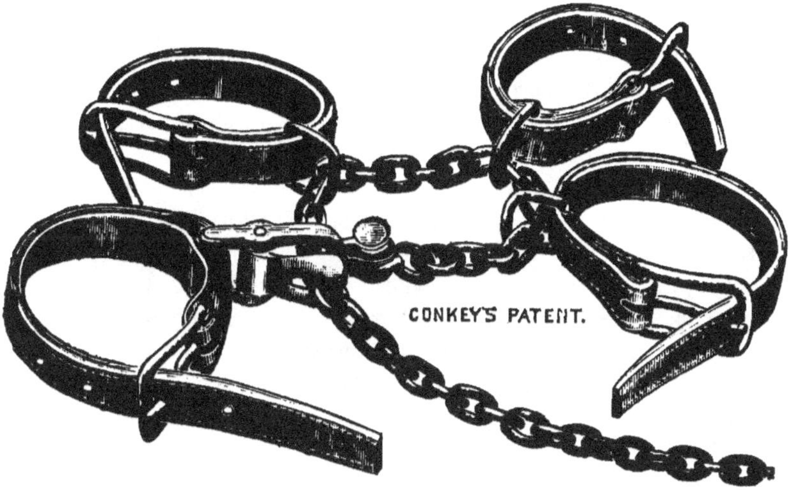

Fig. 47. Baker's Hobbles, used for throwing a horse in common operations.

LOCKJAW. — Lockjaw occasionally follows the operation of castration. It may be brought on by exposure, or by the animal being kept in a damp, filthy stall or lot. Not much can be done for it.

RUPTURE.—It is quite a common thing for certain breeds of horses to be affected with hernia (rupture). Before castrating you should always examine the animal for rupture. Sometimes it may occur after the operation is performed, and the bowels protrude through the opening and may extend to the ground. If seen in time the animal should be thrown, the bowels put back and the wound sewed up. If they protrude to a considerable extent, it is almost useless to try to save the animal. Castration can be performed on a ruptured animal by what is known as the "covered operation," but this shouldn't be undertaken except by an experienced veterinarian.

SEEDY CORD.—This is the formation of a tumor on or in connection with the cord, caused by rough handling or dragging upon the cord, or by leaving it too long, which adheres to the side of the wound and begins a fibrous growth. Castrating with the clamps is the most frequent cause of this, as the clamps hold and stretch the cord down for one, two or three days, and after they are removed the cord has lost its power of retracting and is very liable to adhere to the sides of the wound and cause seedy-cord, or water-seed. These tumors generally keep on growing, and sometimes become of an enormous size, making it almost impossible for the animal to walk. The only remedy for this trouble is to thoroughly dissect them out. If taken before the tumor is very large it can be removed with not much trouble, but when the growth is of several months standing only a qualified veterinarian should undertake the operation.

CASTRATING RIDGLINGS.—A ridgling is an animal where one or both of his testicles has never come down. They are either lodged in the channel (inguinal canal) or in the abdominal cavity. The castrating of these animals is a very difficult task, and one that we can not explain so that the unprofessional mind can understand the operation. The testicle has no certain place to be lodged, but has several places where it is liable to be found. Although it is a serious and severe operation, yet if it is undertaken by a person thoroughly versed in the anatomy of the parts, and who understands the operation, there is no particular danger to the animal. Ridglings are as a rule very mean, ugly-dispositioned animals, and are not at all desirable to have about. Although they can serve a mare, it is only in exceptional cases that they can get a colt. The testicle or testicles that haven't come down are not very thoroughly developed, therefore the reason why the animal is barren.

SPAYING THE MARE.

Castration of the mare is a much more dangerous operation than in thefemales of other domesticated animals. Itisperformed only in those cases where the ovaries (pride) are diseased, and in those mares which are not wanted for breeding purposes. The operation can be performed in the flank or through the vagina. The latter is the best and safest method, but it takes considerable practice and certain costly instruments to be able to successfully perform it. Before thoroughly understanding this operation through the vagina, you must have a thorough knowledge of the anatomy of the parts. In operating in the flank, a hole is cut in the abdominal muscles in the left flank large enough to admit the hand. The hand is introduced into the abdominal cavity and the ovaries brough out and removed with the ecrasure. (Fig. 41.) The wound is then sewed up and the operation is complete. As we said before, this operation is a serious one, and should not be undertaken by any one save an experienced surgeon.

CHAPTER XVI.

DISEASES OF THE MALE ORGANS OF GENERATION.

ORCHITIS.

Orchitis is inflammation of the testicles, and is generally a very serious and painful affection.

Causes.—As a rule it is caused by direct injury, such as blows, kicks, covering mares in an improper manner, etc. It may also be caused by exposure to cold, and being confined in cold, damp lots, stables, etc.

Symptoms.—The parts become swollen and the animal suffers great pain. There is heat and tenderness in the scrotum (bag), and the animal walks in a stiff, straddling manner, and shows all signs of pain and misery. The animal will have more or less fever, a rapid pulse, and generally remains standing.

Treatment.—The treatment must be both local and constitutional. Keep the animal perfectly quiet and bathe the swollen testicles with warm water for hours at a time. Support the testicles by putting on a bandage, the ends of which may be passed between the hind legs and brought around and tied over the loins. Pad the bandage with cotton and keep it moist and warm by pouring on warm water. Apply astringent soothing lotions, such as

Sugar of lead	4 drams.
Laudanum	1 ounce.
Water	1 quart.

Mix, and apply three or four times a day.

Give internally a good physic, as the following:

Barbadoes aloes	1 ounce.
Nitrate of potash	2 drams.
Ginger	2 drams.
Water	1 pint.

Mix, and give as a drench.

After the inflammation has subsided and there is still swelling and accumulation of fluid in the bag, it may be absorbed by giving the following:

Iodide of potassium	1½ ounces.
Nitrate of potassium	2 ounces.
Copperas	1 ounce.

Mix, and make twelve powders, and give one in damp feed every morning.

HYDROCELE—DROPSY OF THE SCROTUM.

This is an affection which the stallion is sometimes afflicted with. It is an accumulation of water in the scrotum (bag), and is often the result of inflammation of the testicles, or may be due to local diseases of the testicles, cord, or walls of the sack.

Symptoms.—The symptoms are enlargement of the scrotum with water, being recognized by fluctuating under the fingers when examined. This is rather a rare condition and is not very serious as a general thing.

Treatment.—If the scrotum contains much serum (water) it should be drawn off with a hollow needle. It may be absorbed by painting the scrotum once a day with tincture of iodine and giving one dram of iodide of potassium every morning for two or three weeks.

ENLARGED TESTICLES.

This condition is occasionally met with in the stallion, and the testicle may enlarge to three or four times its natural size. It may be due to a chronic inflammation, and may increase in size very slowly. When this affection is recognized, the only successful treatment is castration.

PARAPHYMOSIS.

By paraphymosis is understood protrusion of the penis without power to retract it. It is caused by injuries directly or indirectly received. Stallions suffer more frequently than geldings. Too frequent service is often the cause, and we have seen it caused by large stallions injuring the penis by serving small mares.

Symptoms.—The penis protrudes from the sheath and is much swollen, and may or may not be very painful to the animal.

Treatment.—If taken in time it can generally be treated successfully. If swollen to any considerable extent the penis should be lightly scarified by cutting several small holes into it with a sharp knife, to let some of the blood and serum ooze out. After scarifying, bathe it nicely with warm water for an hour at a time, and then a solution of alum water applied. The penis should be supported by a bandage. Give one pint of raw linseed oil as a drench, and give one dram of nitrate of potash morning and night in damp feed. Feed plenty of bran mashes and no corn. If it is caused by too frequent service, give one dram of nux vomica every night for two or three weeks. If the case is too far advanced before treatment is begun and mortification sets in, the penis should be amputated (cut off), and the ecrasure is the best instrument for the operation. (See Fig. 41.)

PHYMOSIS.

This is just the opposite to paraphymosis, and consists of inability to protrude the penis from the sheath. It is generally due to some abnormal growth or contraction of the sheath, making it impossible for the animal to protrude the penis. Warts on the penis or in the sheath may cause it.

Treatment. — If due to warts, they should be removed by throwing the animal and withdrawing the penis from the sheath. If due to the constriction of the prepuce, it should be slit with a pair of scissors. If due to debility, feed well and give our Condition Powders. (See Appendix.)

PARALYSIS OF THE PENIS.

This is generally caused by blows or other injuries to the penis, or from too frequent and exhausting service. The causes are much the same as for paraphymosis.

Symptoms.—This is a local paralysis, and the penis hangs from the sheath in a flabby, pendulous, and often cold condition. The urine is generally passed in a slow, dribbling manner.

Treatment.—The animal should have good care and good, nourishing food. Give one dram of powdered nux vomica in a bran mash morning and night for two or three weeks. If the paralysis is due to an injury, bathe the injured parts with warm water and apply our Healing Lotion two or three times per day.

SELF-ABUSE—MASTURBATION.

This is a disgusting, weakening, vicious habit that some stallions acquire. It is done by stimulating the sexual desire to the discharge of semen, by rubbing the penis against the belly or between the front legs. Some stallions practice this vicious habit so much that they keep thin and poor, no matter how well fed. If in a common stallion of not much value for breeding purposes we would advise castration. It can be prevented by the use of a shield which is attached over the end of the sheath and fastened on by straps over the loins and between the thighs. Shields are generally made of netting or screening, and are so adjusted to the horse as to keep him from protruding his penis.

GONORRHOEA.

This is a disease seen occasionally among both horses and cattle, but more frequently among cattle. In cattle it is sometimes called "bull-burnt." It is an inflammation of the urethra (the canal that conveys the urine from the bladder), and sometimes becomes a very serious affection. Stallions or bulls affected with gonorrhoea will convey it to every female they have connection with. Females will also communicate it to males.

Causes.—It may arise from any cause that has a tendency to irritate the urethra of the male, or the urethra or vagina of the female. Gravel or irritating urine may irritate and inflame the urethra, which may remove the lining membrane and cause chancres or ulcers. Too frequent service is a prolific cause, and it may originate in the female from the whites.

Symptoms.—The animal shows considerable pain in urinating, which is frequently attempted, while only a little urine is passed. The animal evinces a great deal of pain by raising and stamping the hind legs and is disinclined to move. There is a whitish discharge from the penis or vagina. In neglected cases the membranes peel off, ulcers or chancres appear, and the bull or stallion may become totally useless from the sinuses in the penis, and large tumors, which calls for amputation of the penis.

Treatment.—Affected animals should not be allowed to copulate (serve), as the disease is communicated, and the previous sufferer endures greater pain. If noticed in the early stages, give the cow or bull one and one-half pounds of epsom salts, or the stallion or mare one ounce of aloes. Then give a good blood tonic, such as our Condition Powders. (See Appendix.)

Use as an injection the following:

Sulphate of zinc	1 dram.
Glycerine	4 ounces.
Soft water	6 ounces.

Mix, and inject with a syringe once per day. Or 20 grains of permanganate of potash in a pint of water is good.

All heating food should be abandoned and a light laxative diet given. Don't put the animal to hard work or severe exertion during an attack of gonorrhoea. The chancres should be burnt with caustic and then an astringent wash, as the above, applied.

FOULNESS OF THE SHEATH AND PENIS.

This is a very common trouble in geldings, due to their not protruding the penis very often out of its sheath. There accumulates a dark colored, sebaceous substance within the sheath and on the penis, which gets so abundant at times that it causes great uneasiness to the animal. This should be washed out occasionally with warm water and soap, using a soft cloth or sponge. After washing, grease all the inside of the sheath with a little sweet oil or fresh lard. Great care should be taken in washing it out, as the parts can be very easily injured and cause considerable swelling.

More trouble arises from the formation of little "beans" of a soft, clayish color in the cavity in the head of the penis. They sometimes obstruct the passage and cause the horse considerable trouble in staling. They should be removed by carefully drawing out the penis and removing them with the finger.

CHAPTER XVII.

THE FOOT.

The foot of the horse is undoubtedly one of the most important parts of the animal, and it is subject to many injuries and diseases, which, in part or in whole, render the animal unfit for the work he is intended to do. The old maxim, "No foot, no horse," is as true to-day as when first expressed. As the value of the horse depends largely or entirely upon his ability to labor, it is all important that his feet be kept sound. To do this it is necessary not only to know how to cure all diseases of the feet, but how to prevent them. The hard and rough work the horse is compelled to do, and the abuses the foot is put to by defective shoeing, are the fruitful causes of so many diseased and injured feet.

The foot may be said to be composed of the hoof and the structures contained therein. Within the hoof may be found the coffin bone, navicular bone, sensitive laminae, lateral cartilages, planter cushion, and fatty frog. The hoof is composed of the wall, sole, and frog. The wall is that portion of the hoof that can be seen when the foot is placed on the ground. The frog is the three-cornered portion of the bottom of the foot that terminates near the center of the foot in a point. The sole comprises the remaining portion of the bottom of the foot. The frog is composed of a soft, spongy tissue, and serves as a cushion to the foot. The lateral cartilages are pads of cartilage (gristle) placed one on each side of the foot in the region of the quarters. They are just inside the hoof and act as a spring to the heel while the animal is traveling. When they become diseased they turn to bone and are then called side-bones. The coffin-joint is situated deeply in the foot, and is formed by the union of the coffin bone, navicular bone, and os-coronae. When it becomes diseased it is very hard to treat, as the trouble is located so deeply in the foot. The coronary band is situated just to the inside of the top of the wall of the hoof, and it is from it the wall grows. A brief description of the diseases and injuries of the foot will be found below.

CONTRACTION, OR NARROW HEEL.

Contraction is not of itself a disease, but the symptom of disease. It is often called "narrow-heel," as the whole heel and frog waste away. Contraction is due to the atrophy or wasting away of the fatty frog and other vascular substances above the frog and within the heel. When these substances waste away the walls at the heel gradually draw in and form contraction, or narrow-heel. It is generally brought on by coffin-joint lameness or any fever in the heels. Improper shoeing, by cutting out the bars and frogs, and shoeing with high heel shoes, etc., are frequent causes of this trouble.

Treatment.—Dilatation of the hoof by mechanical means (hoof expanders, Fig. 48) is practiced very little in this country to what it is in France. In many cases, no doubt, hoof expanders are found to be beneficial in contraction. But when the contracted feet have to be expanded, there is a far more simple and effective means of attaining that end in the foot itself. By lowering the walls at the heels, so as to restore frog pressure, the latter speedily recovers its lost characteristics, and in a healthy condition gradually and naturally accomplishes one of the very purposes for which nature placed it there. In some cases tips properly applied and persisted in will cure contracted heels.

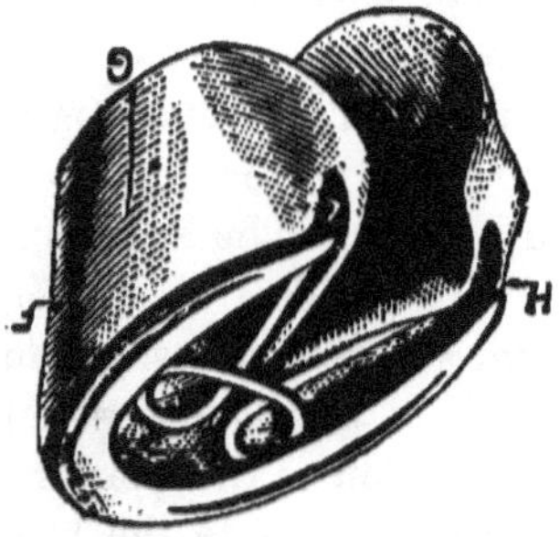

Fig. 48. Hoof-Expander.

FOUNDER—LAMINITIS.

Founder is a very painful disease of the horse and is very destructive to a horse's usefulness unless treated properly and taken in time. Laminitis is the professional name for the trouble meaning inflammation of the sensitive lamina (delicate internal part of the foot). Fever in the feet is another name for the trouble.

Causes.—There are a great many causes for founder, such as driving too hard on hard roads on a hot day; driving through cold streams of water, or giving the animal cold water to drink, while he is too warm; letting stand in a cold wind or storm while hot without protecting his body; eating too much corn or oats, etc. It may also be brought on by diarrhoea, or by giving too strong a physic. If a horse has been foundered, great care should be taken of him, as he will take it again very easily.

Symptoms. — The symptoms vary according to whether one, two, or all feet are affected. In a majority of cases both front feet are the ones affected. In these cases the animal will be found standing with his back arched, the hind feet carried forward towards the center of the body in order that the weight may be borne as much as possible by them and removed from the fore feet. If made to back, he drags his front feet as though he couldn't lift them from the ground. When made to go ahead, he does it with great difficulty, stumbling as he goes ahead. Founder is an excruciatingly painful disease, and the animal may break out in a sweat or shiver with pain. There is a rush of blood to the feet, which, by producing swelling inside of the hard, unyielding hoofs, presses on the many nerves and causes severe pain. The animal may lie down most of the time, which takes the pressure off the feet and affords some relief. There is generally a high fever and the pulse is fast and strong. If the disease is neglected rough rings or ridges grow on the hoofs by the fever interfering with the growth of the hoofs. (Fig. 49.) As founder affects principally the front of the foot, the animal will try to get relief by standing and walking on his heels. In severe cases the sole and wall may separate, and the coffin-bone come down through the bottom of the foot. This is called "pumiced foot." In chronic founder the horse may be very stiff on starting off, but he will limber up and drive very well until cooled off again.

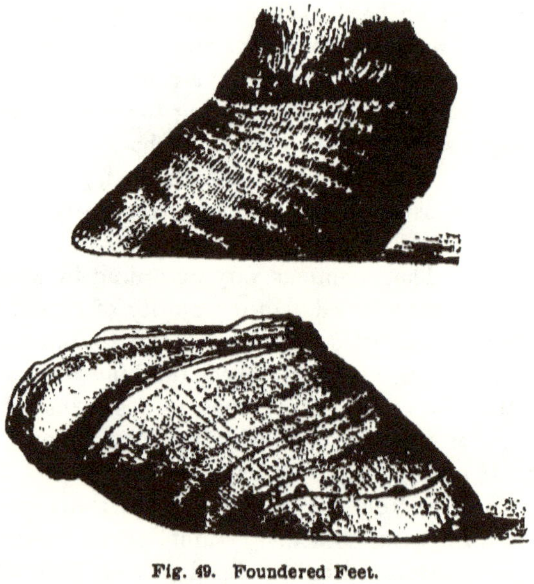

Fig. 49. Foundered Feet.

Treatment.—The treatment of founder should be commenced at once, and varies according to the cause. If caused by eating too much grain, or by drinking water while warm, or by hard driving, give the following physic:

Barbadoes aloes	1 ounce.
Nitrate of potash	4 drams.
Tincture aconite	20 drops.
Ginger	2 drams.
Water	1 pint.

Mix, and give as a drench.

Give 15 drops of tincture of aconite in a little water every four hours until four doses are given. Also give 2 drams of nitrate of potash every four hours for three days. Give bran mashes, etc., to eat. Applications to the feet are very necessary. If the horse can stand, put him in a running stream, or in a hole dug out of a stall, or in a corner of the lot having about four inches of clean water in it. Let him remain in the water two or three hours twice a day. After removing from water apply our Liniment well rubbed in, which is very necessary to draw out the soreness. Wet clay is very good to stand a horse in. In the winter warm poultices of bran and linseed can be tied on the feet with a piece of sack; or the horse may be stood in a tub of warm water. If the disease is brought on by too much physic or from diarrhoea, give the same treatment prescribed above with the exception of the physic. Don't give any physic in those cases. Always remove the shoes, and in some cases pare down the feet. Give walking exercise about the third day, and increase every day, on soft ground, as exercise is beneficial. Have a pair of wide web concave shoes tacked on loosely so as to protect the bottoms of the feet. If, after you have carried out the above treatment for ten days or two weeks, and there is still lameness, then don't put the horse in the water any more, but apply our Spavin Cure (see Appendix) well around the feet in the hair above the hoofs. This will draw out the remaining soreness and limber the horse up all right. If the above treatment is properly carried out, nine out of every ten cases of founder can be cured sound and well.

Old chronic cases of founder may be relieved by taking off the shoes and paring down the feet and standing the horse in water to his ankles five or six hours a day for fifteen or twenty days. Then blister the feet in the hair just above the hoofs well with our Spavin Cure. After blistering oil the whole foot well every day or two for two or three weeks with raw linseed oil or sweet oil.

SEEDY-TOE.

The term seedy-toe has been applied to a peculiar condition of the horn of the toe, which is rendered soft and crumbling.

Causes.—It may be due to an hereditary predisposition, the use of too large toe-clips, or to any irritation causing impaired secretion or interfering with the nutrition of the horn at the toe. It may not in all cases cause lameness, but is, nevertheless, an unsoundness.

Treatment.—Remove the shoe and cut down the toe, removing all the diseased horn. Keep the hoof moist with poultices, and then apply a good blister to the coronet to stimulate the growth of new horn. Continue the poultices, fomentations, etc., and if the sensitive structures are exposed and much irritation exists, the opening should be closed by pledgets of cotton saturated with any of the preparations of tar.

BRUISE OF THE SENSITIVE SOLE.

Causes.—It may be caused by stepping on a rock or other hard substances while traveling rapidly, or by a shoe upon a naturally thin sole, or a sole that has been cut down too much.

Symptoms.—The indications are lameness, heat in the part, and on tapping or pinching the parts the animal flinches, etc.

Treatment.—Remove the shoe, pare down the sole to a certain extent, and apply a poultice of flaxseed meal for two days. Applications of hot or cold water will be useful in allaying any swelling or irritation.

CORNS.

A corn is a bruise of the sensitive sole in the angle of the heel. Corns are of more frequent occurrence in the front feet, and are nearly always found on the inner side. There are three kinds of corns—hard, soft, and suppurating. The latter is by far the most serious, as pus is formed, and unless allowed to escape will cause serious trouble. (See Fig. 50.)

Causes.—Improper shoeing is very often the cause of corns, but horses running on the range may have corns. A bruise in the angle of the heel, from whatever cause, is liable to cause corns.

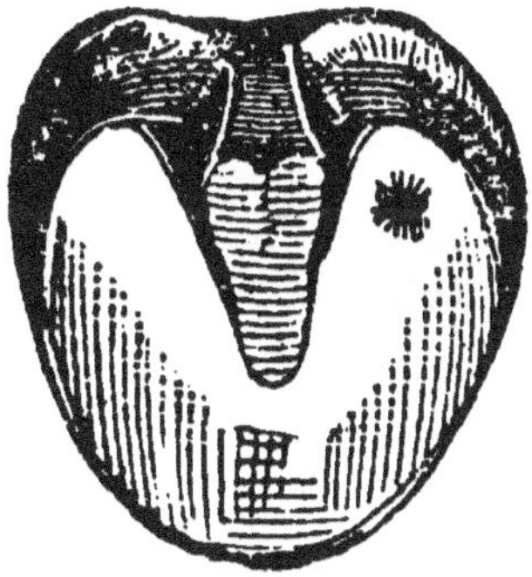

Fig. 50. A Corn.

Symptoms.—The animal is more or less lame, especially when he is trotting. There is a certain amount of heat over the parts. On squeezing the foot with a pair of forceps, or tapping the parts with a light hammer, the animal will evince pain. By paring out the sole over the seat of the corn redness may be seen, and if it is a suppurating corn matter will be found if cut out deep enough.

Treatment.—Remove the shoe, and having decided that a corn is present, cut or pare down carefully, using a suitable knife. (Fig. 51.) When the corn is reached, the pus, if any be present should be allowed to escape and the cavity cleansed out with Dr. LeGear's Healing Lotion. (See Appendix.) The heel should be cut down so as to take all pressure from the affected parts. Put a poultice on the foot, and give a few days' rest; afterwards put on either a bar shoe or a three-quarter shoe, either one of which will take the pressure from the corn. Change the shoes every four weeks and keep the corn well pared out and the horse will travel without much trouble.

Fig. 51. Hoof Knife.

GRAVEL IN THE FOOT.

Whenever a small stone gets into a horse's foot, either through a wound or works into a crevice in the sole or frog up into the quick, it is called "gravel." Some people attribute any matter breaking at the top of the hoof to gravel, which in many cases is merely matter working out from the effects of a bruise of the sole or a corn. If a gravel gets into the foot, and is small enough, it will finally work out at the top of the hoof. The horse is generally lame while it is in the foot, but will get over it as soon as it comes out.

Treatment.—If any soreness in the foot can be found it should be pared down, and if any matter or a gravel is found it should be removed and the cavity washed out for a few days with our Healing Lotion (see Appendix), and the hole protected from all dirt, and it will soon heal.

NAIL IN THE FOOT.

This is a very common occurrence, and though trivial as it seems, at times causes very serious trouble. Unless it penetrates through the sole or frog it never causes any inconvenience. If the nail penetrates the coffin-joint, or injures the bone or tendon, very serious symptoms are presented. When the joint is injured it causes the most painful and serious injury to which the foot is liable. Sometimes a nail enters the foot one or two inches and very little lameness is shown afterwards.

Symptoms.—It is by no means a very easy thing in all cases to detect a nail in a horse's foot, hence a very close and thorough examination should be made in all cases, or mistakes in diagnosis will be very liable to occur. We have known cases where a horse had a nail in his foot, and the owner would blister his hip or shoulders, thinking he had hip or shoulder lameness. In a majority of cases the nail comes out of itself, which is one reason why we are liable to think the soreness wasn't in the foot. Heat may be felt in the foot above the hoof. In all cases of suspected foot lameness the foot should be gently tapped with a light hammer, and if there is much soreness in the foot the horse will flinch and show signs of pain. It is by the hole closing up after the nail comes out, and the matter that forms not being able to escape, that causes the severe pain and lameness. Other objects, such as screws, broken glass, tacks, etc., may penetrate the foot and cause the same trouble that a nail does. Lockjaw is very frequently caused by nails penetrating the feet of horses; the nails being dirty and rusty, carry the germs of the disease into the foot, where they get into the circulation. If by tapping the foot, pain is evinced, the shoe should be taken off and the foot pared down to discover a nail hole if possible.

Treatment.—Having found the nail or whatever it may be, it should be removed at once, and the hole enlarged somewhat to allow a free escape of any pus that may form. The hole may be filled with turpentine, or a solution of carbolic acid, or still better, our Healing Lotion (see Appendix), and plugged with cotton to keep out the dirt. If the hole is found filled up, it should be well opened and cleaned out, and a warm poultice of equal parts of wheat bran and linseed meal be tied on the whole foot, and changed every six hours until four or five poultices have been applied. While the poultice is off, keep the hole plugged with cotton saturated with our Healing Lotion. While you are not poulticing, the cotton should be changed every day and the wound dressed nicely. Keep the horse in a dry, clean place until the sore heals up. Give rest and a laxative diet. Close attention and thorough cleanliness will often ward off an attack of lockjaw.

QUITTOR.

A quittor is a running sore at the top of the hoof, extending down inside of the hoof, sometimes penetrating deeply and involving the bone.

Causes.—Pus occurring in the foot, from any cause whatever, may result in quittor, for the reason that the pus, being unable to escape, extends in various directions, destroying the tissues in its course, increases in quantity, until, finally reaching the top of the hoof, it bursts forth, making an outlet for itself and forming a running sore, when it becomes known as a quittor. Nail in the foot, suppurating corns, or pricks from being shod, may all run into quittor by the matter being unable to get out the bottom of the foot. A gravel will sometimes work out the top of the hoof and form a quittor.

Symptoms.—The animal becomes very lame, and on examining the foot a hard swelling will be found at the top of the hoof, which becomes soft in a day or two and bursts and runs pus. A hole remains which does not heal. Sometimes two or three holes are formed, and then it is a very serious thing. Very frequently matter will burst out at the top of the hoof, and in a day or two will all heal up. Such a case is not a quittor.

Treatment.—Quittor when once well established is very hard to cure. Remove the shoe and thin down the sole and try and let the matter out at the bottom by free drainage. Inject a little of the following solution into the opening: Corrosive sublimate 1 dram, alcohol 2 ounces. Dissect away all the diseased portions above the hoof and cauterize it with a hot iron. In a bad case of quittor a qualified veterinary surgeon should be employed. Treatment is so difficult and uncertain that the average horse owner will not make much headway in the treatment of quittor.

THRUSH.

Thrush is a disease of the horse's foot, shown by a very bad smelling, dark-colored matter coming from the cleft of the frog.

Causes.—The most common cause of thrush is the filthy condition of the stable or lot in which the horse is kept. A sudden change from dryness to excessive moisture may cause the disease. Muddy streets and roads, especially where mineral substances are plentiful, cause the disease. Contracted heels, scratches and navicular disease predispose to thrush.

Symptoms.—There is a discharge of a yellowish or dark-colored matter from the cleft of the frog. This matter has a very offensive smell, and if once smelled will always be remembered.

There may be some tenderness, but it is seldom that the disease causes lameness.

Treatment.—If the animal is standing in filth or mud, remove him to a clean, dry place. Trim off all diseased and ragged portions of the frog and wash all dirt and filth thoroughly from the whole foot and apply a linseed or wheat bran poultice to the affected parts for one or two days. Add a little carbolic acid to the poultice to remove the bad smell. After removing poultice, clean out the cleft of the frog and pour in a little peroxide of hydrogen twice a day and pack a piece of cotton well into the frog to retain the medicine and keep out dirt. Calomel dusted into the frog once a day and retained in it by a little cotton is a good remedy.

CANKER.

Canker is a cancerous-looking fungoid growth in connection with the frog or heel of the horse's foot.

Causes.—This disease is seen more frequently in heavy draft horses. The essential cause of canker is the presence of a vegetable parasite, which gains access to the foot of the horse by standing in filthy stalls and stables. It may also follow thrush, grease, or cracked heels.

Symptoms.—There is a soft, spongy, unhealthy looking growth in connection with some part of the frog or heel of the foot. On being cut it bleeds very freely, and there is generally a mattery discharge of a very offensive odor. The growth may extend and involve the whole sole and frog, and the horse is more or less lame.

Treatment.—The treatment of cankers is tedious, and not very successful, it being in all cases difficult to cure. Unless in a valuable animal we wouldn't advise treatment, as it will take more time and expense than the animal is worth, and then you are liable to fail in your efforts. If treatment is advisable, cut away all diseased parts you can with a sharp knife, and cauterize it with a hot iron to stop the blood and destroy what remaining portions of the disease you can. Keep the foot as clean as possible and apply equal parts of powdered charcoal and calomel twice per day. A weak solution of carbolic acid may be beneficial. Give in the feed 2 tablespoonsful of Fowler's Solution of Arsenic once a day for two or three weeks.

SAND-CRACK.

A sand-crack is a fissure or crack in the wall of the hoof. These cracks may exist in any part of the wall, and receive various names, according to their location. Thus a crack in the front part of the hoof is called a centre-crack or toe crack, and one at the quarter a quarter-crack. (Fig. 52.) The crack may extend part way or all the way from top to bottom. Some cracks begin at the top and extend downward, while others begin at the bottom and work up. The former are much more severe. A crack beginning at the bottom and extending up a short distance seldom if ever causes any trouble.

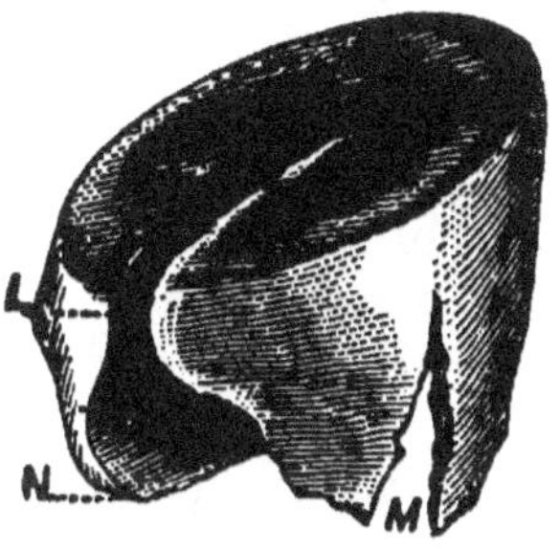

Fig. 52. Quarter-Crack.

Causes.—Horses having thin, brittle hoofs, and being driven on hard roads in dry weather, are liable to have sand-cracks. They are very common among trotting and running horses by being worked so fast on hard tracks. Shoeing with high heels and toe calks may cause sand-cracks. Horses standing on hard, dry floors, with no care being taken of the feet, are liable to have the trouble. Every horse that is worked or ridden during the dry summer should be stood in water for an hour at a time two or three times a week. This cools out the feet and keeps the hoofs moist, pliable and healthy.

Symptoms.—The crack can generally be plainly seen, but at first it may be very small, but still cause lameness. The crack may be very small and just beginning at the top, but it is sore and painful, and causes blood to ooze out. A toe-crack in the hind foot is generally a very serious trouble. Dishonest traders or dealers sometimes fill up the crack with tar, hoof ointment, guttapercha, etc., or walk a horse through the mud to conceal the crack before trading. A horse may have an extensive toe-crack or quarter-crack and not be lame at all. It constitutes an unsoundness, and should be looked upon with suspicion.

Treatment. — Give the animal rest, pare the foot under the crack, and put on a shoe to take pressure off the affected quarter or part of the toe. There are several forms of treatment used in this trouble, all of which are very good if properly carried out. The form of treatment we prefer is to take out a piece of the hoof the shape of the leter V with the base upwards, and right at the top border of the hoof and the point comes into the crack. Have each side of this letter V about one inch long. By taking out a piece of the hoof right across where the crack begins will let the hoof grow solid when it grows in. A good blister of our Spavin Cure should be applied in the hair just above where the crack was after operating on it, to stimulate a more strong and healthy growth of hoof. After blistering, grease well every day with sweet oil. Keep the horse quiet for a couple of weeks during treatment, and then turn him to grass for two or three months, when a cure is generally complete. Another form of treatment is to put on a nice, light brass plate or clinch to prevent motion in the parts. A small cotton rope may be wound around the hoof from top to bottom very tightly, and then paint it with tar, and turn the horse on pasture for a couple of months. Sometimes a nail can be expertly driven through the edges of the crack to hold it together.

COFFIN-JOINT LAMENESS.

This disease is more properly known as "Navicular Disease," as the little navicular bone is the part mostly affected. (See Fig. 53.) The flexor tendon and bursa of the joint are also diseased in most of cases, but the disease more frequently begins in the bone. It is estimated that this disease is the cause of a majority of all serious and obscure lameness in the front feet of horses, and if neglected or not properly treated for three or six months, it becomes incurable by certain changes taking place in the parts.

Fig. 53. Navicular Disease.

Causes.—The most frequent cause of coffin-joint lameness is hard and fast work on hard roads, and sprains of the joint. In some cases the disease is produced suddenly, as by a severe sprain, and at other times it comes on very gradually. The disease is seen more frequently in certain breeds of horses, as those having straight, upright pasterns and a pounding action while traveling. One or both front feet may be affected, but it rarely ever occurs in the hind feet. The disease may be caused by nails piercing through the frog and injuring the flexor tendon or the coffin-joint. Improper shoeing is undoubtedly a very frequent cause of coffin-joint lameness. This is brought about by raising or lowering the heels too much, allowing the toe to grow too long, or any cause of changing the proper adjustment of the foot, etc. The frog is nature's great cushion or support to the foot, and when it is removed from the ground by paring or by high-heeled shoes, the foot is then far more liable to diseases of various kinds. The frog should be allowed to come on the ground, as nature intended it should.

Symptoms.—This disease in most of cases comes on very gradually. The horse is noticed slightly lame, or a little tender, for one, two, or three days or a week, when it will disappear as mysteriously as it came. In a few weeks the lameness returns, but will be a little worse, and last a few days longer than the first attack. It may continue to appear and disappear for three or four attacks, when it is liable to come to stay. The horse points the foot—that is, places it out in front of the other—and contraction may or may not be present. After a time contraction of the heel, wasting of the frog, and in fact the whole foot gets smaller than the healthy one. When both front feet are affected the animal will first point one and then the other. By placing the foot out in front it takes the strain off the flexor tendon and the navicular bone, thus giving relief. The wall of the foot gets hard, smooth, and glassy, and not rough and in ridges as in founder. The animal has a tendency to stumble and wears the toe of the shoe off first. The soreness of this disease is in the heel, and the animal tries to bring his toe to the ground first, while founder affects principally the toe of the foot, and the animal tries to get relief by standing and walking on its heels. If this disease is caused by a severe sprain or by an injury, the symptoms will be more suddenly developed. He may improve after a few days, and then take worse and run much the same course as that described above. The advancement this disease makes depends a great deal on the kind of work an animal has to do. If used regularly on hard roads, they will as a general thing get so lame they are useless in a few months; while for farm work they may go on and work tolerably well for years. When both front feet are affected about alike, an animal can't limp, but will have a peculiar short step, called "groggy action."

Treatment. — The curative treatment of this disease, unless taken in the early stages, is almost useless. There are certain changes that take place in connection with the navicular bone and flexor tendon that can not be rectified when once established. So many horsemen and would-be horse doctors locate every obscure lameness a horse has in front, in the shoulders, and put the poor brute to unnecessary suffering by blistering, burning, seatoning, etc., the shoulder, when invariably the lameness is in the foot. In shoulder lameness the animal has difficulty in picking up the foot and bringing it forward, but if the soreness is below the knee he will have no trouble in this respect. A horse affected in both feet does look, to an ordinary observer, as though it might be in the shoulders, by the animal being so stiff, but this is brought about by the animal trying to keep both feet on the ground all the time; therefore he steps very short. When the disease is first detected the animal should be laid off from all work, the shoe removed, and the foot at the toe pared down, and a shoe with slightly thickened heels put on to tip the foot slightly forward. Then place the foot in a warm water bath. Provide a tub or box, into which put about eight inches of water as warm as the hand will stand, and keep it at about the same temperature by adding hot water occasionally. Stand the horse in the water for two hours at a time twice a day for one week or ten days. If the fever and soreness seem to be pretty well gone by that time, then apply a good blister, using our Spavin Cure (see Appendix) well rubbed into the heels and quarters. This form of treatment thoroughly carried out at the beginning of the disease may form a cure. In place of the hot water bath, warm bran poultices may be kept on the feet several hours a day. After the disease is well established the above treatment will only relieve and not cure it. When the disease becomes incurable, all we can do is to relieve the animal by certain forms of shoeing, keeping the foot soft by bathing, or by nerving the foot. Apply either a bar shoe with slightly thickened heels, or a light, plain shoe with a small heel salk, to raise the heels slightly. (See Figs. 4 and 5, Plate VI., special shoes, page 254.) During the dry summer weather stand the horse either in a mud or water bath to his ankles three or four times a week for an hour at a time, and blister the quarters and heels once a month with our Spavin Cure. After the animal gets so lame he is useless for the work he is intended to do, then the only relief for him is by performing the operation of neurotomy (nerving), which is done by cutting a small hole just above the ankle on each side and removing a portion of the nerve. It is advisable to perform this operation only in animals that have good, strong feet. No matter how sore the foot is, the animal will not limp after the operation is performed, as there is no feeling left in the foot. By being careful what kind of feet we operate on, we have had good success with this operation. In some cases the animal will go on and do its regular work for years without laming at all. This operation, although not successful in all cases, is in some cases an act of mercy to perform, as it instantly relieves all pain from the poor sufferer's foot. As this is a particular operation, we wouldn't advise any one but a qualified veterinary surgeon to perform it, as he can judge whether the operation is advisable, and is competent of perform-it if necessary.

CHAPTER XVIII.

HORSESHOEING.

History tells us that the Romans made horseshoes and used them on their horses about the eleventh and twelfth centuries. The first shoe consisted of a thin plate, with a rim around the outside, which covered the whole ground surface of the foot. Around the outside of this plate rings or loops were fastened, through which small ropes were drawn, and in this way the shoe was fastened to the hoof and pastern. This mode of fastening became unsatisfactory, and a substitute was found in the so-called "Asiatic cap iron sole," which was also made of a plate of iron covering the whole sole, with a rim around the outside of it about one-half inch in height, and upon this rim, on both sides of the shoe, rose three beak-like projections about one inch high, which were fastened into the wall of the hoof in the form of a hook. This mode of fastening also being insufficient, fastening of the shoes by nails, as at the present time, was adopted. The iron plates with rims were too thin to allow nails with sunken heads to be used, so nails with cubical shaped heads were used. A shoe containing a groove made its appearance first in Germany in the fifteenth century, and from this time, as far as we know, ceases the period of the Roman horseshoe. Its influence, however, has even remained until our present day. The science of horseshoeing at the present time is a question of vast importance, not only to mechanics, but to every thinking mind. It is not fully realized the amount of injury being done by poor horseshoeing. The art of farriery is a branch of science which is very valuable to the public. The public ought to support the educated farrier, one who has studied the anatomy of the horse's hoof, is progressive, skilled in his profession, and no other. Practical and scientific horseshoeing is what is needed at the present time, more so than ever before.

THE FOOT.

Preparing the foot for the shoe is of the greatest practical importance in the farrier's art. This is one of the first things he must learn to do, and it takes considerable time, study, and practice to learn how to do it properly. It is advisable at first to get a dead foot, dissect it, and study its anatomy before practicing on the living animal, as most beginners do. You will find the anatomy of a horse's foot an interesting study, and time spent studying it will not be time lost. The structure learned, you will know where to cut and where to stop cutting in the preparation of the foot for the shoe. All extra growth of wall and sole should be carefully removed by cutting or rasping it down to its natural size. (Fig. 54.) Use a great deal of judgment in doing this, as there are scarcely two feet alike. Some grow fast, while others grow slow; some are high-heeled, and some low; some have thick, concave soles, while others are thin and flat. Flat-footed horses have thin soles, while club feet, etc., have the opposite. A good rule to go by is to pare down the foot until you come to what may be called the "white line," or union of sole and wall. All the horn removed in cutting down to this white line is extra growth and should be cut away. In flat feet little paring is

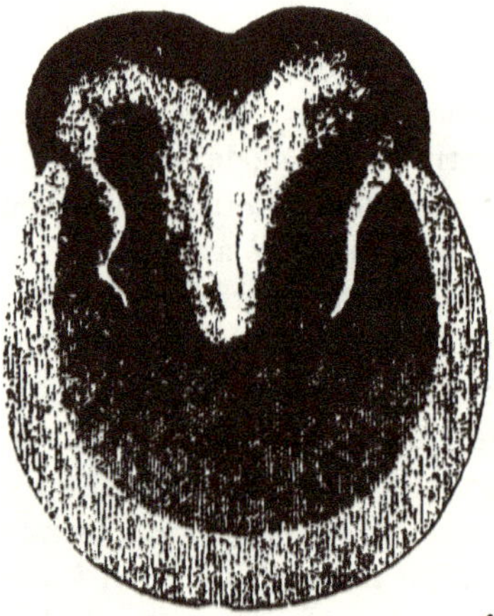

Fig. 54. The Foot, ready for the shoe, showing the frog and bars as they should be left.

necessary, which are seldom afflicted with contraction, while the strong foot is very prone to contraction, and needs considerable paring to prepare it for the shoe. After paring down to the union of sole and wall, care must be taken to leave the foot a perfect level—a dead level fore and aft and from side to side. A foot may be perfectly level on the bottom and yet not be properly balanced. That the angle of the wall varies in different horses is a fact known to all horseshoers. What that angle should be must be determined by a lateral survey of the foot and limb, so as to have the strain or weight equally divided. Step in front or behind the animal and note if the limb tilts in or out. If it does, the hoof is not level on the ground surface, and must be made level and well balanced before the shoe is applied. If this levelling and balancing can not be properly done with the eye alone, a compass for the purpose may be of considerable service in fitting the foot for the shoe.

The object of the frog of the foot is to break concussion, and when in a healthy state should never be touched with a knife, except to pare away the ragged edges, etc. Prof. David Roberge says: "My opinion is that when the dead level of the foot and its perfect balance in all directions is fully understood and generally practiced, we shall hear of greater speed and capacity for endurance among racing and trotting horses than we have yet witnessed; that there will be physical and mental developments in horses not dreamed of in the common philosophy; that lameness will virtually become a reminiscence; horses will enjoy better health and condition; people who own horses will have less plagues and losses from such property, and as a consequence more pleasure and gains; and though last in the list, not the least important result will be a higher respect for horseshoeing as an art—for it must needs be through the instrumentality of improved horseshoeing that these benefits can ever be brought about."

THE SHOE.

The shoe will depend somewhat upon the weight and size of the animal and the nature of the work he has to perform. Draft horses, of course, usually require heavy shoes with calks attached, while driving horses need only light plates. In all cases, make the shoes as light as the nature of the animal's work will admit of. The only mission of the shoe is to prevent undue wear of the walls, and a light one will do this quite as well as a heavy one; it is erroneous to think that a heavy shoe in all cases will wear longer than a light one. This is even true with reference to our heavy draft horses. Let the shoe be of good length, perfectly level on the bearing surface to correspond to the prepared foot, and of a weight to suit the animal; as horses of same size require shoes of different weight. The fore shoes may vary in weight from ten to twenty ounces; the hind ones from eight to twelve ounces, according to the size and requirements of the animal. In cases of deformity, lameness, etc., good results are obtainable from mechanical means, but all such cases should be under the supervision of a qualified veterinary surgeon. In France expansion of the hoof by mechanical means (Fig. 48, p. 230) is advocated and practiced more than anywhere else. They are beneficial, no doubt, in many cases of contracted feet, but there is a far more simple, safe, and effective means of attaining that end, explained in the treatment for contraction.

It would seem unnecessary to say that the shoe should be so shaped as to fit the foot, and not the foot to fit the shoe, as is so generally practiced. Of course it is much easier to make the foot to fit the shoe than it is to make the shoe to fit the foot, but such an excuse is a lazy one on the part of the shoer. The rasp should never be used on the outside of the wall, as by doing so you remove the crust which forms a protection to the hoof. If the shoe is properly fitted, a touch of the rasp under each clinch

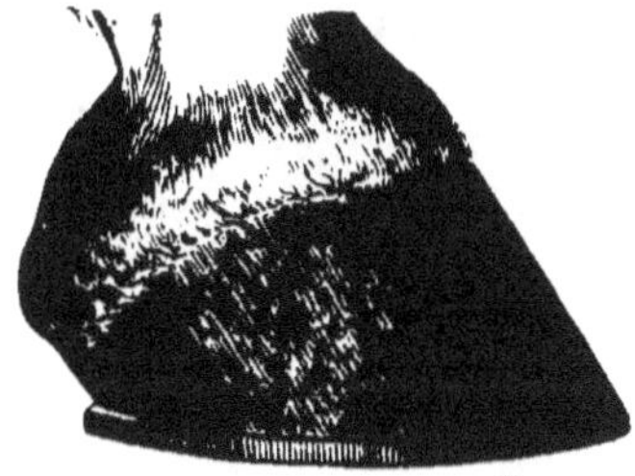

Right fitting. (1.)

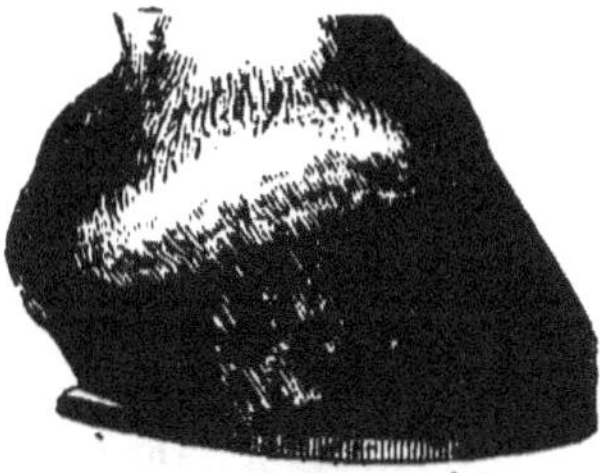

Wrong fitting. (2.)

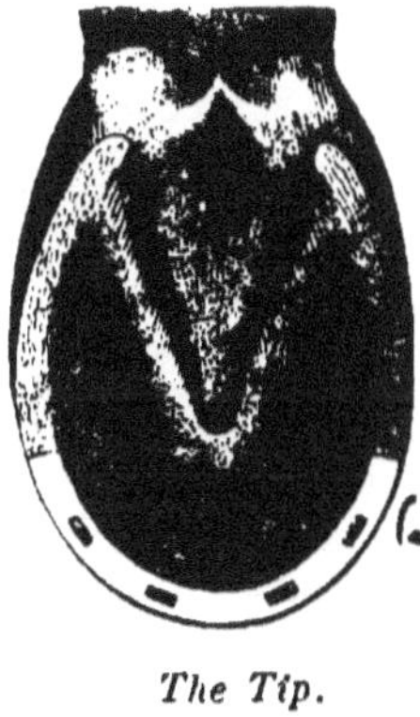

(3.)

The Tip.

Plate V. FITTING THE SHOE.

would be all that is necessary, and even this much might be dispensed with. Plate V., Figs. 1 and 2, will give you an idea of correct and incorrect fitting.

FITTING.

There is what is called hot fitting and cold fitting, either of which being practiced more or less in different countries, climates, etc., according to the objects desired. Systematic experiments a few years ago in regard to hot and cold fitting proved that hot fitting gave the best results. These experiments were carried on in the old country in conection with cavalry horses, where the climate is moist, etc. The advantage of hot fitting consists in the fact that complete contact between the hoof and the shoe can thus be more readily obtained than by any other method; also, the shoes can be made to stay on better and longer, especially in moist climates. Our climate being dry and hot most of the year, cold fitting proves the more satisfactory and is in general use. As a general thing, in our country, the shoes are usually allowed to remain on too long, especially in the agricultural districts. We are acquainted with the fact that if the shoer fails in certain custom work to make the shoes stay on for several months, his employer would be dissatisfied and would transfer his work elsewhere. Such conduct could not be more shortsighted nor more unreasonable. As the horse's foot grows out, it becomes too large on the bottom for the shoe, which should not be left on over a month, or six weeks at the very longest; many animals require to be shod even more frequently. A badly fitting shoe is to a horse as painful as a tight boot is to his owner. The practice of leaving the shoes on too long is a penny-wise and pound-foolish policy.

NAILS.

The following old adage is quite a compliment to the horseshoe nail:

"For the want of a nail the shoe was lost;
For the want of a shoe the horse was lost;
For the want of a horse the rider was lost;
And all for the want of a horseshoe nail."

The fewest nails, and those of the smallest size that will hold the shoe on the proper length of time, is a good rule to follow. The nail holes should not be punched too near the outside edge of the web of the shoe—a very common failing of "keg shoes." Two of the commonest errors in shoeing are, using too many nails, and these of too large a size, and then driving them up too high into the walls. If the foot has been properly pared and a perfectly level bearing secured, it is astonishing how few and how small nails will hold the shoe firmly in its place; but if the fitting has been carelessly done, no matter how the shoe may be nailed on, but a short time will elapse before the shoe works loose. If we could do away with nails altogether, it would be a good thing for our horse's feet. This, however, we can not do at present, and will continue to use nails, which have stood the test so long, until something better is invented. Nailless horseshoes have been invented and patented of late, but don't seem to come into general use. We have been unable to see and examine any of these shoes, so can't speak of their merits.

The "Charlier shoe," invented some years ago by a veterinary surgeon of Paris, France, is no doubt a shoe that has not received the attention that it should. In writing of this shoe, William Dickson says: "I have used both the Charlier shoe and the tip in this country as well as in the East Indies, and I am perfectly

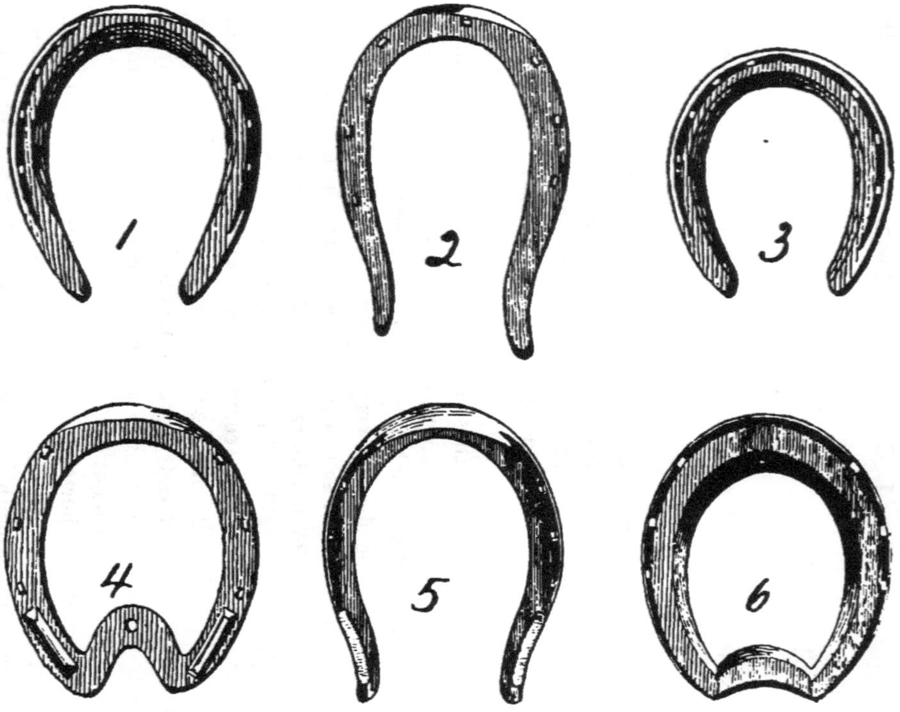

[p. 254] PLATE VI. SPECIAL SHOES.

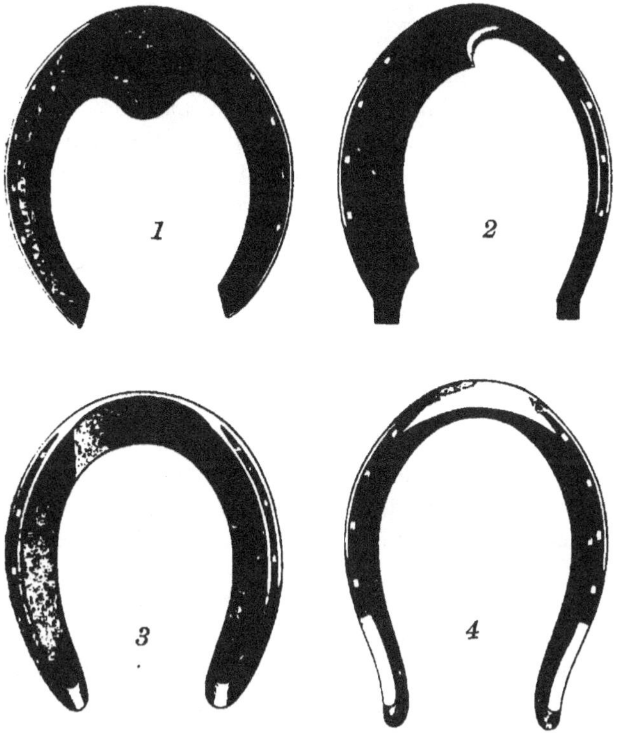

PLATE VII. SPECIAL SHOES.

[p. 255]

satisfied that in many respects they are superior to any other model. They are infinitely lighter, the nails are smaller and fewer in number—all steps in the right direction; but the dominant superiority of the device consists in the fact that the frog obtains pressure to the extent contemplated by nature, and in the case of the Charlier tip particularly, the exercise of its double function as a buffer and dilator is absolutely untrammeled by the shoe." (See Fig. 3, Plate V.)

FINISHING, ETC.

When the shoes have been fitted, the nails driven, drawn up, and clinched, see that nothing is left undone. It frequently happens, however, at this stage that the incompetent workman inflicts serious and lasting injury on the foot. If the wall has not been sufficiently reduced in leveling the foot, or if the shoe used is too small, the rasp is required to reduce the projecting parts. While in some cases the whole outside surface of the wall is rasped and smoothed off. Such finishing touches are very hurtful to the foot, and should never be practiced. Covering the whole outside wall of the foot, from the coronet to the sole level, is a thin protective membrane or crust, which should never be destroyed. Rasping this protective covering away robs the foot of natural protection, moisture, secretion, etc.

SHOEING FOR A SPECIFIC PURPOSE.

There are many styles of shoes, the product of American ingenuity, for the purpose of mitigating or overcoming certain defects, such as interfering, forging, stumbling, etc. Shoeing for a specific purpose has made greater progress in America than in any other country on the face of the globe. The styles of shoes invented for this purpose are without number, and many of them are well adapted for the purpose of overcoming faulty gait and uneven action. Many, however, are only applicable to horses used solely for speed, and in a treatise of this kind an attempt at classification would be out of the question. We will endeavor, however, to lay down a few rules to go by in shoeing horses for certain defects met with in nearly every day practice.

As a majority of these troubles are due to an unbalanced action caused by an unbalanced foot, the one and all-important point is to see that the foot is perfectly level and properly balanced; and as a general thing the horse will travel all right. If you fail to make him go sound by this process, other means (mechanical) must be employed.

OVERREACH, OR FORGING.

This is where the shoe of the hind foot strikes and injures the heel or quarter of the fore foot. It is common in trotting and running horses, or horses that do fast work. The parts injured are usually the outside heels and quarters.

Treatment.—As a general thing, a horse that forges is not properly balanced in build. If he has a low, gliding gait behind, place a heavier shoe on behind than in front, which will have a tendency to slow his action behind, and allow the fore feet time to get out of the way. Give such a horse a long toe behind, and a full heel to the shoe. Tight reining in some cases may stop forging. Another mode of shoeing is to leave the toes long on the front feet, and raise the heels of the hind feet. With many horses this last method will answer, while in other cases nearly the opposite will be necessary, as long toes behind with no heels, and high quarter rolling motion shoes to the fore feet. It will be seen from this that what will do in one case fails in another. Make the shoes as light as possible. If the injury is slight, use cold water bandages for a few days. If the parts are deeply cut, it is well to poultice the parts for a day or two, after which apply our Healing Lotion (see Appendix) and put on a roller bandage.

INTERFERING.

Interfering in animals is where one foot strikes the opposite leg, as it passes by, while traveling. The inner surface of the fetlock joint is usually the part injured, and is seen more often in the hind than in the fore legs.

Causes.—The principal causes are faulty conformation, allow- the feet to grow too long, improper shoeing, weakness from exhaustive labor, etc.

Treatment.—It may in some cases be difficult to overcome. See that the foot is perfectly level and properly balanced before nailing on the shoe. If this does not stop it, lower the inside quarter by rasping down the wall, and then put on the shoe; or weight the shoe on the outside web, to widen his action. (Fig. 2, Plate VII.) Bear in mind that what will overcome interfering in one animal will not in another. So the success of the horseshoer will depend much upon the horse's construction. A glance from the front or rear, or from the side, will tell the man of experience why the horse strikes, or if he is likely to. In very stubborn cases let a natural angle of the foot be obtained, and adjust a tip, which will give the horse the most natural footing. Light shoes are the best in every case to prevent interfering, for they will serve to give the horse confidence, which weight frequently destroys.

When the injury produced by interfering is made on the inside of the fore leg, just below the knee, it is called "speedy cut," and requires about the same treatment as for any ordinary wound in the same region.

STUMBLING.

Stumbling is not at all uncommon among certain horses of faulty conformation, and in many cases is a serious trouble. It may be produced by straight shoulders, short, upright pasterns, high heels, and carrying the head low.

Treatment.—It may be overcome by certain kinds of shoeing. No doubt a rolling motion shoe will prevent tripping and stumbling in more cases than any other kind of shoe. If a full roller shoe is not suitable for the horse, shorten the toe of the foot and give the toe of the shoe a good roll. If the above shoe is properly made, and the foot placed on the natural angle, the worst cases can be prevented.

CHAPTER XIX.

CONTAGIOUS DISEASES.

GLANDERS AND FARCY.

Glanders and its external form designated as farcy, has been known from early antiquity. Probably no contagious disease of the horse is so widely spread, there being but one country—Australia—so far as we can learn, in which the horse is said to be wholly free from the disease. Its prevalence in various countries varies greatly, however, and there are also great variations in the prevalence of the disease in the same country at different periods. It affects not only the horse, but spreads by contact directly or indirectly to the ass, mule, and other solid hoofed animals, and to man. Sheep, goats, and pigs may have the disease, but cattle will resist it entirely.

Scientific investigations in all parts of the world have proven that the two complaints are only different manifestations of one and the same disease. This has been shown time and again through inoculating animals with either the discharge from the nose of a glandered horse or with the matter from a farcy ulcer, and having either or both forms of the disease produced. The term glanders is applied to the disease when the interior of the nose, the lungs or other portions of the organs of respiration are affected, while the term farcy is used when superficial parts, the skin, etc., of the body are invaded. Eminent investigators have definitely established the fact that glanders is a specific contagious disease, due solely to the glanders bacillus, and that the disease is incapable of spontaneous generation, but must at all times depend upon the presence of the bacilli, which in turn must be derived from the parent bacilli of the same kind.

Causes.—The cause of glanders and farcy, as has already been stated, is a living organism belonging to the group known generally as bacteria, under the specific name of bacillus malleus, or glanders bacillus. But even supposing the bacillus mallei is the direct cause of the complaint, we must not forget that improper sanitary surroundings and any weakening, debilitating disease, such as influenza, distemper, catarrhal fever, lung fever, etc., are important factors in the production of the disease by weakening the animal body and making it very liable to become affected with the disease if exposed to the contagion. The germs outside the body retain their life and vitality under ordinary conditions in a moderately dry state for four or five months, although when exposed freely to very dry air with sunlight they probably perish in a few days, and when in water and decomposing fluids they perish in two or three weeks. On the other hand, when large quantities of glanders matter is thickly smeared or spread over stalls or mangers in stables where it is protected from rain and in a measure from light and the deeper parts well excluded from the air the germs seem to retain their vitality for a year or more. The germs are usually spread through careless stable attendants, through public watering troughs, and by the matter discharged drying upon harness, blankets and the like, for after it dries it is readily distributed by currents of air, and this dust, if exposed to a certain degree of heat and moisture, will grow and produce the disease upon susceptible animals with tolerable certainty, if it gets into the interior of their economy.

Period of Incubation.—The period of incubation in the acute form of glanders is short, the disease usually appearing in from four to seven days from the time of exposure, while the chronic form may appear any time in from seven to eight days up to two or three months from the time the animal was exposed to the contagious influence.

Symptoms.—The disease is most frequently seen in the chronic form, there being a discharge from the nostrils which varies in appearance and can not be considered as characteristic; it may either sink in water or float on the surface; usually is somewhat viscid and adheres around the nostrils; may be thin and almost clear and small in amount, or thicker and yellowish with or without odor. The discharge may be from both nostrils, or from only one, either right or left. Glanders may be, and not infrequently is, confounded with other affections somewhat resembling it in some of its symptoms, especially those diseases in which nasal discharge constitute a prominent feature, such as nasal gleet, strangles, pink-eye, acute and chronic nasal catarrh, infectious and epizootic catarrhal fever, disease of the facial sinuses, diseased teeth, tumors in nostrils, etc. The most characteristic symptoms of glanders is the occurrence of ulcers on the partitions between the nostrils, but they are absent, perhaps, in a majority of cases, or situated so high up as to be out of sight. The glands beneath the jaws (sub-maxillary lymphatic glands) become enlarged and hardened, and may or may not be attached to the bone. Discharge from the nose and enlargement of the sub-maxillary glands are nearly always present, but in many cases there may be, for a long time, no other symptoms presented, and such cases can not be diagnosed by mere physical examination, even by an expert.

In acute glanders the course is more rapid, with fever, greater discharge from the nose often streaked with blood and a sudden swelling of one or more limbs; ulcers soon appear upon the lining membrane of the nose, and death is the common termination, but in some cases the acute is followed by the chronic form. In the form known as farcy, they are small nodular enlargements of the size of a pea or larger, which form in different parts of the body, but most frequently along the course of the blood vessels inside the limbs, or on the face and neck. Only a few may be present at a time or they may be numerous. They ultimately burst and discharge a thin yellowish viscid material. They may heal after a time, but are generally replaced by others. Both forms of the disease are incurable, and dangerous to other animals and to man.

Diagnosis.—By reading the above it will be seen that it is impossible to diagnose with any degree of certainty a great many cases of glanders by mere physical examination. In 1891, Professors Kalning and Helman, of Russia, discovered a substance called mallein, which has rendered wonderful service in detecting doubtful and suspicious cases of glanders. During the short time since the discovery of mallein it has been tested by leading scientific veterinarians in every part of the world, and all unite in asserting that its use has at least furnished us with an agent by which we can readily and safely diagnose the disease, not only in suspected cases, but in those animals where the most careful physical examination can detect no signs of the disease. In the annual report of the Bureau of Animal Industry may be found the following:

"Glanders is a contagious and incurable disease of horses, more widespread than is generally supposed. It is also communicated to man from affected horses, and is then nearly always fatal in its results. This disease has been allowed to spread without adequate efforts for its control, until it can now be found in nearly every city of any considerable size and in many country districts. The greatest obstacle to its eradication heretofore existing was the difficulty of making a positive diagnosis in many suspected animals. With many affected horses the symptoms are obscure and indefinite, but the power to communicate the disease is just as marked as those having the most apparent symptoms. Fortunately it has been shown by recent researches that the bacillus of glanders produces a substance during its growth in culture liquids similar to the tuberculin produced by the bacillus of tuberculosis, and that this substance, which is called mallein, may be used for the diagnosis of glanders in the same manner as tuberculin is used for the diagnosis of tuberculosis. The greatest problem connected with the control of glanders is therefore solved, and the question is no longer one of possibility, but of expediency."

Treatment.—As glanders is an incurable and contagious disease, every effort should be made to have the animal destroyed as soon as it is known to be affected, and the carcass burned. The stable, harness, blankets, and all utensils used in connection with the animal should be thoroughly disinfected. Suspicious cases should be quarantined until it is known positively whether the disease exists or not. It is a criminal offense in the State of Texas to sell, trade, or dispose of a horse or mule that is known or even supposed to have glanders or farcy.

LOCO WEED POISONING.

The loco weed grows natural in some of the Western and Southern States. When eaten in large quantities it produces very poisonous effects. Horses and cattle seem to acquire a taste for it, and it is eaten more in the early spring when grass is scarce, as it has a tempting green appearance. It seems to exert its influence on the nervous system, as the animal affected walks like a drunken man. The animal may be very excitable, and loses flesh and gets very poor. They will finally acquire such a taste for it that they will eat nothing else. Delirium comes on, and the animal may die as if from brain fever.

Treatment.—If the animal is removed from the weed before too much injury is done, he will recover. Medicine does not seem to do much good. Good care and good feeding may build up the system and throw off the effects of the poison.

VARIOLA EQUINA (HORSE-POX).

All domestic animals appear to be subject to variola, or pox, in some form or other. It is a disease similar to smallpox in man, but is comparatively simple to what it is in the human family. It is an acute infectious disease, accompanied by fever, producing eruptions or pustules, and, like all febrile diseases, runs a certain length of time.

Causes.—It is caused by a germ. The more common means of contagion is by direct contact, or the virus may be carried by means of the bridle, the saddle, etc. A stallion suffering from this disease may be the means of transmitting it to a number of brood mares, and they in turn return to the farms, where they are surrounded by young animals to whom they convey the contagion.

Symptoms.—Dullness with more or less fever. Soon small red patches appear upon the skin, and these patches are depressed in the center. These little nodules usually appear about the mouth, nose, heels, etc., and soon appear as vesicles, becoming filled with a watery fluid. These vesicles soon become pustules (containing pus or matter) which break and discharge, in some cases, several times in succession. When the mouth is much affected the animal chews his food with considerable difficulty. Variola runs its course in from eight to fifteen days and is not at all serious if treated properly. The virus (poison) is in a fixed form, and the disease may be communicated to man and from one animal to another by contact and by the virus obtaining entrance into a wound or sore. The period of exposure is from six to twelve days.

Treatment.—Keep the animal warm, and carefully guarded from sudden chills, draughts of cold air, etc. Give internally our Condition Powders, and a few doses of sulphur may be beneficial. Apply to the eruptions on the skin the following ointment:

Oxide of zinc	2 drams.
Creolin	20 drops.
Vaseline	1 ounce.

Mix, and apply once a day.

Before applying the ointment each time, bathe the parts nicely with warm water and a clean, soft cloth until perfectly clean, drying afterwards with a dry, soft cloth. If there is much fever, tincture of aconite in 15 to 20 drop doses, or sulphate of quinine in dram doses, may be given. Feed the animal on easily digested food, and of a laxative character, to keep the bowels loose, such as little or no oats, bran mashes, a moderate quantity of sound hay, a few carrots or apples, watermelon rinds, etc. Water may be given often in small quantities, but it should not be cold. A dram of nitrate of potash may be put in the drinking water once or twice a day.

CHAPTER XX.

HABITS.

WIND-SUCKING.

This is a habit similar to cribbing, and a horse affected with the one generally indulges in the other; but they may be separate. A wind-sucker gulps in and swallows a quantity of air and distends his stomach and bowels with the same. It is a very injurious and disagreeable habit. Cribbers and wind-suckers are generally affected with indigestion, hide-bound, and poor in flesh, and may take the colic at any time. We can recommend no treatment for wind-sucking.

CRIBBING.

This is a habit of catching hold of the manger, post, fence, or other object in front of the horse, with the teeth, and bearing down till the neck is altered in position, so as to form a temporary vacuum in the pharynx, when the air rushes in to fill it, making a sound not unlike the hiccoughs. It is merely a habit and not a disease, and is very injurious to the animal. It is claimed by some to be due to indigestion, and by others to be due to an irritation in the front teeth. It is brought on in many cases from idleness. An animal being kept in the stable day after day with no exercise is very liable to acquire this habit as well as others.

There is no satisfactory remedy for the trouble, but it may be checked by buckling a wide strap around his neck quite tight. Another means of breaking up the habit is by smearing the manger, posts, or whatever he cribs on, with some strong irritating mixture, as cayenne or red pepper, kerosene oil, cantharides blister, etc. If due to indigestion, it can be remedied by giving regularly our Condition Powders for one or two weeks. It is claimed by some that sawing between the front teeth with a narrow saw will prevent it. This of course makes the teeth sore and naturally keeps the animal from biting on hard objects for a time. It is a very unsatisfactory habit to break, as all remedies known will fail in most of cases.

LOLLING.

Lolling consists of allowing the tongue to hang loosely out of the mouth, and it dangles about in every direction when the animal is traveling. It can not be considered as a disease, but a habit, and a very ugly one.

Prevention.—It may be prevented, and the animal broken of the habit by the use of a bit with a high center-piece, or a plate, or what is still better the application of a nose-band which should be tight enough to prevent the opening of the mouth.

PART II.

CATTLE DEPARTMENT.

CATTLE DEPARTMENT.

In a work of this kind, with such limited space, we will not attempt to enumerate the different breeds of cattle and their superior qualities, but will merely give the full particulars of different diseases and their treatment, of cattle in Texas and the South.

You will observe, in reading over the diseases of the horse, that we refer to similar diseases in the cow; therefore we will not write on those subjects again in this department. But there are certain diseases and ailments peculiar to the cow and cattle that we will here endeavor to describe, in a brief but plain and simple manner. It must be remembered that owing to the large size of the cow's stomach, and the quantity of food it contains, and to their slow, phlegmatic temperament, that it takes in most cases nearly twice the sized dose of most all medicines for them that it does for a horse. A cow has four stomachs, with a capacity of about 55 to 60 gallons; while the horse has only one stomach, that will hold about 3½ to 4 gallons. A horse's bowels are about 100 fet in length, while a cow's are about 150 feet, but the horse's bowels are larger in diameter than a cow's. A horse has no gall bladder, while of course a cow has. One interesting feature about a cow's stomach is the mechanism by which she can raise the food up into her mouth again and remasticate by chewing the cud. Some people entertain the very foolish idea that a cow's cud is always in her mouth, and that if she loses it by some accident, she will get sick. The cud of a cow is portions of her food which she brings up from her stomach and chews a few minutes, and then swallows it again; and immediately brings up another portion. By rechewing, it prepares it better for digestion. It is almost impossible for a horse to vomit, owing to the small size of the stomach and to the peculiar structure of the oesophagus (gullet).

CHAPTER XXI.

THE DISEASES OF CATTLE.

DISEASES OF THE STOMACH AND BOWELS.

It is well to be remembered by all those interested in cattle and treating their diseases while sick, that a good physic is an important part of the treatment of a majority of the diseases of the cow. Epsom salts is the important ingredient in all cow-physic, while aloes and linseed oil are the best for the horse. Below are formulas for the best cow physics. Before giving, dissolve in one pint of hot water, and when cool give as a drench, using a large long-necked bottle for the purpose:

No. 1:

Epsom salts	1 pound.
Powdered ginger	1 ounce.

No. 2:

Epsom salts	1 pound.
Common salt	1 pound.
Powdered ginger	1 ounce.

No. 3:

Epsom salts	1 pound.
Common salt	½ pound.
Powdered gamboge	1 ounce.
Powdered ginger	1½ ounces.

No. 4:

Epsom salts	$1\frac{1}{2}$ pounds.
Calomel	1 dram.
Croton oil	$\frac{1}{2}$ dram.
Powdered ginger	1 ounce.

The above formulas are intended for ordinary sized cows. You can decrease or increase the dose, according to the size of the animal. No. 1 is a laxative or mild purgative for a cow; while No. 4 is a very strong purgative, given only in very severe cases of constipation or indigestion.

BLOATING, OR HOVEN.

This is a common disease among cows, and is characterized by the formation of gas in the paunch or rumen. It is very similar to wind colic in the horse. In many cases it is a very serious condition, and unless properly treated may cause the death of the animal.

Causes. — Eating green food when not used to it, or eating mouldy or musty food may cause hoven. Green cane is a very frequent cause of this trouble, and it is a common thing for an animal to die in one or two hours after getting into the cane patch. Eating too much of any kind of grain or food which overloads the stomach may cause it. The overloaded stomach becomes paralyzed and inactive, and the large bulk of food lying in there sours and ferments and forms gas which distends the stomach.

Symptoms.—There is more or less swelling of the abdomen, according to the severity of the trouble. The left flank is generally distended the most, and when struck with the tips of the fingers a drum-like sound is heard. The animal is very uneasy, and moans and grunts with pain. Breathing becomes oppressed by the distended stomach pressing on the lungs. If the animal is not relieved in time, it is liable to die of suffocation or of a ruptured stomach.

Treatment.—If the animal is much distended, we would advise the use of the trocar and canula (Fig. 12) at once. The instrument is to be inserted into the left flank, midway between the last rib and the point of the hip and not too near the backbone. Insert it downward and inward, and pull out the trocar, leaving the canula (hollow tube) in until all the gas escapes and gives the cow relief. If the gas forms again, it may be necessary to insert it again, or leave it in two or three hours. Another mechanical means of drawing off the gas is by the use of the probang, which is described under "Choking," which see. After you have drawn off the gas, give a physic, No. 2, to carry off the sour, fermented food. If the case is not urgent enough to use the trocar or probang, or if you haven't a trocar or probang, give as a drench the following:

Aqua ammonia	1 ounce.
Tincture of ginger	1 ounce.
Oil of peppermint	½ dram.
Cold water	1 quart.

If not relieved in one hour, repeat the dose. Give injections of warm water freely. We have known cases of this kind relieved by keeping the cow's mouth open by securing a piece of wood, or such like, between the teeth. In very urgent cases, and as the last resort where no trocar can be had, we would advise a sharp knife-blade to be inserted into the flank at the place advised for tapping with the trocar, and a goose quill or the like put in to allow the gas to escape. If the animal is weak, give liquor acetate of ammonia 4 ounces in 1 pint of water as a drench; or one-half pint of whisky with half a dozen eggs may be given and repeated every four hours. After an animal has suffered from an attack of bloating, great care should be taken that it does not eat too much for several days, as the stomach is weak and a relapse can be brought on very easily.

DISTENTION OF THE PAUNCH WITH FOOD.

This trouble is occasionally seen in cattle, and is due to eating too much of certain kinds of dry food. The stomach becomes paralyzed, and the food lies there in an undigested state. The left flank is seen to be full, but not as in bloating. The fullness will pit on pressure. After a time gas may form, and then very urgent symptoms come on. In treating this trouble every effort should be made to arouse the action of the paralyzed paunch, and work off the large quantity of food it contains. Give as a drench the following:

Sweet spirits of nitre	2 ounces.
Tincture of nux vomica	½ ounce.
Tincture of ginger	1 ounce.
Aqua ammonia	1 ounce.
Cold water	1 quart.

Repeat in four hours if necessary. Give physic No. 3, and if it does not work in twelve hours, give No. 4. If there is much gas present, treat according to directions under bloating. As a last resort, an operation is sometimes performed, called rumenotomy, by which a hole is cut into the left flank and a certain amount of the contents of the paunch is taken out with the hand. This is an operation that is not liable to be successful unless performed by a qualified veterinary surgeon.

LOSS OF THE CUD.

This is merely a symptom of disease, and not a disease of itself. Loss of cud means not chewing the cud, and shows that digestion is not being performed, and that the animal is not well. The cud is a portion of the food that is brought up from the stomach and remasticated. A cow while eating chews its food very little, therefore the greater portion of it is brought up and chewed over again by the animal. Don't force dish-rags or the like into the cow's mouth to give her a cud, as some do, but give her good care and treat her for the disease from which she is suffering, and the cud will come back all right when she gets well.

INDIGESTION OF THE THIRD STOMACH—DRY MURRAIN—GRASS STAGGERS.

This is a digestive disorder affecting principally the third stomach of cattle. It is often called dry murrain, but that is not a proper name for the trouble.

Causes. — It is generally seen among cattle that are eating coarse, dry, indigestible food. It is often seen after the grass becomes dry in the summer. A change from the green grass of spring to the dry, ripe grass of summer will produce it, especially where cattle are not allowed sufficient salt and fresh water. Food with astringent properties, such as acorns, will cause it.

Symptoms.—The animal becomes dull and stupid, with loss of appetite. Constipation is present, and there is generally a fullness of the left flank. The animal loses flesh, becomes weak, and lays down most of the time off by itself. Horns and ears become cold, and there may be some bloating present. In some cases there is partial paralysis, and staggering gait, with general brain symptoms. If relief is not given the animal may live five or eight days and die.

Treatment.—A good physic, as No. 3, should be given at once. If there is much weakness present, give

Whisky	4 ounces.
Tincture of ginger	1 ounce.
Tincture of nux vomica	½ ounce.
Water	1 pint.

Mix, and give as a drench, and repeat in four hours if necessary.

Give injections of warm water freely. After the physic has acted, a good tonic powder should be given, such as our Condition Powders. (See Appendix.)

DIARRHOEA IN CALVES—WHITE SCOUR.

This is quite a common trouble among calves that are not fed regularly or properly. It is seldom seen among calves that run with their mothers, but it is quite common among calves that are fed on cold sour milk and giving them all they can drink only once or twice a day.

Treatment. — Feed the calf often, and a small quantity at a time, of boiled milk. Give one or two ounces of castor oil and one-half ounce of laudanum as a drench, and repeat the laudanum in four hours if necessary. Get the following powders prepared and give:

Bicarbonate of soda	2 ounces.
Powdered ginger	1 ounce.
Carbonate of magnesia	2 ounces.

Mix, and make ten powders, and give one powder three times per day in a little new milk and one ounce of good whisky.

Feed the calf carefully for some time after an attack of diarrhoea, as the stomach and bowels are weak and it can easily be brought on again.

DIARRHOEA IN CATTLE.

Diarrhoea in cattle is generally caused by eating some indigestible food, or a change of food. Stagnant or foul water may cause it, or some irritant in the bowels. It may follow constipation or strong physicing.

Symptoms. — There is a copious fluid discharge from the bowels, which has a very offensive smell. The animal is dull, stands with its back arched, and shows thirst. It is often accompanied by high fever, great loss of flesh, and sometimes death in a remarkably short time.

Treatment.—When the trouble is due to some irritating food, give 1 pint of raw linseed oil and 1 ounce of laudanum as a drench. The following may be given:

Powdered opium	2 drams.
Carbonate of magnesia	1 ounce.
Powdered ginger	½ ounce.
Prepared chalk	2 drams.

Mix, and shake up with 1 pint of warm water and three fresh eggs, and give as a drench; and give three times per day until the bowels become natural.

After an attack of diarrhoea give our Condition Powders (see Appendix) according to direction, to tone up the stomach and bowels.

CONSTIPATION.

This is due to much the same causes as in the horse, and may be relieved by giving either formula No. 2, 3 or 4, page 272.

WORMS.

Stomach and bowel worms are sometimes very troublesome to cattle, and can be relieved by giving our Worm Remedy (see Appendix) according to directions on each box.

DISEASES OF THE RESPIRATORY ORGANS.

Cattle are occasionally sufferers from diseases of the respiratory organs, such as catarrh, laryngitis, bronchitis, pneumonia, etc., but the remarks on these diseases in the horse department of this book will sufficiently explain them for cattle; so you can know the trouble and give a course of treatment; remembering that a cow takes from one-half to once again as much for a dose of nearly all medicines as a horse does.

CHAPTER XXII.

OPERATIONS.

DEHORNING.

This is an operation by which cattle are deprived of their horns. It has received a great deal of controversy through the stock and farm papers and veterinary journals as to the advisability and cruelty of the operation; some claiming it to be very cruel and unnecessary; while others assert that it is not cruel, but a humane act, to deprive cattle of their fierce and dangerous weapons—horns. We claim the operation is not cruelty to animals. Cruelty to animals is defined as the infliction of unnecessary pain. Of course it is more or less painful to the animal, but not more so than the operation of castration or branding, to which we regularly subject animals. The pain of a few minutes during which the operation is performed is nothing to be compared to the severe and lasting torture inflicted as a matter of every day occurrence, by animals upon each other, when left to wear in confinement their weapons of offense, which, although doubtless of utility in a wild state, are in a state of domesticity a menace to their companions and a dangerous encumbrance to themselves. How cruel it looks to see a bunch of long-horned steers, shut up in the feeding pens, in the stock yards, or worse still, in cars for shipment. There are always some restless, vicious ones goring the quieter ones with their long, sharp horns, and causing a commotion all the time among them. Still another plea in favor of dehorning is for the safety and protection of mankind. Often do we read of men, women and children being gored to death by the sharp horns of vicious bulls. Cows and steers are dehorned chiefly to protect them from each other, but bulls should be dehorned to protect ourselves. Animals that are dehorned are more quiet and contented, fatten faster, and do better all around.

As the exportation of cattle is quite extensively carried on, the removal of their horns will then not only lessen the owner's risk, but will also add materially to the comfort and safety of the animals themselves. The operation may be performed at the age of two or three days or at any time through life. With the bull it is better to let him get old enough to learn the use of his horns as weapons of offense, and then deprive him of them. If taken out when a mere calf he will learn to use his head in butting, as a "moolly," but if dehorned after he grows up, it will generally make him very docile and peaceable. You can very easily and with very little pain to the calf, prevent his horns from growing by applying the caustic potash treatment when but a few days old. This is done by putting the calf over on its side and holding it, while the operator clips the hair off the spot where the horn is to grow. Then with a stick of caustic potash he dips one end into cold water and rubs it gently on the spot for about ten or twelve seconds. The calf is then turned over and the operation repeated on the other side. By this time the first side is dry and ready for a second application of the caustic, which is done exactly as the first. When both sides have been treated twice the calf can be let go and he will grow up a hornless animal. Dehorning of grown cattle should be done in the spring or late fall—between fly-time and cold weather. The operation is comparatively simple, and can generally be performed by the owner. A good saw or a pair of dehorning clippers (Fig. 55) is necessary to take the horns off with. The animal can be secured by tying down or by being put into a contrivance made for the purpose. The head must be securely fastened so the animal can't move around too much while the operator is removing the horns. It is well to take them off close, and even remove a portion of the skin about the horn so as to make a clean job. Bleeding seldom ever amounts to anything, and about the only after-treatment needed is to see that no screw worms get into the wounds. If care is taken in performing the operation, very few losses, if any, will be had.

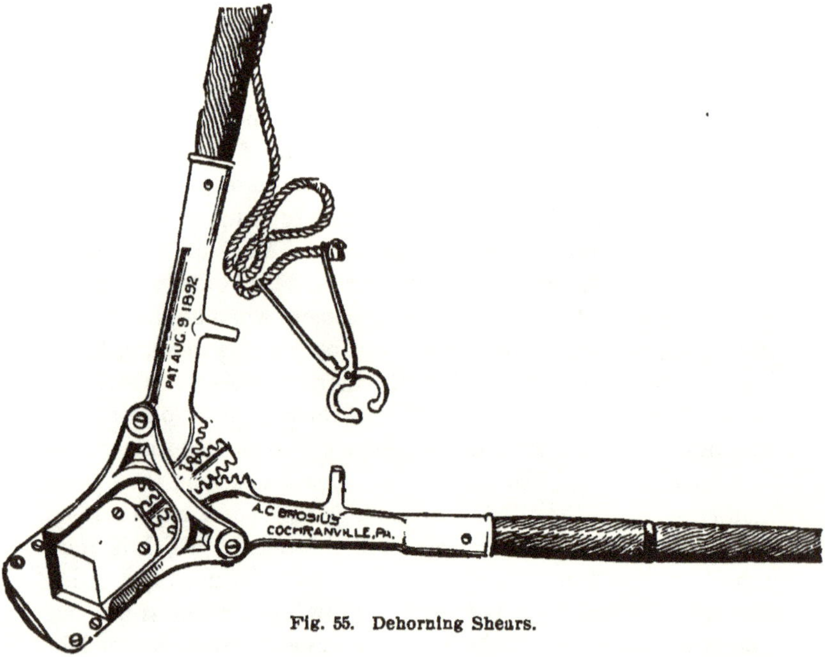

Fig. 55. Dehorning Shears.

SPAYING COWS.

Spaying is castration of the female animal, and was practiced extensively in Texas and the Western States a few years ago on cows and heifers. The fashion has rather died out in most breeding districts, one reason being that they are using all their heifers for breeding purposes. The object of spaying heifers and cows, as practiced by most stockmen, was to keep them from going in heat, and by so doing they would grow larger, fatten easier, and take on flesh faster. Dairy cows, for city purposes, are sometimes spayed to keep them giving a good flow of milk for two, three, or five years continuously. For these purposes she should be spayed in her prime of life, and while giving her greatest flow of milk. She should be in good health and in moderate flesh, but never should be operated on while pregnant or in heat.

This operation in the cow is not a serious one, and if properly performed, there is little danger to the life of the animal. The operation may be performed in two ways, as in the mare, namely, by the flank or by the vagina.

By the vagina operation is meant, to insert the hand into the vagina and by cutting a hole through the upper part of the vagina near the womb, the hand is inserted into the abdominal cavity and the ovaries (prides) found and brought into the vagina, where they are taken off by a pair of forceps made specially for the purpose. This operation is less dangerous than the flank operation, but it requires some costly instruments and a thorough understanding of the anatomy of the parts before it can be performed with safety and ease.

In the flank operation, after the animal is secured, an incision is made in the left flank large enough to insert the hand and arm. The ovaries can be found by finding the womb and then tracing it up, one ovary being found at the end of each of the two branches of the womb. When found they should be drawn out, one at a time, and removed with the ecrasure. The wound should be closed by strong silk or linen thread, being first cleansed with clean water containing a little carbolic acid. It is very important that the instruments and hands of the operator should be perfectly clean, as the animal could be very easily inoculated with some poisonous germs adhering to them. The instruments should be scalded with boiling water each time before using, and the operator should pare his finger nails closely and thoroughly wash his hands and arms with soap and water and then rinse them and his instruments frequently in clean water containing a little carbolic acid. In this, as well as in all other surgical operations, absolute cleanliness is the great secret of success.

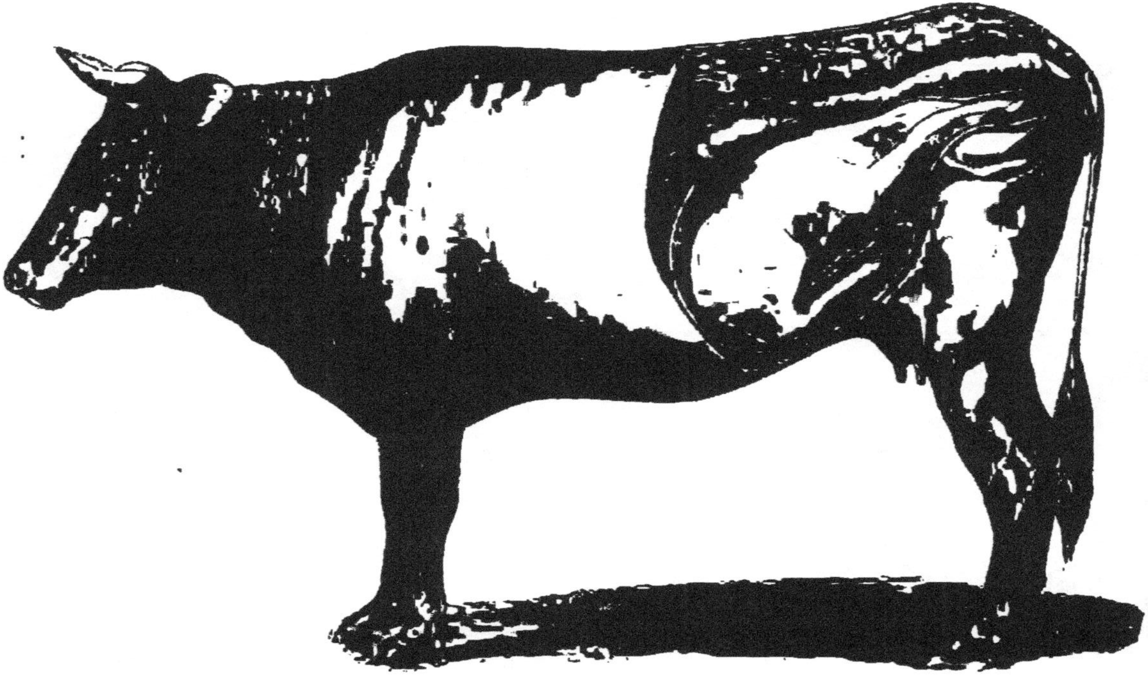

PLATE IX. NATURAL PRESENTATION IN THE COW.

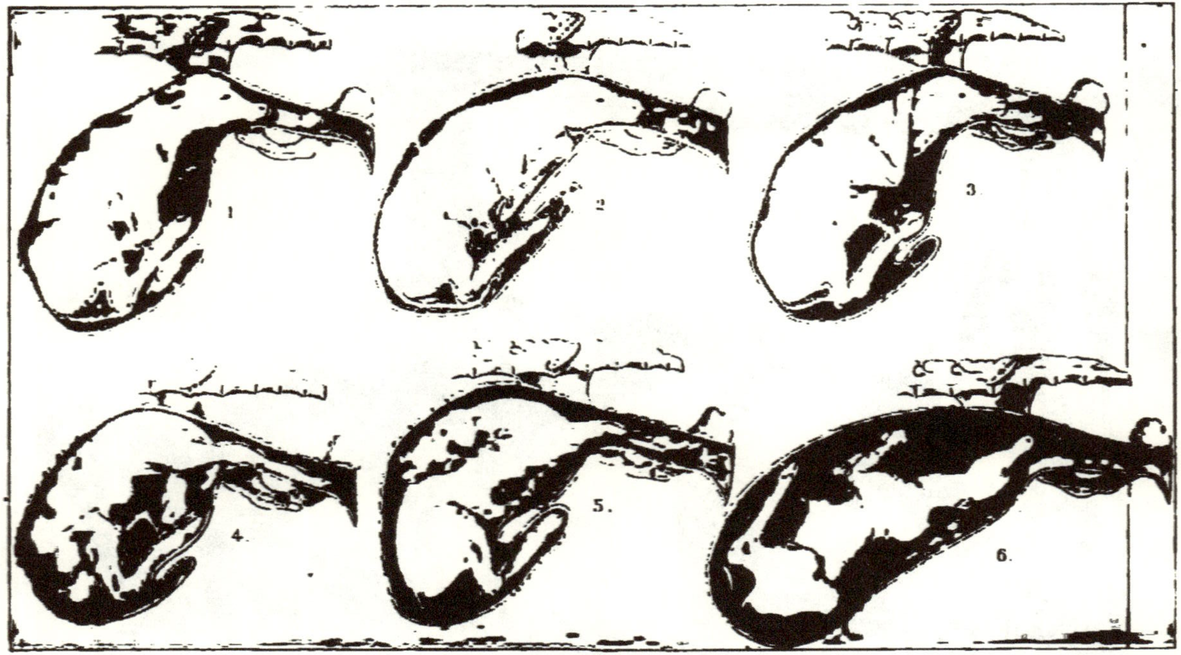

PLATE X. UNNATURAL PRESENTATIONS IN THE COW.

CHAPTER XXIII.

PARTURITION—PARTURIENT DISEASES.

For a description of the general remarks on parturition in the cow, we will refer you to those given under this heading in the Horse Department.

All such troubles as abortion, barrenness, natural presentations, unnatural presentations, retention of the afterbirth, inversion of the womb, inflammation of the womb, bleeding after parturition, whites, etc., are fully described under their respective headings in the Horse Department, and can be referred to there.

MILK FEVER.

There are three or four diseases that follow calving, such as parturient paralysis, parturient apoplexy, garget, etc., and the name Milk Fever is applied to them as a whole by most dairymen. We will describe them later on. All animals, and more especially cows, have more or less fever after delivery of their young. It is due to the nervous shock and the agonizing pain they have to endure at this time.

Symptoms.—The animal is somewhat dull, and has more or less fever according to the severity of the case. The appetite may be impaired, and the bag sometimes becomes swollen and feverish.

Treatment.—Give the cow a physic, as No. 1, and give ½ ounce of nitrate of potash and 25 drops of tincture of aconite in one pint of water as a drench three times a day for one or two days. Milk her often, and bathe the bag well two or three times a day with warm water; then apply our Liniment well rubbed in. Feed on bran mashes and green food.

PARTURIENT PARALYSIS.

Paralysis occasionally follows parturition, generally coming on in from one to three days after calving, but it is not a dangerous trouble as a general thing. It is due to a rush of blood to the spinal cord or to pressure on the large nerves in the hind quarters.

Symptoms.—The cow on being made to walk is seen to be unsteady in her gait, perhaps staggers from side to side, or has what is known as a paddling gait. The animal may soon grow worse, and, being unable to stand, falls to the ground, the loss of motion becoming better marked. Although not able to rise, there is not much, if any, pain present, and the appetite generally remains good.

Treatment.—A good physic, as No. 2, should be given, and if necessary stimulants may be given every four or six hours. Blankets wrung out of hot water should be applied to the spine and across the loins, and the loins bathed well two or three times a day with our Liniment. Prepare and give the following powders:

Nitrate of potash	3 ounces.
Powdered copperas	2 ounces.
Powdered nux vomica	2 ounces.

Mix, and make twelve powders, and give one powder morning and night in damp feed.

The cow will generally recover, although it may take a couple of weeks to get her on her feet. While lying down, turn her over once or twice a day.

PARTURIENT APOPLEXY.

This is a disease peculiar to mature, fat cows, at or a day or two after calving. It is seldom if ever seen in the common breeds of cows, but the well bred, heavy milkers that are big fat at the calving time are the ones that suffer more frequently from this disease. It is seldom if ever seen in cows that are poor in flesh, or at first calving; nor ever seen after a case of difficult calving, as the severe labor, loss of blood, etc., have a tendency to weaken the system to a certain extent and prevent the disease. It invariably follows an easy calving, and the large amount of blood which after delivery of the calf should go to make milk, instead of doing so is thrown back upon the system, and causing congestion of the brain and spinal cord, gives rise to the various symptoms of parturient apoplexy. It is one of the most serious and rapidly fatal diseases with which the Veterinary Surgeon has to deal. High feeding, with the animal fat and full of rich blood, and an easy delivery, are the main causes of this terribly fatal disease. It is more prevalent during very hot weather, as the heat helps to bring on the fever. Heavy milking cows that are in good flesh and fed heavily up to the time of calving are very liable to this disease, if they come in during a very hot spell of weather.

Symptoms.—The disease comes on from one hour to several days after calving, it being seldom seen before calving. The nearer to the time of calving the disease comes on the more fatal it is. All cases that come on within two days after calving generally die, while a majority of cases can be cured that come on after the third day. The animal is generally first noticed to be somewhat dull, with unsteady, staggering gait. There is a peculiar paddling action of the feet which is characteristic of parturient apoplexy. In severe cases the paralysis increases rapidly, and the animal is soon unable to walk or stand alone, therefore goes down. It may, in a fit of excitement, try to rise, but fails, and soon quiets down into a comatose (sleepy) condition, with the head turned to the side with the nose resting on the ground. Occasionally the animal will stretch out at full length with the head on the ground. She is now in a dead sleep, as it were, with no signs of life except a weak, slow pulse and very slow breathing. You can touch the ball of the eye without her even batting the eyelid. The animal may live in this condition for several hours, but as a general thing they will die in from two to four hours after it comes on. Many valuable cows have we been called to see in this comatose condition, but all we could do was to watch them die. The animal has no power of swallowing, neither is there any digestion going on. Medicine put into the stomach with a stomach pump does no good, as there is no digestion or absorption.

Treatment.—If the cow is seen before she falls and before the power of swallowing is lost, a good physic should be given, as No. 4. If the physic is given six or eight hours before the comatose condition comes on you may save her. But if she goes off to sleep before you give the medicine, or shortly after, the case is hopeless, and she will die. The head should be kept cool by applying ice or cloths wrung out of cold water. The animal should be protected from the sun or cold wet weather. All milk should be removed from her bag often. If the animal can yet swallow give:

Tincture of aconite	20 drops.
Nitrate of potash	½ ounce.
Bromide of potash	1 ounce.
Water	1 pint.

Mix, and give as a drench every four hours.

Prevention.—Prevention is of far more value in this disease than all the treatment you can give. Cows that are heavy milkers and big fat should be cut short on their feed for a couple of weeks previous to calving. Plenty of salt and all the water they will drink is beneficial. A dose of epsom salts, as No. 1, should be given about one day before the cow is expected to come in. If she comes in unexpectedly, don't delay to give her the physic as soon as found, if she is fat and a big milker. One ounce of nitrate of potash may be given every day for several days instead of the salts. If the udder (bag) becomes much distended before calving, it should be milked every day, as it gives relief to the cow and wards off disease. Plenty of exercise, light feed, and a dose of salts, are the great preventatives against this dread disease. Many a poor cow is killed through kindness by her owner feeding her very heavy previous to calving, so she will give a good flow of milk when she comes in.

MAMMITIS—GARGET.

Garget, more properly known as Mammitis, consists of inflammation of the mamary gland (bag), and is brought about in various ways. Some cases are very mild and pass off in a day or two, while others are more severe, and may either destroy the udder or kill the cow. Any one or more of the quarters may be affected, and sometimes the whole bag is involved. Garget generally comes on shortly after calving, but may take place even before calving, or any time while the cow is giving milk.

Causes.—Garget may be caused by an injury to the udder, such as kicks, blows, wounds from briars or thorns, lying on sharp objects, etc. A frequent cause of the trouble is irregular milking, and not completely emptying the bag at each milking. Over-driving with distended udder may cause it, and also it very often follows calving by the fever in the system settling in the udder. Sudden changes of temperature, as hot days and cold nights, may be a cause of garget.

Symptoms.—There is a swelling of a part or the whole of the udder, with heat, tenderness, and a hard feeling. It is in some cases so tender and sore that the animal will refuse to have it touched or handled. Instead of natural milk, a thin, yellowish fluid is drawn from the teat, which soon becomes thicker and in curdled lumps, and has a bad smell. The animal is more or less stiff and lame in the hind quarters and especially on the side where the swelling is. The animal is restless, feverish, and has lost her appetite. Milder cases generally yield readily to treatment, while in some of the severer forms the udder becomes mortified and great portions of it slough off. In other cases abscesses form in the affected quarters, which have to be freely opened to let the pus escape. If a cow recovers from a case of garget she seldom regains her full flow of milk until after her next calf. Where abscesses form, or where mortification and sloughing sets in, the quarter or whole udder is generally destroyed.

Treatment.—Give the cow a physic, as No. 2, and give the following:

Tincture of aconite	20 drops.
Nitrate of potash	4 drams.
Water	1 pint.

Mix, and give as a drench, and repeat every four hours until four or six doses have been given.

If the udder is much swollen it should be supported with a large bandage padded softly with cotton and such like. Cut holes in the bandages for the teats to come through. Bathe the bag well for an hour at a time, and apply the following, which is undoubtedly the most effectual remedy to remove the cake (hardness) from a cow's bag:

Fluid extract of belladonna .... 1 ounce.
Soft soap .... ½ pound.

Mix, and use only what you need at a time, and apply twice per day.

Fig. 56. Milking Tube.

Another way this can be done is to wet the bag with the belladonna, and then with a piece of strong lye soap make a thick lather on all the swelled, caked portions of the bag, and let remain for six or eight hours, when you can wash off with warm water and apply again. Keep this up as long as there is any fever in the bag. Long continued, gentle hand-rubbing and kneading the affected parts is very beneficial. Strip out all the milk you can four or five times a day, or the milking tube (Fig. 56) may be inserted to drain off the milk as fast as it forms. If, after the fever leaves the udder, there are hard places still remaining, apply the following:

Tincture of iodine .... 6 ounces.
Tincture of opium .... 2 ounces.
Soap liniment .... 4 ounces.

Mix, and apply with friction, two or three times per day.

Also give 2 drams of iodide of potash as a drench in 1 pint of water every morning and night before feeding. If abscesses form they should be lanced and let the matter out; and syringe out the cavity once a day with a weak solution of carbolic acid.

BLOODY MILK.

Cows occasionally give bloody milk, which may be due to some injury to the udder, or to congestion or inflammation of the same. It may be due to some diseased condition of the udder, or from eating some acrid or irritant plants.

Treatment.—If it is due to congestion or injury of the udder, give physic No. 1. Bathe the bag well with warm water twice a day, and each time after bathing apply our Liniment well to all affected parts. After the cow has physicked out, give our Condition Powders in bran mash for a week or ten days. If due to eating certain kinds of weeds, change the pasture. Don't use the milk while it is bloody or for several days afterwards, for it may be due to some poison or from tubercular disease (consumption) in the udder.

BLUE MILK.

Cows sometimes give bluish or watery milk, which is generally due to the presence of a germ in the teat or udder that infects the milk and changes its color and character. Give internally physic No. 1, and give 2 drams of hyposulphite of soda twice a day in the feed or as a drench. Our Condition Powders given regularly for one or two weeks will be beneficial.

STRINGY MILK.

This is a condition in which the milk gets in a stringy white or yellowish condition. Its causes and treatment are about the same as for Blue Milk, which see.

BLOCKED OR CLOSED TEATS.

This is quite a common trouble among dairy cows, and is due to various causes, such as warty growths, fleshy growths, thickening of the mucus membrane, calculus, etc. In some cases the little warty or fleshy growth can be felt by squeezing the teat. Many a valuable cow has been made to lose one or more quarters by this trouble. It is generally first noticed when the cow comes in. On trying to milk her, no milk can be gotten from the affected quarter, and the general procedure is to run a knitting needle or the like up the teat to try and force an opening. You can generally force an opening, but it will close right up again. You may get a little milk from the teat, but it swells up for a few days and then gradually dries up and withers away, and will not fill up again until the next calf.

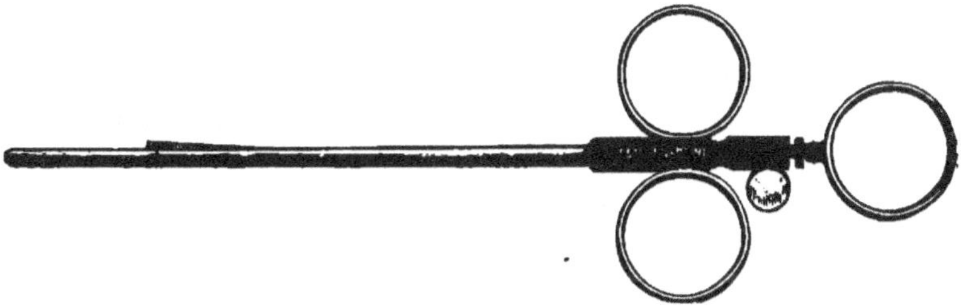

Fig. 57. Teat Slitter, for opening closed (blind) teats in cows.

Treatment.—The milking tube should be inserted, but if there is a fleshy or warty growth in the teat, the teat slitter (Fig. 57) should be inserted and an opening be made through the growth with the little knife on the side near the end, and then the milking tube inserted and used until the cut surface heals around the cavity. If this is done in time a great many cases can be saved. But as a general thing treatment is not successful, and the teat will dry up.

OPENING IN THE SIDE OF THE TEAT.

This trouble is occasionally met with, and is very unpleasant to the milker while milking. It is generally caused by an external wound, as a barb-wire cut which penetrates the milk canal, and when it heals it leaves a hole by which the milk escapes at the side of the teat. Most of cases of this kind can be cured by scarifying (making raw) the edges of the hole with a sharp lance, and then stitch the raw surfaces tightly together by the use of the quilled suture (see quilled suture in Horse Department). If the cow is giving milk, draw off the milk two or three times per day with the milking tube. Leave the stitches in for eight or ten days, when they can be removed with safety.

SORE TEATS.

When sores exist to any considerable extent on cows' teats, they make it very painful to the cow and unpleasant to milk her. They are caused in various ways, as from barb-wire cuts, scratches from thorns and briars, chapped from cold winds, lying down in filthy places, etc.

Treatment.—There is nothing that will heal up sores of this kind as fast as our Healing Lotion. After each time of milking wash the teats all off nicely with soap and water, and wet the sores with the Healing Lotion. Remove all the scabs at each time of washing, as you will heal the sores faster by so doing.

CHAPTER XXIV.

INSECTS AND THE STIFF DISEASE.

TICKS.

There are several species of ticks that attach themselves to cattle. The most common in this country, and the one we will describe here, is the *Boophilus bovis*. It is important and interesting to know something of the life history, development, and habits of this parasite on account of the important part it plays in its relation to Texas fever, and the annoyance it causes stock when they infest them in countless numbers. It was not until about 1889 that any attention was paid to this tick. Experiments show that the life of a tick, or of one generation (from the time the eggs are laid until the tick is matured and full grown), is from 45 to 70 days. It will be found that by taking mature female ticks from cattle and putting them in a glass vessel, they will remain quiet for two or four days, when they will begin to lay their eggs, and continue to lay them for several days. Statistics gathered at experiment stations show that the average full grown mature tick will lay a little over 2000 eggs. All female ticks at any age after maturity, that have been fertilized by the male, will begin laying eggs in a few days after being taken from or fallen off the host (cattle). The eggs will hatch out in from three to four weeks, according to the temperature, moisture, surroundings, etc. They will hatch out much quicker in hot, damp weather than when it is cool or dry. These young ticks will remain on the ground alive for several months in favorable weather, but will not grow or mature unless they can get upon an animal. By having the power of living so long in this larval state, they are very liable to get upon an animal if they are in a pasture frequented by cattle. When the larval tick gets upon an animal, it at once begins to grow, and in about one week it has its first moulting (shedding its skin). At the end of the second week it moults again and becomes sexually mature, when fertilization is liable to take place, as a male and a female tick are generally found together. After fertilization, the female tick enlarges very slowly until from the nineteenth to the twenty-second day, when she swells up very rapidly, and in a day or two loosens her hold and falls to the ground, where the laying of eggs begins in a few days. It will be seen by the above that the length of time a tick remains on an animal is about three weeks. Ticks are more numerous on uncultivated land, prairies and woodland. They bore into the skin, and when in large numbers cause considerable irritation and annoyance to the animal.

Treatment.—The subject of a cheap, reliable and convenient remedy that will eradicate ticks from cattle has received a great deal of thought and investigation during the past few years. If such a remedy could be worked out it would be of great benefit to the cattle and farming industry of the whole country. The danger of infecting northern territory in the transfer of southern cattle would be overcome; a market previously closed would be opened to summer feeders in the north, in seasons when there occurs an abundance of corn and grass and a scarcity of native cattle. This surplus food stuff could be turned to the profit of the farmer. The present necessary though burdensome quarantine regulations would be greatly eased; foreign countries could no longer exclude these animals on the grounds that they are liable to introduce a dangerous disease. In some parts of the country ticks are so bad that stock owners have to resort to some means by which they can rid their cattle of the tick, for they are a great curse to the comfort, welfare, and growth of the animal. There have been various remedies and modes of application advocated, but none seems to be so effectual or easily applied as by dipping. A large vat or tank is constructed, leading to which is a narrow chute and trap door, by which the cattle are plunged into the solution in the tank and made to swim out at the other side. Various preparations have been tried, to make the solution in the tank, such as crude carbolic acid, tobacco, chloro-naptholeum, cotton seed oil, etc. With some, the oily preparations have proven very satisfactory, while others claim it is not a sure remedy.

For dairy cows and for gentle farm cattle the ticks can be destroyed by painting the cattle with 15 parts crude carbolic acid dissolved in 80 parts of crude cottonseed oil.

Extensive experiments have been made with the dipping of cattle for the eradication of ticks by Dr. Francis, at College Station, Texas, and by Mr. R. J. Kleberg, of Alice, Texas. We think we can not do better here than to quote some of Dr. Francis' remarks on dipping cattle:

"The destruction of these parasites on the bodies of our cattle has engaged a large share of our attention for several years. It is evident that whatever means be adopted, it is of first importance that every tick be reached. This is accomplished by forcing the cattle to swim through a large dipping vat, somewhat similar to the dipping process employed against certain parasites of sheep. The device consists of a large wooden vat, about ten feet deep and forty feet long, having a working capacity of about five thousand gallons. It is constructed in a large trench so that the lower two-thirds is below the ground line. The entrance is through a narrow chute at the end of which there is provided a trap door balanced over the end of the vat, so that when the animal passes through the chute and arrives on the trap, the latter tilts, and the animal, losing its balance, plunges into the vat. The animal is almost always completely submerged, thus bringing the solution in contact with its entire body. On rising to the surface it swims to the exit, which is provided with a cleated inclined floor to enable it to make its way out and reach an inclined dripping platform where the cattle are detained a short time. This device has a working capacity of about one thousand head per day. It is, perhaps, not desirable to burden this report with the details of the construction of the vat. Those who are seriously interested in the subject will be provided with plans and dimensions. In our earlier studies of the subject we began testing the different varieties of sheep dips, with the view of finding a suitable and efficient commercial preparation that could be supplied in large quantities and be of uniform quality. We selected a certain one which seemed to be typical of the carbolic acid group. Of this we made up 4000 gallons of a 5 per cent strength. The cattle were then forced to swim through it. The results were not satisfactory, because it irritated the animals considerably and did not kill all the ticks. We also tried other carbolic preparations in a similar manner, but found ourselves confronted with this condition: That some of the ticks would survive solutions that would probably be fatal to the cattle if immersed in it. On one occasion we seriously scalded about ninety animals by using a too concentrated carbolic preparation. We found, also, that carbolic emulsions are very unstable, and undergo changes very rapidly, which makes them almost worthless for dipping purposes. Our attention was next engaged with an arsenical sheep dip, which we used in a 1 per cent solution. Of this we made up 4000 gallons and forced cattle to swim through it. This preparation was stable, uniform, and non-irritating, but its action on the ticks was so indifferent that it was discarded. Emulsions of kerosene and decoctions of tobacco were also tried in a small way with no practical results. We next began using oils. The first season we used cottonseed oil to which had been added 10 per cent crude carbolic acid and 5 per cent pine tar. We filled the vat with water and added about 100 gallons of the oil mixture, which made a layer on the surface of the water three-fourths to one inch in depth. The cattle were forced through the chute and plunged into the vat. On rising to the surface and coming out they became covered with oil, which was exceedingly fatal to the tick without causing any positive injury to the cattle. We noted, however, that such a coating of oil in the vat soon became greatly altered in appearance and quality, from contact with the water, which eventually induced us to seek a substitute. We next tried a cheap natural or mineral oil, called "Winter West Virginia." We used this in the same manner as the cotton oil. It bears agitation with water quite well, but it occurs to me that it is not so fatal as the cotton oil to the tick. We sometimes use it alone, and sometimes add carbolic acid to it. In some instances we have dipped a bunch of cattle with absolutely perfect results, and sometimes we notice an animal on which the work was imperfect. There is yet a third condition of affairs for which we have no satisfactory explanation. It sometimes occurs that half-grown ticks will be noticed several days after dipping. This has caused us great annoyance and much study. At present we attribute it to the condition of the tick at the time of dipping, viz., that it was moulting. These young ticks sometimes increase in size, and may have the appearance of healthy ticks, but we have invariably failed to hatch their eggs, which seem to have been aborted, though the conditions were suitable as proven by eggs of other ticks hatching under the same conditions. This has led us to be somewhat guarded of late, in claiming that one dipping will offer sufficient safeguard against Texas fever, if the dipping process be adopted on a commercial basis. For purely experimental purposes it may, but in our judgment it would be somewhat risky for general use. It occurs to us then, that if a change in the present Federal regulations be contemplated, it would be wise to require two dippings with an interval of several days. This we believe would be absolutely safe."

By reading the article in this book on Texas Fever, it will be seen that the tick is without a doubt the sole transmitter of the disease, and a large dipping vat is now being constructed at Fort Worth, Texas, where cattle will be dipped under State and Federal inspection, and if pronounced free from ticks they will be admitted into the State of Kansas for feeding purposes, thus opening a market from Texas to summer feeders in the North. This is a long stride in the direction of breaking down quarantine barriers, and will be watched with interest.

HORN FLY.

This is a little black fly which infests certain districts of the United States and causes great annoyance to cattle. They have received the popular name of "horn fly" from the fact that they collect upon the horns of cattle while they (the flies) are at rest. This fly first made its appearance in any great numbers in the United States about ten years ago, and at that time some very wild stories were told about it. It was claimed that the fly ate through the horn, caused it to rot, and laid eggs inside, which, after hatching, penetrated the brain. This, however, is not the case; but they do cause great annoyance to cattle by biting them. They prevent thrift in beef cattle and milk production in dairy cows. When they are present in large numbers they collect upon the base of the horns, along the top of the neck, or under the belly. They attack cattle in the field by piercing the skin and sucking the blood. Certain cattle will be covered with the flies and mind them very little, while others lose flesh very rapidly. But as a general thing they are not very injurious to stock and will never cause death to the animal. They will not make sores on cattle, but sores will form by the cattle rubbing themselves against trees, fences, etc., to get rid of the flies.

Treatment.—The only thing to be done is to keep the cattle in dark stables during the day or apply some greasy or oily substance to the skin. Crude cottonseed oil 1 gallon, and crude carbolic acid 4 ounces, thoroughly mixed and painted on the cows with a large brush, will keep off the flies for four or five days at a time. The female fly lays its eggs in the droppings of cattle, which soon hatch out and form a new generation of flies. These droppings by being burned when a little dry will destroy the eggs.

SCREW-WORMS.

The maggots from the screw-worm fly (Lucillia macellaria) are the greatest curse to stock, and cause the stockmen of Texas more trouble than any other thing. The flies deposit their eggs on sores on stock, and these eggs hatch out in a remarkably short time; and then the maggots grow very rapidly, and in two or three days there are dozens, or perhaps hundreds, of good-sized screw-worms burrowing and boring into the healthy flesh; and unless killed, they will in many cases kill the animal. Dogs and pigs will drown them out if they can get to water, but they have to be killed by the use of medicine as a general thing on horses, cattle and sheep. The best and safest remedy we know for killing screw-worms is chloroform 1 part and alcohol 2 parts, to be injected into the sore. After killing them out, dust the sore with Dr. LeGear's Screw Worm Powder, which is a fine healing preparation and keeps out the screw-worms.

THE STIFF DISEASE.

This is a fragilitis (brittle) conditon of bone, and is variously known as "the stiffness," "the cripple," etc. It appears to be more or less dependent upon a peculiarity of soil, being common to that of a porous or sandy nature, and more or less sterile.

We have been confronted with similar trouble in Texas, counties of Burnet, Lampasas, Tom Green, etc., where the disease seems to be quite common, and appears to be due to a lack of phosphates, and amonia in the soil.

Symptoms.—The animal has a depraved appetite, the milk decreases and becomes thin, watery, and of a bluish color, yielding but little cream. The animal soon gets poor, becomes stiff and weak, rises with difficulty, drags the hind limbs in walking, and usually lies down a great deal; the joints swell, the animal evidently suffering much pain; fracture of the bones are common; paralysis of the limbs may take place. The disease may continue for months, or even as long as a year, but may be arrested in the early stages.

Treatment.—Remove the affected animals from the soil on which they contracted the disease to a pasture where the character of the land is entirely different, and make a change in the water supply also. Nutritious food, those rich in phosphates, are most important, for the assimilation of which common salt should be given. If the drinking water is soft (rain water), give water that contains carbonate, sulphate, or phosphate of lime, and chlorate of magnesia, etc. Not much can be done for advanced cases, and treatment is almost useless. We believe it is generally due to the influence of the drinking water, and consider that the relation between lime-salts in the water and softness of bone deserve far more consideration on the part of stock owners than is generally done.

CHAPTER XXV.

CONTAGIOUS DISEASES.

CHARBON OR ANTHRAX.

Anthrax may be defined to be a malignant and contagious disease of the blood, attacking particularly cattle, horses, mules, sheep and goats, but communicable to all domestic animals. It may be communicated to man, and is then known as "malignant pustule." On account of it attacking such a variety of the domesticated animals it is one of the most dreaded scourges of animal life.

History.—This disease dates back to the siege of Troy, in Asia Minor, and was a terrible plague of the cattle of Egypt in the time of Moses. And in response to the casting forth of ashes from the furnace by Moses, the modern name of charbon, anthrax and carbuncle, all signifying burning, would seem somewhat remarkable. The Greeks in writing about it in regard to man called it anthrax, while the Latin writers termed it carbuncle. In Germany it is called milzbrand; in Australia, cumberland disease. In the Middle Ages it was frequently confounded with another plague, rinderpest, but the outbreaks of it in 996 A. D. and 1090 A. D. in France, clearly identified it as a different disease. In 1617, at Naples, Italy, numbers of human beings died from eating the flesh of animals which were affected with the disease. Serious outbreaks constantly occur in the United States, and it has a great tendency to spread. In recent years the most noticeable outbreaks have occurred in Delaware, New Jersey, New York, Illinois, Louisiana and California. Between June 15 and October 15, 1893, 970 animals succumbed to the disease in five counties in Illinois. In July, 1895, 222 died in one county in New Jersey. And it is reported that thousands of animals have died during the recent outbreak in Louisiana. It is quite common among the mules of Mexico. Generally speaking the germs of anthrax seem to exist wherever the soil is of a marshy nature, and outbreaks are always likely to take place where such soil is found.

Causes. — The causes of anthrax were at one time attributed entirely to climatic influence, the soil, etc., and no doubt they are important predisposing factors in the development of the disease, for it is most prevalent in low, damp, swampy districts during the warm season, especially when outbreaks over any number of animals occur. Decaying vegetable matter seems most favorable for nourishing and preserving the virus, while it is more frequent in districts where low-lying swamp lands dry out during the heat of summer and are then covered with light rains. The direct cause of anthrax is the anthrax bacillus (bacillus anthrax), which is a rod-like, vegetable organism. These bacilli are very small, and require a powerful microscope to see them. The bacteria multiply very rapidly in the blood by becoming elongated and then dividing into two, and each of these dividing, and so on indefinitely. Outside of the body, however, when under conditions favorable to growth, they multiply in a different way. Small round bodies appear within the rods, called spores (seed germs), which remain alive after years of drying. They also resist extreme heat, so that boiling water is necessary to destroy them. The bacilli themselves, on the other hand, show only very little resistance to heat and drying.

The spores may remain in the ground for years and then produce an outbreak of the disease. They may be carried to land on skin scraps which are used as fertilizers. Weather, rainfall and temperature in particular govern the source of the contagion.

Heavy rains may wash the seed into the ground as deep as the water itself goes, but as long as they remain there of course they are harmless. Now during dry weather the water is drawn up through good soil from a very considerable depth, evaporated and deposits on the surface whatever it brings up in it. Or during light rains after a dry spell earth worms in seeking moisture may bring the spores to the surface from the same depths. This places the seed in suitable soil and temperature to sprout and multiply at once, or they may find their way into the animal's body still in the form of seed, therein germinate and develop an epidemic. This explains why a long drouth followed by light rains is characteristic of anthrax weather.

The first discovery of the specific virus of anthrax was made by Davaine in 1851. But it was left to M. Pasteur, the great French scientist, who in 1877 defined the exact nature of the bacillus, the manner of its production, and its exact relationship to anthrax, as the real cause of the disease. The anthrax bacilli may be introduced into the body in three different ways: either through the mouth or alimentary canal, through the respiratory organs, or through the skin. When the infection takes place through the skin it is usually introduced by the sting of some insect, especially the large horsefly. This fly carries the poison from the carcasses of the animals which have died of the disease and simply inoculates it into the skin of live animals. The germs may also be introduced into the system by coming in contact with a wound or abrasion of the skin or mucous membrane. And when it affects the digestive organs the germs of the disease are usually taken into the body with the feed or water.

Symptoms.—The symptoms as a general thing are suddenly developed and very alarming in character. An animal may be left at night in apparently a state of perfect health and found the next morning dead. Milk cows have been milked in the morning and at noon found dead. Horses and mules will succumb to the terrible disease while working in the field. Pigs eating at a trough have been known to step back, turn around, squeal, tumble down and die in a minute. This may properly be called the apoplectic form of the disease, and the most thrifty animals in the flock or herd may become victims of the disease, contracting it usually in its most acute and malignant forms, while the poorer animals may escape entirely or take it in a mild form. As this form is so suddenly developed, death takes place before any symptoms are noticed. But in other forms it runs a somewhat longer course. The symptoms are different in different animals, and may differ in the same class of animals.

As has been stated before, the disease germs may gain access into the animal in several ways, viz., on the feed or in the water, thus gaining access into the alimentary canal; through the air, passing into the lungs; and by inoculation into the skin or mucous membrane, by coming into contact with diseased animals or infected pastures, premises, etc. When the infection takes place through the skin a hard, warm, painful swelling with well defined margins form under the skin and spread rapidly over the surface. The infection is usually accompanied by fever, loss of appetite, and quickened respirations. The swelling becomes cold and painless in a few days, and either may be absorbed or the disease spreads to the intestinal organs and proves fatal to the animal. But when the disease gains access through the alimentary canal or the lungs, there is a very high fever, a small, rapid pulse, the visible mucous membranes of a bluish red color, and in some cases symptoms of congestion of the brain, also of colic and diarrhoea often mixed with blood. Chills and muscular tremors may appear, and the skin show uneven temperature. The animal becomes dull and stupid, the eyes staring, and manifests great weakness. There is also loss of appetite, labored breathing, and the region of the throat may become swollen to such an extent that the breathing becomes roaring, and may be followed by suffocation. The disease usually lasts from a few hours to two or three days. Recovery is very rare. An examination of the blood shows a dark fluid, which is not clot, and which remains black after exposure to the air. After death the bodies putrify very rapidly and bloat, the tissues are filled with gases, and a bloody foam exudes from the mouth, nostrils, etc. The spleen becomes enlarged from two to five times its natural size, and the pulse is blackish and soft. The liver has a cooked appearance, and the kidneys are congested and also soft.

Treatment.—When the animal becomes affected with charbon it almost invariably dies, as there has been no reliable treatment discovered as yet. Nearly every drug in the pharmacopoeia has been tried with negative results. There is only one form of the disease in which treatment is of any avail, and that is the form in which the disease germs gain access through an external wound or abrasion of the skin. In such cases the swellings should be opened freely by long incisions with a sharp lance and the wound dressed several times a day with strong antiseptic solutions. No matter whether treatment is adopted or not, a few of the affected animals may recover, but recoveries are doubtful.

Pasteur in 1881 very fortunately discovered a protective vaccine, which has been thoroughly proven to be a sure preventive against the disease. It is well known how human beings are protected from smallpox by vaccination. All domestic animals can in the same way be protected from anthrax by the use of Pasteur's anthrax vaccine. It is a specially prepared liquid, a few drops of which are injected under the skin by the use of a hypodermic syringe. Vaccination consists of two inouculations, the first with a very weak virus, while the second is somewhat stronger and injected about twelve days later. Pasteur's vaccine is not, and is not intended to be a cure for charbon, but animals after being vaccinated enjoy immunity from the disease in nearly every case. Vaccination of the domestic animals against this disease is being practiced quite extensively in various parts of the United States and receives the highest approval of our leading veterinarians. In a locality where charbon has appeared all stock should at once be inoculated with Pasteur's anthrax vaccine. By vaccinating all unaffected animals and immediately burning all dead bodies, a check can very quickly be made in the spread of this dread disease.

TEXAS, OR SPLENETIC FEVER.

This is a specific fever communicated by cattle which have been moved northward from the infected district, or which is contracted by cattle taken into the infected districts from other parts of the world. It is characterized by a high fever, greatly enlarged spleen, destruction of the red blood corpuscles, escape of the coloring matter of the blood through the kidneys, giving the unrine a deep color; by a yellowness of the mucus membranes and fat; by a rapid loss of strength, and by fatal results in a large majority of cases. This disease has various names in different parts of the country, as Spanish fever, acclimation fever, red water, bloody murrian, etc.

As early as 1814 the people of Virginia prohibited cattle from a certain district in South Carolina from passing through their State, on account of these cattle so certainly diseasing all others with which they mix in their progress to the north; while these cattle were in perfect health, they gave to all others, whether from Europe or the Northern States, a disease that generally proved fatal. Similar observations have been made in regard to nearly all of the Southern States, and it is now known that the infection is not peculiar to Texas or even the Gulf coast, but that it extends far inward and northward almost to the southern limit of Maryland. On account of the frequent and severe losses following the driving of cattle from the infected districts in Texas into and across the Western States and territories, the name of Texas fever became attached to this disease.

Northern cattle taken into the infected district contract this disease usually the first summer, and if milk cows or fat cattle, nearly all die. Calves are much more likely to recover than adult cattle. Calves which survive are not again attacked, as a rule, even after they become adult. Experience shows that the disease is not communicated by animals coming near or in contact with each other. Cattle from the infected district first infect the pastures, roads, cars, etc., by the mature cattle-tick dropping from their bodies; and susceptible cattle obtain the virus (poison) from the young ticks which hatch out from eggs deposited on the ground, and which crawl upon them. But if sufficient freezing takes place during the winter season, these infected pastures, etc., will be free from any attack next season, as all the ticks have been killed.

The investigations made by the Bureau of Animal Industry prove that ticks which adhere to cattle from the infected district are the chief means of conveying the infection to non-infected cattle; that the disease is never transmitted by the saliva (spittle), the urine, or the manure through eating of foods contaminated by these excretions. The feet of cattle are not capable of carrying the germs. Grasses and pond water of the infected districts of the Southern States do not cause the disease when given to cattle. In studying the causation and prevention of this disease, the tick theory has attracted the most attention, and it stands to reason that if cattle could be freed from this parasite when leaving the infected district, they would not be able to cause the malady. That this is true has been conclusively proven by recent experiments in connection with the Texas Experiment Station near Bryan in co-operation with the Missouri Experiment Station at Columbia. Ten Texas cows covered with ticks were forced to swim through a large dipping vat made for such purposes, and afterwards sent by car to Columbia, Missouri. Missouri cattle were put in the pasture with the Texan cattle, and remained there for a period of 79 days, but failed to contract the disease. And throughout this period not a tick was found on the Missouri cattle; nor could any be found on the Texas cattle, save a few brought with them, which soon disappeared. It would appear from this experiment that great benefits would accrue to the cattle and farming industry of the whole country from the dipping process; the danger of infecting northern territory in the transfer of these animals would be overcome; a market previously closed would be opened to summer feeders in the North, in seasons of abundance of corn and grass and a scarcity of cattle.

Nature and Cause.—Texas fever is caused by a micro-parasite (little animal living on another) which lives within the red blood-corpuscles and destroys them. It is therefore a disease of the blood. The little organism is carried and introduced into the blood of animals by the cattle tick (boophilus bovis) which may be found on nearly all Texas cattle. It is not, therefore, a microscopic plant, but it belongs to the lowest form of animal life. This very little animal multiplies very rapidly in the body of the infected animal, and in severe cases causes great destruction of the red blood corpuscles in a short time.

All the disease processes which go on in Texas fever, as seen by examining the organs after death, all result from the destruction of red blood-corpuscles. When this destruction is rapid, we have the acute, usually fatal, type of Texas fever, usually witnessed during the latter weeks of August and the early weeks of September. Cases of the mild type occurring early in the season usually become acute later on and terminate fatally.

Symptoms.—The disease first shows itself in dullness, loss of appetite, and a tendency to leave the herd and stand or lie down alone. The temperature of the body, taken per rectum by a fever thermometer (Fig. 19), shows an elevation, in acute cases, to 106-107 degrees Fahrenheit. When the temperature does not rise above 104 degrees Fahrenheit, the disease is milder and more prolonged. The bowels are usually constipated, and toward the fatal end the feces may become softer and tinged with bile. The urine near the fatal termination is deeply stained with the coloring matter of the blood, while during the course of the disease it may be quite natural in color. The pulse, as well as the breathing, is also quickened. As the end approaches the animal becomes very weak and stupid, the blood is thin and watery, and the poor sufferer may lie down most of the time, or until death takes place.

Examination after Death.—It is very important at times to know whether an animal died of Texas fever or some other disease. This can as a rule be determined at once by a thorough microscopic examination of the blood. But as this method is entirely in the hands of experts, the general reader will have to depend on certain changes caused by this disease, which may be detected by the naked eye when the animal is opened. These changes in the internal organs are as follows: The spleen or milt is much larger than in a healthy state, weighing three or four times as much, and its contents or pulp consists of a mottled blackish mass. The liver is also found to be enlarged, has lost its natural brownish color, and has on its surface a paler, yellowish hue. The gall bladder is found to be fully distended with bile of a cloudy or flaky consistency. The contents of the bladder should be examined. This usually contains urine which varies in color from a deep port wine to a light claret. These are the principal changes and sufficient proof of the trouble.

Prevention.—According to the latest experiments, Texas fever is carried north only by the cattle tick. Hence, to prevent Texas fever north of the quarantine line, the pastures, etc., must be kept free from cattle ticks, and to do this, no Southern cattle with ticks must be allowed upon them. Cattle cars may also be the means of conveying ticks from one part of the country to another. Knowing that Southern cattle when free from ticks are harmless to Northern cattle, various experiments have been going on as to the best means of destroying these ticks. The dipping process, up to the present time, has proven the most effectual. All cattle, before being shipped North, should be dipped in a vat made for the purpose, when they can be safely taken into non-infected territory.

Treatment.—When once the disease has broken out, the healthy should be separated from the sick animals and put upon non-infected pastures. While this may not cut short the disease, it may save the lives of some by removing them from the possibility of being attacked by more young ticks; also prevents a second later attack in October or November, which is caused by another generation of ticks. As far as possible, remove all ticks from the sick and well animals. To accomplish this, apply some oil, as cottonseed oil or black machine oil, with a paint brush, to those parts usually affected. The giving of sulphur is said to cause the ticks to loosen their hold and drop off. Medicinal treatment, so far, has been useless, as nearly all animals having the acute form of the disease die. It is quite probable that the blood serum (sero-vaccine) treatment by vaccination, lately coming into use, will produce immunity from the disease. This is a departure from all the methods previously employed in this disease. It is simply a test of a law laid down by Behring, namely, that if an animal has acquired immunity against a disease producing micro-organisms or its toxins, the serum from the blood of the immunized animal will prevent the disease in another susceptible animal.

How well we know that immunity (proof) from smallpox is acquired by vaccination; also the anti-toxin treatment in the cure and prevention of diphtheria. So we believe the same results can be obtained by what may be called the "anti-toxin" or "serum" method of treatment in Texas fever. It is true that Texas fever is caused by an animal parasite (protozoon); while in diphtheria, the cause is a vegetable parasite (bactera). This difference in the nature of the cause of these two diseases, has led most investigators to the belief that there must be a difference in the process by which immunity is acquired. But the simple law of immunity will teach us that there can be no essential difference in the process by which immunity is acquired against micro-organisms and poisons of any kind. Immunity against Texas fever is certainly acquired, and is fully as effective as that acquired against any of the bacterial diseases. In naturally acquired immunity against Texas fever the ticks have taken the place of the hypodermic syringe in the way of inoculation. The animal may while young, if the dam is immune, gain immunity through the milk; and on Southern soil the ticks keep up the natural inoculations from year to year by which immunity from the disease is obtained.

The serum used in this preventative treatment must be obtained from a Texas steer or cow, or any other animal that has had the disease and recovered, or is naturally immuned. It is injected or inoculated by a hypodermic syringe under the skin of the animal to be treated. This blood serum sets up a slow process of disease in the animal, and after sufficient has been injected to make the animal safe from an attack, the ticks that infest her body from year to year afterwards continue to keep the animal in a state of immunity. The serum is meant to tide them over the acclimation period, and can be prepared and used by any one having the apparatus and proper instruments. It can be obtained at the Texas Experiment Station, where they keep it on hand or prepare it fresh on short notice.

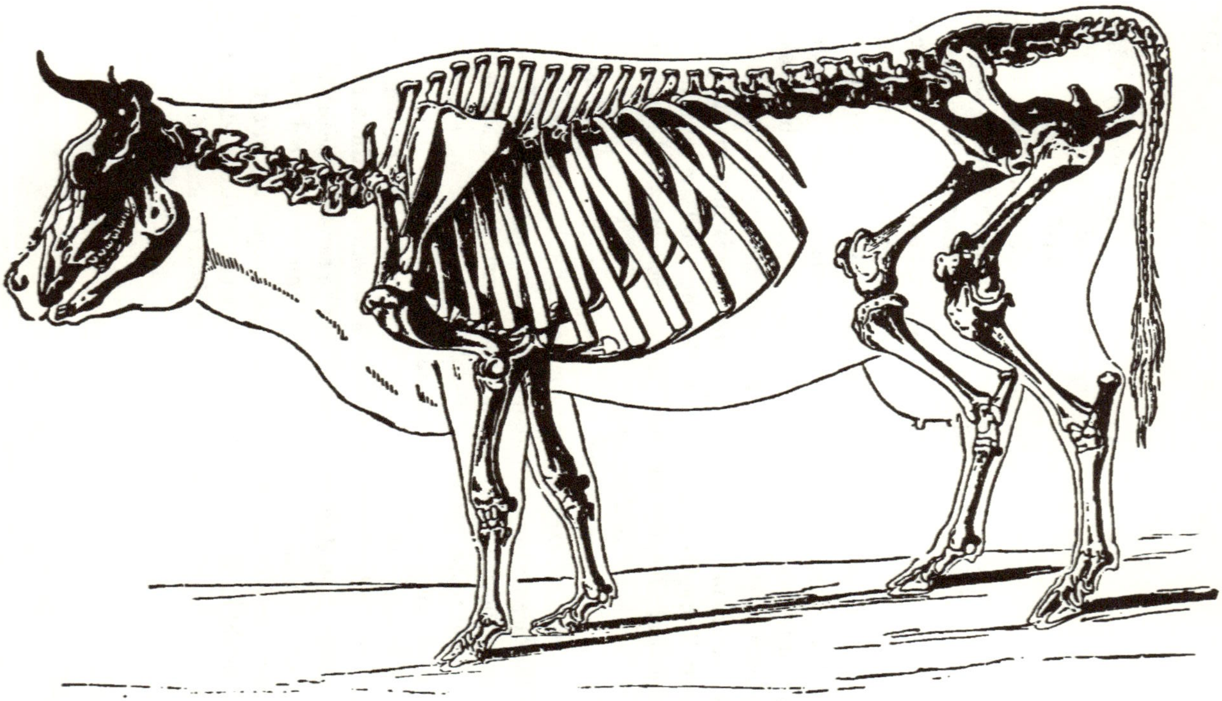

Plate XI. SKELETON OF THE COW.

[p. 314]

BOVINE TUBERCULOSIS, OR ANIMAL CONSUMPTION.

In speaking of consumption, it is generally understood to mean a disease of the human family characterized by an affection or "wasting away" of the lungs. But we may have consumption of other organs of the body as well, and so are the lower animals subject to this same disease.

We are not sure of the exact time that this disease made its first appearance, but it has been known for many centuries, and legislative enactments having reference to the destruction of affected animals and forbidding the use of the flesh date far back into the Middle Ages.

Nature and Cause.—All kinds of theories prevailed as to the nature and cause of consumption until Robert Koch, in 1882, proved it to be a disease due to a germ (bacillus tuberculosis) and that this germ caused the disease in all the lower animals and in man. This wonderful discovery at once put an end to all disputes and controversies as to it causation. The germ is a slender, rod-like body, so small that it can not be seen with the naked eye. When it has become lodged in any organ or tissue it begins to multiply, setting up an irritation which leads to the formation of little nodules or tubercles; these, when full grown, are about the size of a millet seed. When these tubercles continue to form in large numbers they run together, forming masses of various sizes.

There are several ways in which these germs may find their way into the body: First, by inhalation into the lungs; second, into the digestive tract in the milk of consumptive cows. Other ways could be given, but the two named are the most common modes of infection.

It has been shown by thousands of experiments that the discase is transmissible from one animal to another of the same species, and from one species to another. No matter how the germs may enter the system, whether inhaled, taken in with food or inoculated, the disease is liable to ensue. A consumptive animal placed among animals communicates the disease to those previously healthy. Milk from an affected cow fed to cats, calves, hogs, guinea pigs, etc., produces the disease in them. Inoculating the infected milk into other animals produces the disease. Sputa coughed up by man and carelessly spit out has been licked up and devoured by animals and produced the disease in them.

When the stomach, intestines and mesenteric glands are diseased, it is probably the result of food infection. The germs of the disease may have been scattered upon the feed by diseased animals. But the milk of consumptive cows is the most common source of such infection. Calves may become infected in this way, and the disease may not develop until the animal becomes older.

Up to a recent period the opinion prevailed that it was only milk from cows with diseased udders that was extremely dangerous, but the experiments of Professor Ernst of Harvard University and many others have demonstrated the fact that milk from a consumptive cow may contain the germs, even though the udder is absolutely free from disease.

While we believe in the germ theory, yet there are conditions which must be recognized as almost necessary to an attack of the disease. Unsanitary conditions, such as overcrowding in poorly ventilated and lighted stables, and feeding of food that is not nutritious are conditions which favor the germs in their attack. Any injury to the lungs such as inhalation of dust and smoke and all conditions which may induce chronic inflammation of the bronchial tubes.

Of all points in the subject none seem to be more assailed than heredity. There has been no positive proof of the disease having been inherited, but it is a fact nevertheless, and one of almost daily occurence, that the disease reaps its harvest among the offspring of consumptive parents. A weakly, consumptive parent generally transmits a similar constitution, which is extremely liable to the disease; and when it appears at an early age those who believe in heredity think that there has been an "hereditary infection" instead of an early "direct infection." Among the wild herds of the plains consumption is practically unknown, while among the cows of closely confined dairy herds it is quite common.

Prevalence, etc.—Consumption, whether in man or the lower animals, is a disease prevalent in all civilized countries. In some countries, such as the northern part of Norway and Sweden, on the steppes of eastern Europe and Russia, in Sicily and Iceland it is said to be quite rare.

Where cattle are few, or absent, consumption is relatively less in man. Dr. Burich pointed out the fact in countries like Australia and the Sandwich Islands consumption among the people did not exist until after dairy cattle were introduced. He also called attention to the fact that consumption prevails in all countries where the dairy products are derived from cattle. He further says: Morocco, where there are no European dairy cows, is exempt from consumption, while in Spain and Portugal, where dairying is carried on in European style, the disease exists.

In most countries an effort is now being made to determine more accurately the prevalence of the disease. Statistics show that 75 per cent of old dairy cows in Germany have tuberculosis. In Denmark nearly 40 per cent of the cattle have been found to be consumptive. Some herds tested in the United States showed that 32 per cent were affected. Some herds tested proved to be entirely free from the disease. Of all the cattle killed in Germany at the slaughter houses from 16 to 25 per cent have been found affected.

In the West and Southwest of our country, where cattle are reared mostly in the open air, the disease is apparently quite rare, as most of the animals are able in a measure to resist the contagion, and only occasional animals in a herd show any physical signs of the disease.

Symptoms.—In the first stages of the disease it is very difficult to detect. It is a disease slow in its course, and at first unnoticed; many cases never show any symptoms, and are found only to be tuberculosis when killed. In those animals showing symptoms there is generally a dry, hoarse cough, at first slight, occurring after feeding or drinking; it may be easily excited by running the animal. As the disease progresses, the animal grows thin and has an unthrifty appearance of the coat, etc.; this persists in spite of good feed. The cough now becomes more frequent and the breathing more rapid, especially on slight exertion; the breath becomes offensive, and usually there is a discharge from the nose. Weakness continually increases, followed by disorder of digestion—bloating and diarrhoea—and the animal finally dies from exhaustion. Often all symptoms are wanting in spite of the existence of the disease, and in such cases the tuberculin test must be used.

Tuberculin Test.—Tuberculin is a glycerine extract of the culture of the bacillus tuberculosis (germ of the disease), and when injected under the skin it has the property of causing a rise in temperature in all animals suffering from this disease. It is also known as Koch's lymph. In animals free from the disease no reaction takes place after the use of the tuberculin. It is therefore a valuable agent for detecting all tuberculous cattle in an infected herd, and is the only means by which this can be accomplished.

In 1890 Koch, under pressure, made public his work on tuberculin. This resulted in a tremendous and intense excitement all over the world, and consumptives undertook journeys of hundreds of miles for the sake of being treated with the new cure for consumption. It was noticed by several observers that when a person suffering from consumption received an injection of the lymph, it invariably caused a rise in temperature; and in 1891 Gutman, a Russian, took advantage of this fact and began to make experiments with it as a diagnostic agent in cattle; and as a result of which, we are able to detect the slightest forms of the disease.

On account of the deep-seated tubercles usually existing with superficial ones, they render tuberculin almost useless as a curative agent, since, to eradicate the disease, the deep-seated tubercles must be afterwards removed by surgical means.

But this action which renders tuberculin so objectionable as a curative agent, makes it of the highest value as a test of tuberculosis in cattle. The minute (small) dose which has no effect on a healthy cow, sheep or goat, when employed on the slightly tuberculous one, produces an acceleration of the disease process, and in eight to fifteen hours a material rise of temperature.

This has been now employed on thosuands of cows, and those who have used it most value it the most highly; whereas many who at first reported reactions in non-tuberculous animals are now acknowledging with Nocard, one of the best veterinarians in Europe, that the fault has been mainly their own, for the tubercles were present, but were overlooked through careless and faulty post mortems.

The explanation of the reaction under tuberculin may be simply stated as follows: The dose is so small that it will not affect a healthy cow under ordinary conditions. In the slightly diseased cow the system contains a certain amount of tuberculin produced by the bacillus (germ) in the tubercles, or nodules, but to this the system has become accustomed and it causes no appreciable fever. But when, in addition to this, we introduce into the body of the cow the small amount of tuberculin used for the test, the increased dose acts on tubercle and nerve centers alike, and a fever is produced.

. *Post Mortem.*—An examination after death of internal organs should always be made on any animal that dies, or which has been slaughtered, presenting the above symptoms, which will generally enable even the inexperienced to recognize this disease if present. In advanced cases the principal changes are usually found in the lungs and the lymphatic glands or in connection with the same. The surface or substance of the lung will generally show solid cheese-like masses of varying size. A favorite situation for these tubercular masses is in the glands between and at the root of the lung. They may also be found in the abdominal organs; in fact, the germs of the disease may find lodgment in any organ of the body.

Treatment.—Inasmuch as there is no specific for this disease, it is of the utmost importance that all animals, as far as possible, be protected from the contagion. The difficulty of knowing when cattle first become affected makes it impossible (except by the tuberculin test) to prevent the possibility of infection. Too much care can not be bestowed upon the breeding, the surroundings, and the food of the animal so that the latter may be the more able to resist infection even when exposed to it. A rigid exclusion of tuberculous animals is all that is necessary to prevent the appearance of the disease, provided consumptive persons or other animals do not infect the cattle.

The carcasses of all animals which have died of consumption should be burned or buried deeply, so that other animals can not eat them. Hogs, dogs, cats, etc., eating such carcasses and contracting the disease, may in turn give the disease to other animals and man.

Danger in Milk.—It is plain that the only means we have to insure a safe milk supply to consumers is the inspection of the source of the milk—the cow. The examination of the milk itself would be a farce, for the simple reason that the time required for microscopical examination and chemical analyses of all milk sold would make such tests utterly impossible and impracticable. We need not fear intentional or criminal adulteration of milk by the dairyman; he will add nothing harmful to human health; it is the cow we must fear, and in order to make inspection of benefit to humanity, the cow should be ascertained to be free from consumption beyond all doubt. Happily for mankind, this is being done all the world over with perfect success. The "tuberculin test" applied to the cows at regular intervals will enable the disease to be kept out of the herd. People who have had no experience with tuberculin may talk against it and argue against it, but their idle boasting, wild statements, and pretended knowledge do not do away with the fact that tuberculin is a reliable diagnostic for bovine (cattle) consumption, and has been proven to be such in proper hands so invariably that all civilized governments, including our own, employ it in their official work in connection with consumption.

Cattle consumption is a question that must come under State supervision sooner or later. There can be no doubt of the contagious and infectious nature of the disease, and hence the State and local boards of health should have their powers enlarged to be able to handle the question. There is no reason why consumers of milk should continue to daily run the risk they now do, when it is only necessary for the city council to pass an ordinance creating the office of dairy inspector, whose duty it should be to test all cows in dairies supplying milk to consumers and see that no milk is sold which does not come from cows proven to be free from consumption.

Danger in Meat.—The flesh is not so dangerous as the milk of tuberculous cows. It is quite rare to find tubercle in the substance of the muscle of cattle. They are common, however, in the lymphatic glands lying between the muscles; but in swine they are common, even in the red flesh. The flesh of tuberculous pigs is therefore far more dangerous than that of consumptive cattle.

A further safeguard against the eating of the flesh of animals is that it is cooked before it is eaten, while milk as a general thing is not. In meat that is thoroughly cooked, all the germs of the disease are destroyed. Thoroughly cooking or boiling the milk renders it entirely safe to be used as an article of food.

BLACKLEG—BLACK QUARTER.

Blackleg is a very fatal and infectious disease of young cattle, which is at the present time causing considerable mortality among calves and young cattle in various portions of Texas, as well as in other States of the Union. It is a world-wide disease, causing large losses among young cattle in Germany, France, Italy, Belgium, Australia, England, etc. In this country it is known by various names, such as blackleg, black quarter, quarter evil, quarter ill, symptomatic anthrax, etc. Until within the last few years it was considered identical to anthrax, but it is now proven to be a specific disease produced by bacilli (germs), which are easily distinguished from anthrax bacilli. Cattle between six months and four years of age are most susceptible to the disease. Certain pastures and districts are more favorable to the growth of the bacillus, therefore the disease is more common there. Swamps, bottom lands, or any low lands along streams that are subject to inundations and floods are the most frequent places for outbreaks of the disease, although it will occur in any locality regardless of soil, location, altitude, etc.

Causes. — Blackleg is causd by a bacillus, which is a microscopic organism, or bacteria, visible only by the use of a powerful microscope. The bacilli are cylindrical or rod-like bodies and have the power of indefinite multiplication, and in the body of an infected animal they produce death by rapidly increasing in number and producing substances which poison the body. In the body they multiply in number by becoming elongated and then dividing into two, each new germ continuing the same process indefinitely. They will grow and multiply outside the body when in a favorable locality and position for growth. Oval bodies appear within the bacilli, which are called spores (seeds), and which remain alive and grow and produce the disease after several years of drying. They have a wonderful power of resistance against heat and cold, as it takes boiling water to destroy them. These spores often collect in sufficient numbers in feed and cause serious outbreaks of blackleg among stall-fed cattle.

There is practically no danger of a transmission of this disease from one animal to another, since it is contracted on the pastures from the ground and in the stables from the food. The bacilli, if not already in the soil, finds its way on to a farm or ranch in what appears at times to be the most unaccountable way. Throwing carcasses of animals that have died of blackleg into running streams, or shallow burial near running streams, is a fertile source of infection to pastures along such streams below. Dogs or wild animals may dig up carcasses not buried deep and scatter the bacilli and spores over the pastures. M. Pasteur by a series of experiments has proven that earth worms bring the spores to the surface which remain a source of danger to all young cattle that graze in the vicinity. Before the disease can be produced the germs must gain entrance to the animal's system by some means. They may enter the system through sores and abrasions on the feet or legs of animals as they walk over the pastures or through mud and water. The most common source of entry of the bacilli is with the food and water. There may be small sores or abrasions on the lips, tongue, checks, throat, or any abraded surface, or ulcers in the stomach or bowels through which the bacilli gain entrance to the blood, and when once in the blood they multiply very rapidly and cause death quickly.

Symptoms.—The disease is generally produced in from one to three days after the animal is infected, and death most always follows in from one to three days after the disease sets in. The first symptom of the disease shown is loss of appetite and rumination, with dullness and debility and a high fever. The most noticeable symptom is the appearance of a tumor or swelling under the skin, which may appear before the animal is noticed sick, or shortly after. This tumor may be located on the neck, shoulder, breast, thigh, rump, flanks, etc., and when in connection with the limbs causes stiffness and lameness. When the tumor is handled a peculiar crackling sound is heard under the skin, due to a collection of gas formed by the bacilli as they multiply. The animal's breathing becomes difficult; there may be attacks of colic, and the animal's weakness increases until death ends the scene, which may all take place in a few hours or in two or three days.

Treatment.—Up to the present time medicinal treatment for Black Leg has been almost an utter failure. Nearly all animals attacked die. As the disease runs such a rapid course, the animal is too near death before noticed sick for medicine to relieve. Since medicinal treatment is of little or no avail, prevention is the most important subject demanding consideration. When the disease breaks out, the healthy ones should at once be removed from the diseased. Those that die should be at once burned or buried deeply. All well animals under two years of age should be vaccinated with Pasteur's Black Leg Vaccine, which has proved to be a sure preventative against the disease. It is well known how human beings are protected from smallpox by vaccination. Young cattle can in the same way be protected against black leg by the use of a special vaccine which is a preparation of weakened virus discovered by Louis Pasteur, the great French scientist. This preventative inoculation is being extensively practiced in Texas and other States in the Union with very gratifying results. In some districts the death rate from year to year has reached upwards of 30 per cent, but since Pasteur's Black Leg Vaccine has been used it is almost entirely overcome. Statistics show that out of 75,000 head of cattle vaccinated against black leg in Texas and other portions of the United States with Pasteur's Black Leg Vaccine, less than one-third of 1 per cent died from the disease, while over 10 per cent of unvaccinated cattle died in the same districts from black leg.

Vaccine is put up in a fine white powder to be dissovled in a little water at the time of using. Vaccination consists of two inoculations about ten days apart, by the use of a graduated hypodermic syringe. The most suitable and convenient places for the inoculation are in the shoulders, ears or tail. The most convenient time for vaccinating is at branding time, when one inoculation can be given, and the second given ten days later. The operation can be easily and quickly done in the chute, and when once properly vaccinated the animal is proof against the disease through life. All spring and summer calves should be vaccinated at the fall branding, as black leg generally begins late in the fall and is liable to break out at any time during the fall, winter, or spring. The operation is perfectly harmless to the animal and causes no sore or sickness. It is not advisable to vaccinate during very hot or very cold weather, but at most any other time it is perfectly safe.

[Any one wishing further particulars regarding the use, price, etc., of this vaccine can address Dr. L. D. LeGear, Austin, Texas, who is Texas agent for Pasteur's Black Leg Vaccine.]

VARIOLA VACCINA (COW POX).

This disease, commonly known as cow pox, is more common among cattle than any other class of animals. It is an eruptive pustular disease, usually found in connection with the udder (bag).

Cause.—It is caused by contagion, which exists only in the fixed form.

Symptoms.—There is usually a slight fever, the flow of milk is arrested, and the appetite is impaired. The skin of the udder and teats presents a reddened appearance, and soon red patches occur, known as papulae. This is the papular stage and lasts three or four days. The papulae gradually take on the character of vesicles, becoming filled with serum (a watery fluid), and, like the vesicles in horse pox, are depressed in the center, as though bound down. This stage is the vesicular or second stage of the disease. The vesicles gradually become pustules, and the third or pustular stage of the disease is now reached. As many as five of these pustules may be upon one teat, and each the size of a finger.

Treatment.—As a general thing but little treatment is necessary. The animal should be fed upon food of a laxative nature. Great care must be taken not to expose the animal to draughts of cold air, taking cold, etc. If the teats are so sore as to be very painful in milking, use the teat syphon, which should be nicely oiled and gently passed up the teat, when the milk will come away of itself. Anoint the sores on the teats and udder nicely twice a day with carbolized vaseline. Separate the animals from other animals, and the milk should not be used. The attendant should not be allowed to attend to animals unaffected, as the disease can in this way be carried from one animal to another. The lymph or vaccine matter used to vaccinate people for purposes of protection against smallpox is obtained from cattle suffering from this disease. One attack gives proof against subsequent attacks.

ACTINOMYCOSIS—LUMP-JAW.

Lump-jaw is the formation of a peculiar tumor on the head, more often the lower jaw. In some cases the soft tissues only are affected, while in others the bone is diseased, the latter being far more serious. In these latter cases the bone swells out and becomes porous and honeycomb-like, and later on the jaw teeth will become loose and fall out from the results of the bone spreading away from the teeth.

Causes. — Lump-jaw is caused by a germ or fungus (actinomyces or ray-fungus) which gets into the body from the food or by an abrasion of the skin. It generally gains access through a hollow tooth, and the germs, once in the jaw-bone, begin to grow and multiply and disease the bone to such an extent that it begins to swell and enlarge, causing the regular lump-jaw tumor. These germs have frequently been found on the straw of certain kinds of grain and grasses.

Symptoms.—The first symptom noticed in an enlargement on the jaw. It may appear suddenly and grow rapidly, or it may come on gradually and grow very slow. After a time they generally break and discharge a thick matter, and soon form into a raw, unhealthy-looking sore. The matter that comes from the tumor contains great quantities of the germs, and if discharged on the pastures or in the feed troughs is dangerous to the other cattle. The disease is far more prevalent in certain districts and localities, as the germs are more prevalent in these places. An animal affected with lump-jaw is unfitted for human food and is rejected by inspectors in all stock yards; therefore, as soon as they are noticed with the disease, they should either be thoroughly treated or killed, as a recovery seldom, if ever, takes place without treatment.

Fig. 58. Two Cases of Lump-Jaw.

Treatment.—This is a disease unless properly treated, very seldom if ever recovers. If the tumor is just in the soft tissues about the head, it can be cured by thoroughly cutting it out. This operation should be undertaken only by a qualified man, as there are many large and important blood vessels about the head, which, if cut, would cause serious trouble. If the tumor affects both the bone and soft tissues, it can be cured in the majority of cases, if taken in time, by thoroughly cutting it out and giving the animal iodide of potassium in 1-dram doses twice per day for one, two, or three weeks, as the case demands. The United States Bureau of Animal Industry has made extensive experiments with iodide of potassium in treating this disease, with gratifying results. The best treatment we have found is to thoroughly dissect out the tumor and all the diseased portion of the bone that can be easily removed, and give iodide of potash internally. The wound should be left open and washed off every day with soap and water, and some good antiseptic dressing applied, as Dr. LeGear's Healing Lotion or Dr. LeGear's Screw Worm Powder. For an ordinary sized cow, give one dram of iodide of potash morning and night as a drench in 1 pint of water, or give 1½ drams once a day. Give the medicine before feeding. After you have given the iodide for six or eight days you may notice a discharge from the nose and eyes and a scurf forming in the skin. When that is noticed, just stop giving for two days, when you can continue again as before.

FUNGUS HAEMATODES, OR BLEEDING CANCER.

This consists of a dark-colored, bloody-looking or vascular fungoid tumor protruding from the cavity of the eye. It is a malignant disease, and, fortunately, is very rare. The tumor, being removed, always has a tendency to return, and in fact does reappear in nearly every case.

Causes.—It may follow several attacks of ophthalmia, by which it is thought to be caused; but, on account of its malignant nature, it is due, no doubt, to a certain morbid (unhealthy) condition of the blood.

Symptoms.—First, there is a slight irritation of the eye, causing a flow of tears; a small fungoid tumor soon puts in an appearance, growing steadily and rapidly, so that it soon pushes the eye aside and hangs down over the cheek. It gives an unsightly appearance to the eye.

Treatment.—With a sharp knife remove the tumor, and if necessary the eyeball as well, and touch the parts with caustic potash, nitrate of silver, or the hot iron. To stop the bleeding, which is apt to be very profuse, use tincture of iron, acetate of lead, or the hot iron. To be successful, the operation must be performed as soon as possible, and even then it is nearly always useless. The bones may become diseased also. In such cases, treat the same as that indicated for caries. It is very essential that all diseased structures be removed, or the treatment will not be successful.

CHAPTER XXVI.

MEDICINES.

It is very necessary that every stock owner, more especially farmers that live some distance from town, should keep a few of the more important drugs and medicinal preparations on hand for cases of necessity and immediate use. Many a poor animal is ruined or dies for the want of proper medicines, used at the time the injury was inflicted or the disease commences; time saved is money saved in treating diseases of stock.

MEASURING MEDICINES.

60 drops make 1 teaspoonful.
1 teaspoonful makes 1 dram.
4 drams make 1 tablespoonful.
2 tablespoonsful make 1 ounce.
16 ounces make 1 pint.
2 pints make 1 quart.
4 quarts make 1 gallon.
A wineglass will hold about two ounces; and an ordinary sized teacup will hold about 4 or 5 ounces.

Below will be found a dose table, giving the average size doses of the more common drugs used in treating stock. Colts at one month old take about one twentieth of what a horse does; three months old, about one tenth; six months old, one fifth; one year old, one third; two years old, one half. Medicines given to suckling mares transmit the effects of it to the colt through the milk.

Doses for the Horse of Drugs Commonly Used.

Name of drug.	Action and uses.	Dose.	Antidote.
Aconite, tincture of.	Febrifuge and sedative	10 to 20 drops	Alcohol, atropine, ether.
Alcohol	Stimulant and antiseptic	1 to 2 ounces	
Aloes, Barbadoes	Purgative and tonic	½ to 1 ounce	
Alum	Astringent	1 to 4 drams	
Ammonia, Aqua	Stimulant and antacid	2 to 4 drams	Milk and oils.
Arnica	Stimulant and alterative	½ to 1 ounce	
Arsenic	Tonic, stimulant, and alterative	2 to 5 grains	Sesquioxide of iron.
Antifebrin	Febrifuge	2 to 4 drams	
Arsenic, Fowler's solution of.	Alterative and tonic	½ to 1 ounce	
Belladonna, Fl. Ext.	Antispasmodic and anodyne	1 to 4 drams	
Camphor (gum)	Stimulant and anodyne	1 to 2 drams	
Cannabis Indica	Anodyne and antispasmodic	1 to 4 drams	
Carbolic Acid	Antiseptic and disinfectant	10 to 30 drops	Sulph. of soda, eggs, gruel.
Castor Oil	Laxative	1 pint	
Calomel	Purgative and alterative	1 to 2 drams	
Catechu	Astringent	1 to 3 drams	
Charcoal	Antiseptic and deodorant	2 to 3 drams	
Chloral Hydrate	Anodyne, hypnotic, anæsthetic	½ to 1 ounce	
Chloroform	Stimulant, antispasmodic, and anodyne.	½ to 1 ounce	
Croton Oil	Powerful purgative	10 to 15 drops	Opium.
Digitalis (leaves)	Sedative and diuretic	10 to 30 gr'ns	
Ergot	Astringent	½ to 1 ounce	
Ether, Sulphuric	Stimulant, carminative, and antispasmodic.	1 to 2 ounces	
Gentian	Tonic	2 to 3 drams	
Ginger	Carminative and stomachic	½ to 1 ounce	
Iodine	Antiseptic, alterative, diuretic	20 to 30 gr'ns	
Iron, Sulphate (copperas).	Tonic and astringent	½ to 1 dram	
Linseed Oil, raw	Laxative and purgative	1 to 2 pints	
Laudanum	Anodyne, antispasmodic, and astringent.	1 to 1½ ozs	
Morphine	Antispasmodic and anodyne	3 to 10 grains	Atropine, strong coffee, brandy, belladonna.
Nux Vomica	Nerve tonic	½ to 1 dram	Chloral hydrate.
Opium	Anodyne and astringent	1 to 2 drams	Atropine, brandy, belladonna.
Potassium, Chl'rate	Diuretic, alterative, antiseptic	1 to 2 drams	
Potassium, Iodide	Alterative and diuretic	½ to 1 dram	
Potassium, Br'mide	Nerve sedative	4 to 6 drams	
Quinine	Febrifuge and tonic	½ to 1 dram	
Saltpetre	Diuretic, alterative, febrifuge	1 to 2 drams	
Soda, Bicarbonate	Antacid and alterative	1 to 3 drams	
Soda, Hyposulphate	Antiseptic	2 to 4 drams	
Sweet Nitre	Stimulant, diuretic, diaphoretic	1 to 2 ounces	
Turpentine	Stimulant and diuretic	1 to 2 ounces	
Tar, Oil of	Antiseptic and expectorant	1 to 3 drams	
Dr. LeGear's Colic Cure.	Antispasmodic, anodyne, astringent, and stimulant.	1 to 2 ounces	
Dr. LeGear's Condition Powders.	Tonic, diuretic, and alterative	1 dram	
Dr. LeGear's Worm Remedy.	Worm destroyer	1 dram	

Doses for the Cow of Drugs Commonly Used.

Name of drug.	Action and uses.	Dose.	Antidote.
Aconite, tincture of.	Febrifuge and sedative	20 to 30 drops	Alcohol, ether, [atropine.
Alcohol	Stimulant and antiseptic	2 to 4 ounces	
Ammonia, Aqua	Antacid and stimulant	3 to 6 drams	
Antifebrin	Febrifuge	3 to 4 drams	
Belladonna, Fl. Ext.	Anodyne and antispasmodic	3 to 6 drams	
Carbolic Acid	Antiseptic	15 to 30 drops	Eggs, gruel, oils.
Castor Oil	Laxative	1 to 2 pints	
Catechu	Astringent	2 to 4 drams	
Charcoal	Antiseptic and deodorant	3 to 6 drams	
Chloroform	Anæsthetic and anodyne	1 to 2 ounces	
Croton Oil	Powerful purgative	½ to 1 dram	Opium.
Digitalis	Heart sedative and diuretic	½ to 1 dram	
Ergot of Rye	Astringent and ecbolic	1 to 2 ounces	
Epsom Salts	Purgative and febrifuge	1 to 2 lbs	
Ether, Sulphuric	Stimulant and antispasmodic	1 to 2 ounces	
Gamboge	Purgative	½ to 1 ounce	
Gentian	Tonic	3 to 6 drams	
Ginger	Carminative and stomachic	1 to 2 ounces	
Iodide of Potash	Diuretic, absorbent, alterative	1 to 2 drams	
Iron, Sulphate (copperas).	Tonic and astringent		
Linseed Oil	Laxative and purgative	1 to 2 quarts	
Laudanum	Anodyne, antispasmodic, and astringent.	1 to 2 ounces	
Morphine	Anodyne and antispasmodic	5 to 10 grains	
Nux Vomica	Nerve tonic	1 to 2 drams	
Opium	Anodyne and astringent	2 to 4 drams	Atropine, brandy, belladonna.
Potassium, Chl'rate	Diuretic, antiseptic, alterative	2 to 4 drams	
Potassium, Bromide	Nerve sedative	4 to 6 drams	
Quinine	Febrifuge and tonic	1 to 2 drams	
Saltpetre	Diuretic and febrifuge	2 to 4 drams	
Soda, Bicarbonate	Alterative and antacid	2 to 4 drams	
Soda, Hyposulphite	Antiseptic	3 to 6 drams	
Sweet Nitre	Diuretic, stimulant, diaphoretic	2 to 4 ounces	
Sulphur	Laxative and alterative	1 to 4 ounces	
Turpentine	Diuretic and stimulant	1 to 2 ounces	
Dr. LeGear's Colic Cure.	Anodyne, antispasmodic, stimulant, and astringent.	1 to 2 ounces	
Dr. LeGear's Condition Powders.	Tonic, diuretic, and alterative	2 drams	
Dr. LeGear's Worm Remedy.	Worm destroyer	2 drams	

PART III.

SHEEP DEPARTMENT.

SHEEP DEPARTMENT.

In this department, as in the cattle department, we will not attempt a lengthy discussion of the various breeds of sheep, but will give the more common diseases that the sheepmen of Texas have to contend with. Texas has about 1,843,678 sheep at present, and Western Texas is one of the best sheep districts in America. Owing to the free trade that was in force during Cleveland's administration wool dropped down to such low prices that most of the sheepmen had to quit the business and look to some other business for a livelihood. This of course decreased the number of sheep in America a great deal. Since a tariff has been levied on wool, the prices of wool and mutton have nearly doubled, therefore the sheepmen are enjoying good times again.

Below will be found a few of the more common diseases of sheep:

CHAPTER XXVII.

THE DISEASES OF SHEEP.

SCAB, OR SCABIES.

Scab, or scabies, is a very common disease in some countries, causing serious loss to sheep owners. It is very contagious, and the insects which cause the disease may remain in the pasture for years and then cause the trouble. Every precaution should be taken to keep the infection out of the flock.

Causes.—This disease is purely of a local nature, and due to a parasite. This parasite or insect is of the class "dermatodectes," which simply hold on to and prick the skin. This parasitic insect is very small, and does to a certain extent burrow beneath the outer layer (cuticle) of the skin, but never burrows very deeply.

Symptoms.—Scab is easily detected, as the symptoms are very plain. The animal is very restless and uneasy, and will rub and scrach itself on some object or with its hoofs until the wool begins to fall off in patches. Examine the skin and it will be found to be considerably reddened and inflamed, with the formation of blisters which break and discharge a watery fluid (serum). These finally dry up and form sores or scabs, a characteristic sign of the disease. The whole fleece may drop off, or nearly so, and leave the poor animal a sight to behold. The animal loses flesh and spirits, becomes weak and debilitated, etc.

Treatment.—It is not difficult to cure, if the treatment is thorough and of the proper kind. It is of the utmost importance to keep all animals that are free from the disease away from those affected, or off from infected pastures, as those free from the disease will contract it from those that have it. Also the pens should be thoroughly disinfected.

A good effective remedy, though poisonous, is the following:

White arsenic	5 pounds.
Pearl ash	5 pounds.
Soft soap	5 pounds.
Sulphur	5 pounds.
Boiling water	20 gallons.

Mix, but don't inhale the fumes, and when cold add 180 gallons of cold water, and stir until well mixed.

This mixture must be put in a tank or dipping vat prepared for the purpose and the sheep dipped in it. Dip the sheep in such a way, back foremost, that the head will remain out, and leave in for at least one minute. As soon as the sheep is brought out of the bath, its wool should be thoroughly squeezed to rid it of all the liquid preparation possible before turning into a clean yard to dry. To reach every part not touched by the dip, go over the heads of the flock with the following:

Mercurial ointment	1 pound.
Oil of turpentine	½ pint.
Rosin	1 pound.
Lard	3 pounds.

Mix, and apply to all parts of the head not touched by the dip.

A tobacco dip as the following is a very good preparation:

Tobacco leaves	20 pounds.
Sulphur	6 pounds.
Pearl ash	6 pounds.
Soft soap	6 pounds.
Hot water	90 gallons.

Mix.

In preparing the above, put the tobacco in the water and boil, and stir in the other ingredients while the liquid is still hot. In this dip the head may be dipped occasionally, while dipping the rest of the body. The sheep may remain in the liquor, as hot as can be borne, four or five minutes.

A dip very much used in Australia, where immense flocks are kept, is the following:

Tobacco leaves	10 pounds.
Sulphur	10 pounds.
Water	50 gallons.

Boil the tobacco in the water, and add the sulphur while hot.

THE SCAB LAW.

The following is the new scab law passed by the Texas Legislature, May 7, 1897:

An Act to prevent the introduction of scab disease among sheep in the State of Texas, and to prevent the spread of and secure the eradication of same, and providing a manner of examining such animals, together with the manner of taxing and collecting costs therefor, and making it a misdemeanor to violate the provisions of this act, and prescribing penalties for such violation.

Section 1. Be it enacted by the Legislature of the State of Texas: That from and after the passage of this act, it shall be unlawful to import into this State, or to move from one county to another, or to move from their accustomed range on to lands owned or leased by any person, without permission of such person, any flock of sheep in which one or more such animals are infected with scab, and any person or persons violating any of the provisions of this section shall be deemed guilty of a misdemeanor, and upon conviction thereof, shall be fined in any sum not more than two hundred dollars for each such offense.

Sec. 2. Any person having knowledge or notice of the existence of scab on any sheep owned or in charge of such person, who shall fail or refuse to dip in some preparation known to be effectual in curing scab, all flocks of sheep in which one or more such are so infected, within twenty days after such knowledge or notice has been received, shall be deemed guilty of a misdemeanor, and upon conviction thereof shall be fined in any sum not less than one hundred nor more than two hundred dollars; provided, that every successive twenty days of failure or refusal to dip such sheep, under the provisions of this section, shall be considered a separate offense.

Sec. 3. For the purpose of determining the existence of scab, under the provisions of this act, and to serve notice on persons as provided in section 2, the justice of the peace having jurisdiction, upon complaint of any person owning or having charge of sheep, supported by affidavit as to his belief that a flock of sheep within such jurisdiction are infected with scab, shall forthwith issue order to a constable or some peace officer of his county, directing such officer to summon to his aid two persons having knowledge of scab, and to proceed with such persons and examine the sheep so designated, and to notify in writing the owner or person in charge of said sheep, of the result of such examination, and to return to the court of issue such order, showing how he has executed the same.

Sec. 4. Any person refusing to permit the examination provided for in section 3 of this act, or to place the sheep in pens for such purpose, shall be deemed guilty of a misdemeanor, and upon conviction thereof, punished by fine of not less than one hundred nor more than two hundred dollars.

Sec. 5. Upon return of the order provided for in section 3 of this act, the justice of the peace shall, if it states said sheep are not infected, or that they have been dipped, within ten days next preceding such examination, dismiss such cause. But if such order states said sheep are infected with scab and have not been dipped within the ten preceding days, said justice of the peace shall issue warrant of arrest forthwith against the owner or person having said sheep in charge, and proceed as in other misdemeanor cases; provided, should defendant show, by competent testimony, that such infected sheep were held only on his own or accustomed range, and that he had dipped all flocks so infected, as provided in this act, within twenty days after receiving notice, or within ten days next preceding the serving of such notice, he shall upon payment of all accrued costs be discharged.

Sec. 6. The constable or other peace officer and the person summoned to assist, shall receive as compensation for services performed under the provisions of this act, and for attendance at court as witnesses in such cases, the sum of two dollars and fifty cents per day for each day actually and necessarily so engaged, and such fees shall be taxed as costs against the owner of such sheep, and execution shall be issued; provided, in all cases where it is found such sheep are not infected or have been dipped within the ten days next preceding the examination so made, the costs and fees shall be taxed against the person who made the complaint, and execution shall so issue.

Sec. 7. All laws and parts of laws in conflict with the provisions of this act be and the same are hereby repealed.

FOOT ROT.

Cause.—It is now believed to be caused by a parasite, and the other so-called causes, such as irritant soils, damp pastures, foul yards, etc., are believed to be only indirectly concerned in causing this disease, from the fact that they probably constitute favorable grounds for the parasites to harbor in.

Symptoms.—Lameness is noticed, and at the top of the cleft of the hoof it becomes red, moist, warm and rough, soon followed by a discharge, which soon becomes offensive and purulent, and the whole foot becomes a mass of corruption. The animal loses its appetite, and at length dies of exhaustion.

Treatment.—Treatment should be begun early, and the first thing to do is to cut away all diseased parts, after which the affected part may be touched with the following solution:

Chloride of zinc	2 drams.
Water	1 pint.

Or,

Butter of antimony	1 part.
Compound tincture of myrrh	1 part.

Or, the following may be found very useful:

Sulphate of copper	½ pound.
Acetate of copper	¼ pound.
Linseed oil	½ pint.
Tar	1 pint.

Solutions of carbolic acid, nitrate of silver, oil of vitriol, etc., may be found very useful also.

If so desired, a foot bath may be used instead of the above, as follows:

White arsenic	1 pound.
Sodium carbonate	1 pound.
Water	50 gallons.

Or,

Sulphate of copper	1 part.
Water	50 parts.

The sheep may be walked through a trough or vat containing either of the above solutions.

The sheep should be kept in perfectly dry pens, and dry upland pastures.

ROT, OR LIVER FLUKE.

This condition is due to the presence of a parasite (Distoma hepaticum), or common liver fluke. These flukes, or parasites, are the cause of the disease, and have a peculiar life-history. The fluke worm lays the eggs in the ducts (vessels) of the liver; these ova, or eggs, descend into the bowels and pass out with the feces; after which they gain entrance into the soft-bodied mollusks found in stagnant water. The sheep, on drinking the water, take into the stomach these mollusks, which contain the parasites of the disease. They soon gain access to the liver, and when developed deposit their eggs, to go the same round of existence again. These parasites, when full grown, vary in size from one-half to one inch in length, and may be two-thirds of an inch wide.

Symptoms.—The animal is dull and inactive; there is yellowness of the lining membrane of the eye, best seen when the eyelid is pushed back; the abdomen becomes large and pendant (pot-bellied), the back becomes razor-like, the flanks tucked up, usually with dropsical swellings in different parts of the body. The breathing becomes quick and short, and the animal suffers from diarrhoea and great weakness, followed by stupor and death.

Treatment.—Remove the sheep to a high, dry pasture, and give them water to drink from a deep well. Feed on highly nutritive food. Prepare and give the following:

Epsom salts	2 ounces.
Oil of turpentine	2 drams.
Water	1 pint.

Mix the salts and water together, add the turpentine, and give as a drench. Repeat every other day until three doses have been taken; then prepare the following:

Oatmeal	40 pounds.
Powdered gentian	2 pounds.
Powdered anise seed	2 pounds.
Common salt	4 pounds.
Sulphate of iron	1 pound.

Mix. Give of the above half a pint to each sheep once a day; wait three weeks, and repeat. Or, our Condition Powders may be given twice a day in the feed, instead of the above tonic.

GRUB IN THE HEAD.

This disease is one of the most serious the sheep owner has to deal with, and one that needs close attention on the part of the farmer.

Causes.—It is caused by the egg of the gadfly (Oestrus ovis) being deposited in the nostrils of the sheep during the summer months. From the eggs hatch maggots, which find their way up into the chambers (sinuses) of the head, causing much pain. Each larva (grub) is supplied with a pair of hooks on its head, by which it attaches itself to the lining membrane of the cavity where it is lodged. It remains there nearly a year, when it falls to and buries itself in the soft ground, and in from thirty to forty days it hatches out into a gadfly.

Symptoms.—When the sheep are attacked by gadflies, the animals will crowd together, with their noses to the ground, stamp violently at times, or run from one part of the pasture to another. At other times they will lie down, with their nostrils buried in the dust, etc. When the grubs get up into the head, and begin to mature, the animal soon shows signs of dullness, stands or lies down in one place nearly all the time, and notices but little. The appetite is gone, the head lowered to and resting on the ground, or turned to one side (usually the side affected), and there is a discharge from the nose. If the animal can keep up its strength until the grubs are dislodged, or come away of themselves, recovery may take place; otherwise, death usually ends the scene.

Treatment.—The grubs may be extracted by a qualified veterinarian, but scarcely pays, except in the case of a valuable animal. For this operation, a special instrument, called a trephine (see Fig. 3), must be used. With a sharp knife make an incision through the skin over the cavity (sinus) that contains the grub, large enough to let the trephine down upon the bone. With this instrument a piece of the skull can be removed, after which the grubs may be easily taken out through the opening. The grubs should all be removed, the opening in the skin stitched and dressed as an ordinary wound. The grubs may often be dislodged, when they are not firmly fixed, by injecting up the nostrils equal parts of sweet oil and turpentine, but care must be taken not to strangle the sheep. Another means is to cause the animal to inhale smoke of some kind, to induce sneezing, which may dislodge them. But when the grubs are well up, and firmly attached, inhalations of smoke, or injections of liquid preparations, are useless.

Prevention.—The preventative mode of treatment in this disease is of the utmost importance. Smear tar on the nose of each sheep, around the nostrils, which is distasteful to the fly, and death to the egg. Where the sheep are pasturing, always keep a piece of ground well plowed and pulverized, so that they can go at any time, when attacked by the gadflies, and bury their noses in the soft earth, to protect themselves from the insect.

STURDY, OR GID.

This disease is not so common in America as it is in England, probably from the fact that there are fewer dogs in proportion to the population here than there. It is also known as turn-sick, hydatid of the brain, etc.

Cause.—This dangerous disease is caused by the bladder worm—a form of tapeworm preceding the true or sexually perfect worm—which is developed from the tapeworm of the dog. This parasite (coenurus cerebralis), if given to the dog, will produce a tapeworm, which, becoming fully developed, leaves the dog in pieces (segments), each ripe piece containing a large number of eggs. The eggs are picked up by the sheep whilst grazing or drinking. In the stomach its shell is dissolved, setting free the minute parasites, which soon find their way to the brain; it becomes encysted (enclosed in a sac), and sets up a considerable amount of irritation. The disease is apt to be more common where dogs and sheep mix. The hydatid may attack any part of the brain, but usually locates itself in the upper part of one of the great lobes, or between them.

Symptoms.—The affected animal is found off by itself, walking in a circular manner, with the head carried to one side, if the hydatid is located in one of the lobes of the brain; when it is situated between them, the head is carried in an elevated position. If the animal turns to the right, the hydatid will usually be found in the right lobe; if to the left, in the left lobe. If deeply situated in the middle of the brain, the animal will be apt to lower the head, instead of elevating it, as in the upper part. Sometimes the entire brain may become affected before death takes place.

Treatment.—About all that can be done is to make an opening down upon the hydatids (if they can be found) and draw them out in the water they are in, with a syringe; or, inject into the cyst containing the hydatid one-half teaspoonful of the following solution:

Iodine	1 grain.
Iodide of potash	5 grains.
Water	1 ounce.

Mix.

PART IV.

SWINE DEPARTMENT.

SWINE DEPARTMENT.

CHAPTER XXVIII.

THE DISEASES OF SWINE.

HOG CHOLERA, AND SWINE PLAGUE.

These are two separate diseases, but resemble each other very closely in their symptoms, and it requires an examination of the internal organs after death to clearly distinguish between them. They are not only similar in symptoms, but in their effect upon the bodies of diseased animals. It is not so important to the stock raiser to know whether his hogs are dying of hog cholera or swine plague, as the agents which destroy the germs that cause the disease in the one will generally destroy them in the other. The difficulty of distinguishing between the two diseases is, therefore, not a matter of much importance in controlling them. It is important, though, to know that one or the other of these maladies is present among the herd, because such knowledge will lead us to adopt proper treatment for such infectious diseases.

The annual losses from hog cholera in the United States alone must be very heavy, although all diseases of swine are called cholera by most people, yet the researches of the Bureau of Animal Industry have shown that there is another disease, known as swine plague, which is almost as common and fatal as hog cholera. Hog cholera and swine plague affect hogs in all parts of the United States, and cause heavy losses, estimated to reach from $10,000,000 to $25,000,000 annually.

Causes.—Both hog cholera and swine plague are caused by bacteria (vegetable parasites), which may be easily identified by persons accustomed to such researches. The hog cholera germs are slightly larger than those of swine plague. They are provided with long, thread-like appendages, which enable them to move rapidly in liquids, while the swine plague germs have no such organs, and are unable to move in like manner.

Both diseases are produced by injecting cultures (growths) of their respective germs directly into the blood vessels.

From results of experiments with these two diseases, it has been found that the germs of hog cholera find their way into the bodies of swine mainly with the food and drink, and with the air; while those of swine plague are taken almost entirely with the air, or, in other words, they gain entrance through the lungs in nearly every case.

Hog cholera germs are very hardy and vigorous, while those of swine plague are very delicate and easily destroyed. Hog cholera germs are able to multiply and live for a long time in the water of ponds and streams; they may live in the soil for at least three months, and amongst straw and litter for a much longer time; they withstand drying in a remarkable manner. Swine plague germs, on the contrary, soon perish in water or by drying; the temperature for their growth must be more constant, and every condition of life more favorable, than is required for the hog cholera germs.

Symptoms.—In the most severe forms of the disease the animals die very suddenly, either before sickness has been observed or after they have been ill but a few hours. Such cases are usually seen at the beginning of an outbreak. In the majority of cases the progress of the malady is slower, and, fortunately, giving an opportunity to observe the symptoms. There are noticed signs of fever, shivering, unwillingness to move, loss of appetite more or less, elevation of temperature, which may reach 106 to 107 degrees Fahrenheit; the animals appear stupid and dull, and have a tendency to hide in the litter or bedding and remain covered by it. The bowels may be natural at first, but later there is generally a liquid and fetid (bad smelling) diarrhoea, and persisting to the end. At first the eyes are congested and watery, but soon the secretion thickens, becomes yellowish, collects in the angles and sticks the lids together. The breathing is quicker than usual, acompanied by a cough, which, however, is not very frequent, and generally heard when the animals are driven from their bed. The skin may be congested and red on different parts of the body, varying from a pinkish red to a dark red or purple. Sometimes there is an eruption, which leaves crusts or scabs of various sizes over the skin. There is a rapid loss of flesh, the animal grows weak, stands with arched back and the belly drawn up, and walks with a tottering, uncertain gait. There is less and less inclination or ability to move, and the weakness and exhaustion increase until death takes place. The course of these diseases vary from one or two days to two or three weeks.

Diagnosis.—When a disease breaks out among swine it is very important to know what it is. If several animals show symptoms similar to those already given, and the same disease has been affecting the hogs, on neighboring farms, we may be safe in saying that it is one or both of the diseases in question, since no other such disease has been recognized in this country.

In anthrax districts there may be occasional outbreaks of the disease, in which there is great inflammation and swelling of the tongue, or of the throat, or simply a fever with no visible swellings. If the disease is anthrax, other animals, such as horses, cattle and sheep, will also be affected.

The carcasses should be examined after death, and if projecting, button-like ulcers are found in the large bowels, we know that hog cholera is present. It must be remembered, however, that these ulcers are not found in the most acute cases, but only in the sub-acute and chronic, where life is prolonged a sufficient time for them to form. If there is inflammation of the lungs, and particularly if cheese-like masses are found in these organs, the disease is probably swine plague.

Small blood spots in the tissues or scattered over the internal organs indicate hog cholera, while inflammation of the serous membranes indicates swine plague.

The germs of hog cholera collect or grow in clumps in the blood vessels, which leads to a plugging of the smaller ones, with frequent rupture and escape of blood. This causes red spots to form where the blood leaves the vessels and collects in the solid tissues. In swine plague the bacteria are evenly diffused through the blood, never form plugs, and, therefore, bleeding from this cause is not seen.

In hog cholera the first effect of the disease is believed to be upon the bowels, with secondary invasion of the lungs; in swine plague it is the reverse of this.

Notwithstanding the difference in typical cases of the two diseases, there are many outbreaks where it is impossible to distinguish betwen them, as both diseases may be affecting the same animal at the same time, or the changes may somewhat resemble both diseases. In such cases a diagnosis can be made only by microscopic examination and cultivation of the germs.

Prognosis.—The result of an outbreak of this malady is important to know, but difficult to state, as the losses will depend partly upon the susceptibility of the hogs to the disease and partly to the virulence of the contagion in the particular outbreak. If the animals are very susceptible and the contagion very virulent, the loss even in large herds may reach 90 to 95, or even 100 per cent in those cases where the disease is allowed to run its course. In milder outbreaks, or with the animals more capable of resisting the contagion, the losses vary from 20 to 60 per cent. More animals recover toward the end of an outbreak than at the beginning. A portion of those recovering will fatten, but others remain lean, stunted in their growth, or never become really healthy animals.

Treatment.—Like all diseases of this class, preventive treatment is far cheaper and in every way more satisfactory than medical treatment. Our great aim should be, therefore, to prevent the spread of infectious diseases. Every swine raiser should use the utmost precautions to prevent the introduction of these plagues into his herd. As soon as the hogs are found to be affected with hog cholera or swine plague, the lot or pens where they have been confined should be disinfected by dusting plentifully with dry, air slacked lime, or by sprinkling with a 5 per cent solution of crude carbolic acid. The animals should then all be moved into new quarters. If possible, the sick and apparently well should be separated before they are moved and put into different lots. This is not essential, but an aid to the treatment. Keep them in dry lots or pens where there is no mud, and above all no stagnant water. It is also advisable to keep these lots disinfected with carbolic acid or air slacked lime.

The medical treatment must be begun as soon as possible, and the following formula will be found as good as any:

Wood charcoal	1 pound.
Sulphur	1 pound.
Sodium chloride	2 pounds.
Sodium bicarbonate	2 pounds.
Sodium hyposulphite	2 pounds.
Sodium sulphate	1 pound.
Black antimony	1 pound.

Mix.

These ingredients should be completely pulverized and thoroughly mixed. The dose of this mixture for a 200-pound hog is a large tablespoonful given once a day. For feed, corn alone is not sufficient, but they should have at least once a day soft feed, as bran and middlings, or middlings and corn meal, or ground oats and corn mixed, and then stirring into this the proper quantity of medicine. Animals that are very sick and that will not come to feed should be drenched with the medicine shaken up with water. Great care should be exercised in drenching hogs or they will be suffocated. Do not put the hog on its back to drench it, but pull the cheek away from the teeth so as to form a pouch, into which the medicine may be slowly poured. From this pouch in the cheek the medicine will flow into the mouth, and as soon as the hog finds out what it is it will stop squealing and swallow.

This medicine may also be employed to prevent an outbreak of the disease, and for such purpose should be put into the feed of the whole herd. See that each animal gets its proper share. Give this medieine a fair trial, and it will cure most of the animals that are sick and will stop the progress of the disease in the herd. It is an excellent appetizer and stimulant of the processes of digestion and assimiliation, and when given to unthrifty hogs it increases the appetite, causes them to take on flesh and assume a thrifty appearance.

TRICHINOSIS—TRICHINA.

Perhaps no other parasite has attracted so much attention as the Trichina Spiralis, which lives rolled up in flesh; it is very small, nearly microscopic, varying from one-eighteenth to one-sixth of an inch in length. Trichina may be found in all animals, but usually in man, the hog, and the rat. If any of the flesh containing trichinae is eaten, the parasites are set free during the process of digestion. Their growth is extremely rapid, and each female lays an immense number of eggs. From each egg the little worm is hatched, which bores through the walls of the stomach, or of the bowels, and buries itself in the flesh, where it lies hidden until it is eaten and introduced into another stomach.

Man obtains this disease through eating of the flesh of swine. The trichinae are not always destroyed by the ordinary methods of roasting, cooking, pickling, and smoking. Pork should always be thoroughly cooked, as in this way the parasites will be destroyed; but there is always danger in eating partially cooked or raw pork and sausage. The use of the microscope is the surest and most reliable preventive against all danger. It appears that the heart, liver, kidneys, brain and fat of the pig are seldom, if ever, affected with trichinae. As a general thing, swine obtain trichina from rats, to which latter man, as the natural bearer, conveys them.

Symptoms.—In man there is swelling and soreness of the muscles affected; great pain, emaciation and exhaustion; it is often mistaken for rheumatism. In the lower animals the symptoms are the same, but not so well marked; there is loss of appetite, the muscles are sore, stiffness in the hind quarters, and the animal is not inclined to move. If those affected live through the six weeks (the time it takes the little worm to become lodged in the muscle, after being set free from the egg in the stomach) they will recover.

Treatment.—Not much can be done. During the six weeks, stimulants, such as alcohol, in tablespoonful doses, may be given three times a day in gruel, and a teaspoonful of sulphur in the food morning and night. In the first stages of the disease, give our Worm Remedy in the feed night and morning, to rid the bowels of the worms before they find their way into the muscular system.

MEASLES.

Measles in swine is a different disease entirely to that called measles in man.

Causes.—In swine, measles are caused by a parasite (the bladder worm) from eating the eggs of the tapeworm of man (taenia solium) in its food; dogs also carry and void the eggs of the tapeworm, and hence care should be taken that swine do not eat their excrement. If the flesh of measly pork is not thoroughly cooked before being eaten by man, he is sure to be affected by tapeworm. Since there is always danger that some of the cysts may escape death in cooking, it is never safe to eat measly pork.

This hydatid, or bladder worm (cysticercus cellulosa), is what forms measles in pigs; it becomes encysted in the muscles, brain, liver, lining membranes, etc.

Symptoms.—The symptoms of the disease are a cough, running from the eyes, discharge from the nose, and weakness of the hind quarters, with general debility. The cysts, some of which are about the size of a grain of barley, may be seen scattered through the muscles and other tissues of the pig. Their presence may sometimes be detected in the eye or under the tongue. When once encysted, further annoyance to the animal is stopped.

Treatment.—But little can be done for this disease. If recognized at the beginning of an attack, the following powders might pass the eggs from the bowels:

Sulphur	4 drams.
Saltpetre	½ dram.

Mix, and give as one powder every day for two weeks.

Swine should never be allowed to feed upon human excrement, nor pastured on land manured with the same.

Some prefer turpentine in the treatment of measles. Two teaspoonsful may be given in swill if the hog can swallow; if he can not swallow, swab out his throat with equal parts of turpentine and oil.

PART V.

DOG DEPARTMENT.

IMPORTED JOE FLOCKMASTER.

DOG DEPARTMENT.

CHAPTER XXIX.

THE DISEASES OF DOGS.

DOG DISTEMPER.

This a very common affection of the canine race, and it is often very fatal, especially among the finer breeds, where there has been close in-and-in breeding. It is usually seen in puppies under one year old, although age is no preventive. Distemper is a specific fever, and very contagious and wide-spread in its prevalence. It is of a catarrhal nature, usually affecting the mucous membranes of the head and digestive tract. Distemper usually runs a definite course, and generally terminates favorably when not accompanied by other diseases, but when complicated it is not very satisfactory to treat. Frequently dogs pass through life without contracting the disease, and one attack does not render the animal proof against a second one. The period of incubation (exposure) is from four days to three weeks, and that of duration from ten days to two or three months.

Causes.—That dog distemper is caused by a germ is quite certain, although this specific microbe (germ) is not as yet very well understood. The virus (poison) of the disease has great vitality, and can be communicated from one dog to another by immediate contact or through the air, or from a kennel in which the diseased dog has been kept. We are satisfied it is due to a specific virus, although the surroundings have a great deal to do with it, such as improperly ventilated, damp kennels, etc., or improper feeding, especially that of a meat diet. Spring and fall are the most common seasons of the disease, and, as the annual bench shows are held then, we have more distemper than at other seasons of the year.

Symptoms. — The principal symptoms in an uncomplicated case are catarrhal discharges from the eyes and nose, thin and watery at first, finally becoming muco-purulent; high fever, rapid pulse, sneezing, dry hot nose, dullness, loss of appetite, etc. Complications usually accompany the disease, the most common ones being those of the respiratory organs, such as congestion, broncho-pneumonia, etc.; those of the digestive organs, such as gastritis, jaundice, enteritis, etc.; and those of the cerebro-spinal system, such as mengengitis, myelitis and chorea. There is a hard dry cough; bowels may be constipated, but diarrhoea is usually present, the discharge being very offensive. When skin eruptions occur, they are usually seen on the belly.

Treatment.—There is no specific for distemper in dogs any more than there is in the horse. Good nursing is all important. Make the patient as comfortable as possible by placing him in a warm place, free from draughts of cold air, and feed him on nutritious food, such as eggs and milk beaten up together, beef tea, mutton broths, etc. Bulky food of any kind should be avoided. If the patient will not eat he should be fed with a spoon. The importance of pure air can not be over estimated, but cold air must be avoided. It is advisable to disinfect the kennel, or where the patient is kept, with a preparation of carbolic acid or lime. If constipation is present, give injections per rectum of warm soapsuds, oil, or glycerine; either will be found very useful in such cases. If a physic is necessary, give the following:

Buckthorn syrup	4 drams.
Castor oil	2 drams.

Mix, and give at once with a large spoon.

If there is still a tendency to constipation, the bowels may be kept regular on a diet of liver, oatmeal, etc.; also continue the injections per rectum.

To reduce the high fever, from 5 to 8 grains of quinine may be given in a capsule at once, and follow up with the following in case of lung trouble:

Quinine sulphate	2 grains.
Muriate ammmonia	2 grains.

Mix, and give in a capsule three times a day.

A constant supply of pure drinking water is very essential, to which add two teaspoonsful of the chlorate of potash to every quart of water.

In case of irritability of the stomach and bowels, and the tendency to vomiting, milk and limewater, beef tea, etc., are indicated; or give subnitrate of bismuth in 5-grain doses four times a day in case of persistent vomiting.

If diarrhoea is present it may be relieved by teaspoonful doses of paregoric combined with twice that quantity of prepared chalk and given as needed.

The discharge from the eyes and nose should be washed off every day with clean borax water, and oftener if necessary.

All changes in diet should be made cautiously. In convalescence, tonics, such as cod liver oil, will be found especially valuable. Other diseases setting in should be treated according to the nature of the complication.

The following is a simple but a good remedy in most cases of distemper:

Tincture of iron	1 ounce.
Tincture of aconite	½ dram.
Whiskey	3 ounces.

Mix, and give one teaspoonful three times per day.

Continue this as long the the fever and hard breathing lasts.

ECZEMA IN DOGS.

Eczema is a non-contagious disease of the skin, characterized by formation of scabs with more or less irritation and itchiness. The skin becomes reddened, moist, and swollen, and the disease has a tendency to spread over the body.

Causes. — Eczema may be caused from any irritation of the skin, as applying caustic medicines, scratches, etc., but comes more frequently from indigestion, injudicious feeding, want of exercise, and bad blood. Eczema is not contagious, but in certain stages it may be transmitted to another dog by sleeping together for some time.

Symptoms.—There will be noticed great itchiness and a scurfiness and scabby condition of the skin, with falling out of the hair. Continuous scratching may form thickened rough portions of the skin devoid of hair. In some cases the skin becomes very much reddened and inflamed and causes the animal a great deal of discomfort.

Treatment.—Great cleanliness is very essential in the treatment of eczema. Give the dog a clean bed to sleep on, and keep his kennel as clean as possible. Make a complete change in the food. If the animal is fat, reduce the food and give a light, cooling diet. If the animal is thin in flesh, give a good nutritious diet. In some cases it is advisable to clip the hair all off short so as to be able to apply the external applications more easily and more effectually. Wash all affected parts thoroughly every morning with cold water and carbolic soap. After washing, dry off the skin and apply the following ointment:

Oxide of zinc	1 ounce.
Oil of tar	1 ounce.
Flour of sulphur	1 ounce.
Vaseline	4 ounces.

Mix.

Give internally 5 drops of Fowler's solution of arsenic morning and evening. The following may also be tried:

Creolin	1 ounce.
Water	4 ounces.

Mix, and apply every morning after washing.

Some cases of eczema will be found very difficult to cure, but patience and continued treatment will be rewarded with success.

MANGE—ITCH.

Mange is a contagious disease of the skin, due to the presence of insects which burrow into the skin and cause irritation, and in some cases severe inflammation of the skin.

Causes.—The disease is caused by the mange insect, which gains entrance into the skin, multiplies rapidly, and spreads over various parts of the body. Although the insects (mites) must be present to produce the disease, filth and unclean beds, kennels, etc., are important factors in causing the disease. One dog in a kennel affected with mange will soon infect all the others.

Symptoms.—In certain stages mange is very hard to detect from eczema without a microscopical examination. There is intense itching, falling out of the hair, rough, scabby, scaly skin, etc. When the insects burrow into the skin they cause a pimple or pustule, and on being scratched by the dog the pustule opens up and a small quantity of matter with the insect runs out. Eczema more commonly occurs in poor, debilitated dogs, while mange has no preference. The disease may attack any part of the body, but more commonly the head is first affected. In some cases the hair falls out and the animal emits a very offensive odor. The appetite is rarely lessened. As the disease progresses, loss of weight, debility, and impoverishment of the general system results.

Treatment.—The bedding of the infected animal should be destroyed and the animal removed from all healthy ones. Wash the kennel, woodwork, etc., where the dog sleeps, with hot whitewash, into which put 1 ounce of pure carbolic acid to every gallon of whitewash. Wash the infected animal thoroughly with carbolic soap and water, and apply either of the following lotions once a day for six or eight days:

Creolin	4 drams.
Methylated spirits	4 drams.
Water	3 ounces.

Mix.

Or,

Trikresol	30 drops.
Water	6 ounces.

Mix.

Or,

Sulphur	2 parts.
Carbonate of potash	1 part.
Oil of tar	1 part.
Benzine	2 parts.
Lard or oil	10 parts.

Mix, and apply to all affected parts.

Or,

Iodide of sulphur	1 part.
Glycerine	8 parts.

Mix, and apply as above.

Long hair must be closely clipped or shaved; the affected parts freely rubbed with soapsuds, allowed to remain on for twenty minutes or half an hour; crusts and scales are thus softened and removed by subsequent thorough scrubbing with warm water. As mange is a local affection, there is very little use in giving internal treatment.

SPAYING BITCHES.

This is an operation that is being quite extensively practiced among dog fanciers. If you have a bitch that you don't wish to breed from, you can prevent the unpleasantness and trouble of having her coming in heat (rutting), by having her spayed. A bitch can be spayed any time in suitable weather, except when they are in heat or with pup, after they are six months old. The operation can be performed in the side or in the centre of the belly. We prefer the last-named place of operating. A bitch should not be too fat, as it makes it much harder for the operator and more dangerous to the bitch. If she is big and fat, shut her up for several days and feed her very little; or, let her run out, and feed nothing at all, to reduce her flesh. Feed nothing for at least eighteen hours before operating, so the bowels will not be full.

Some recommend hanging a bitch up by the hind legs, and others strap them upon a rack, but we prefer putting them to sleep on a table by the use of 1 part chloroform and 2 parts sulphuric ether. If the bitch is large and strong, tie her legs and muzzle her, so she can't bite. If a small bitch, one man can hold her legs. Saturate a small, new sponge with the anaesthetic (chloroform and ether), put it down in a funnel made of tough paper, and shove her head down into the funnel and hold it there tight until she goes to sleep. Care should be taken not to give her too much, or she will never wake up. If she stops breathing, take the sponge away and throw water on her head and work her front legs. When she is asleep, the hair, if long, should be clipped from the place of operation, which is best done between the last four teats. Wash off the skin with a weak solution of carbolic acid, and with a sharp, perfectly clean lance, cut through the skin and flesh into the abdominal cavity. Make a hole about two inches long; insert the finger and bring out the ovaries (prides), and remove them one at a time with a pair of dull scissors. Sponge off the blood nice and clean and draw the wound together by the use of silk sutures. The wound will heal in six or eight days, when you can remove the stitches. It is well to wash the skin and wound nicely every day with soap and water, and apply a little of our Healing Lotion to cleanse the wound and heal it quickly. Feed the bitch on light diet for four or five days after the operation, and keep her from running around a great deal. A spayed bitch will make the very best kind of a dog; they will be smart, quick, and intelligent. Occasionally, it will be noticed that a bitch, after being spayed, will come in heat once or twice, but this will pass off and not bother them any more.

RABIES, OR HYDROPHOBIA.

Rabies, which prevail chiefly among animals of the canine species, as the dog, wolf, fox, etc., is at the present time accepted as being an acute, infectious disease of the central nervous system, characterized by fever, a high degree of irritability and excitement, the presence of a spasm, generally a disposition to bite, great prostration, and finally death. Man, and all warm-blooded animals, are liable to this malady. It was called hydrophobia because it was supposed that the rabid (mad) animal had a dread or fear of water, which is not true, for it will drink water greedily to the very last, providing the power of deglutition (swallowing) is not lost. Rabies, which means "to rave," being a far better name for the disease.

History.—The antiquity of rabies is not exactly known. Aristotle, Xenophon, Virgil, Horace, Ovid, and many others, in their writings, mention it as one of the maladies in their time. Then come the writings of Caelius Aurelianus, who treated all the important questions relating to it in a most masterly manner. After him, centuries passed, during which time but little or nothing was added to the present knowledge of the subject. But toward the end of the last century investigations were renewed, and since then a great deal of light has been thrown upon the subject, especially by M. Pasteur, Koch, Williams, and many other noted men of our day. Rabies has recently been quite prevalent in England and in some of the United States of America, while in Australia and New Zealand it is very rare. Until lately, it has been comparatively rare in Canada and in the United States, while in Peru, Chili and some other countries it is very common. It has occurred in every State in this Union at some time or another during the present century, but, fortunately, never to any alarming extent.

Causes.—The theory of a spontaneous development of rabies is still a question of controversy among our best authors. It is now universally accepted that the poison is communicated almost invariably by means of the bite of a rabid or infected animal. Climate does not appear in the least to exert any amount of influence over its production. It is very generally imagined by people that dogs are more liable to have the disease during very hot weather. Experience, however, proves that hot weather has not the slightest influence, so far as being the actual cause or producing the disease is concerned. Statistics show that January and August, the coldest and hottest months, furnish the fewest cases. In Egypt and Syria, both very hot countries, the disease is unknown, and Greenland, on the other hand, being a very cold country, is also exempt. So far as is known, the contagious principle or virus exists only in the fixed form, and is found in every tissue of the body. In the brain, spinal cord, and saliva, it is found in its most potent forms, but its vitality is soon lost after death. We are justified in saying that hydrophobia is a specific blood disease, due to an unknown germ. As yet, the germ has not been isolated or cultivated, but, by the process of inoculation, sufficient proof has been found of its presence in the blood of an affected animal. This virus, without doubt, is developed in the saliva of all affected animals, and is inoculated by a bite or by its coming in contact with an abrasion of the skin or mucous membrane, thus producing the disease in other animals and in man. The virus seems to be weakened in its transmission from one animal to another, so that the first bites of a mad dog are said to be the most dangerous. French authorities go to show that not one-third of those bitten by rabid animals die of rabies, while only 1 per cent of those bitten through the clothing die. Some people think the bite of an angry dog will produce hydrophobia, and all the more so if the animal should go mad, even years after. M. Pasteur, the noted French scientist, says: "The bite of a dog is only dangerous when he is suffering from rabies. The non-rabid animal, however enraged, can not give rise to hydrophobia by his bite." No doubt a great many persons die from mental derangement (delirium) caused by fear of taking the terrible malady. The period of incubation is extremely variable—from a few days even up to a year or more. In man, nine days was the time generally accepted to elapse between the infliction of the bite and the first symtoms of the disease.

Symptoms.—In giving the symptoms of canine madness, two forms will be noticed: the furious or violent, and the dumb or sullen. About the first thing noticed in the first form is a period of dullness, showing that the brain is affected. This period of dullness is followed by a period of restlessness or excitement, and after a time may again be followed by a period of coma. The animal has a tendency to seek confinement in out-of-the-way places, where he can lie undisturbed. When disturbed, he becomes very much excited, and may become furiously enraged without any apparent cause. Now the countenance becomes anxious and appalling, the eyes become bloodshot, with a sparkling, bright appearance, and a tendency to distorted vision or squinting. A very prominent symptom is a depraved appetite, the animal eating or swallowing pieces of wood, stones, coal, leather, and even pieces of iron, lead, etc.—in fact, any kind of filth or dirt that comes in his way is swallowed seemingly with great relish. Prof. Lagarris, of the Pasteur Institute, Chicago, Ill., says this symptom alone is characteristic of rabies, and is sufficient to justify any man giving his opinion as such, who also adds that in making post mortems on animals supposed to be affected with rabies the contents of the stomach always plays an important part in his decision, and always, where rabies are found, the stomach is partly filled with stones, gravel, pieces of wood and other indigestible material. An intense thirst is early acquired, and in his endeavors to quench it he will push his head up to the eyes into the vessel containing the liquid, and drink eagerly, unless prevented by a spasm of the larynx, when he becomes enraged and furious at the sight of drinking liquids.

The animal now becomes very restless and irritable, and if allowed his liberty will seek seclusion as the disease advances. He will leave his home and a kind master and go off in nearly a straight line along the street. He travels in a peculiar, long, swinging trot, the tail hanging down and often with the tongue hanging out of his mouth. He looks neither to the right nor to the left, and keeping his head in a straight line with his body hastens on as if in search of something he doesn't seem to find. This is characteristic of the rabid animal, and nothing else. An excessive secretion of saliva, called frothing at the mouth, usually takes place, and flows from the mouth. He seems to take no notice of any one or anything until pursued and bodily hurt, when he will wreak his vengeance on the offender, or anything else that comes in his way. Still, he will not go out of his way to do any mischief, and will even pass through crowds of people without attempting to bite them, but, instead, he tries to escape his pursuers and hide. When by himself, he will bite at imaginary objects, and will attack only real ones when placed in his way. His snapping at the open air is a very characteristic sign.

The inclination on the part of the mad dog to wander about seems to be an instinctive attempt to get rid of the disease by muscular activity, as rabies, if spontaneous, is only so in non-perspiring animals. A rabid dog when at large always alters his course, when compelled, by turning at right angles, and never breaks this rule unless compelled to by a furious mob. It is nothing unusual to see a dog hounded about the streets, and said to be mad, when he is not, but is only excited or frightened. He never thinks of going out of his way to clear any object, attempting to go over, under or through it, and never giving up until he is completely exhausted. The wound from the bite of a rabid animal heals very rapidly, and is rarely accompanied by inflammation; but when the disease itself has set in, the wound may show evidence of irritation or inflammation, which causes the animal to gnaw or bite it, without feeling the slightest pain therefrom. If the animal is confined by a chain, he attempts to bite it in two; if by a door, he vents his fury on that. At this stage he has not the slightest sense of pain, as he will bite a red-hot iron exactly as if it were cold, if presented to him. If allowed water to drink, he will usually upset the vessel in his hurry to quench his thirst. At the appearance of some stranger he will bark as if angry, suddenly changing to a voice of joy and ecstacy, then he will whine as if desiring something, then change again into a lonely, dismal howl, as if lost, or that approaching trouble was at hand; then he may become really natural for a few minutes, followed with the same symptoms, only increased until the whole muscular system is completely overcome with hideous, tetanic convulsions, which, however, soon disappear, and the characteristic howling commences again, which is readily recognized by an expert as that of a mad dog.

The constitutional symptoms are increased temperature, nervous excitability, respirations of a sobbing or sighing character, etc. One peculiarity of the disease is that the affected animal shows a great antipathy to animals of its own species. After two or three days of terrible suffering the animal succumbs, death taking place either from a paroxysm of choking or in a tranquil manner from nervous exhaustion. The power of swallowing usually returns shortly before death, which generally takes place in from two to five days.

The second or dumb form is but a peculiar type of the disease, which runs a much shorter course and without the violent or irritative stage. The animal is quiet and depressed and has but little disposition to bite or run away. Paralysis of the lower jaw early sets in, appetite perverted, changed voice rarely heard, progressive emaciation and exhaustion, and the poor sufferer seldom lives beyond the third day.

Treatment.—Medical treatment, after the disease has become manifest, is of little or no avail, hence the affected animal should be destroyed at once. In case of a valuable animal, or a member of the human family, being bitten by a rabid animal, the wound should, as soon as possible, be well cleansed and freely cauterized. One of the first things to do is to endeavor to prevent the absorption of the virus into the system. This may be accomplished by complete excision of the part bitten, or by suction by means of a cupping glass, or even by the mouth if practicable, after which the part should be thoroughly cauterized with nitrate of silver, caustic potash, nitric acid, or the actual cautery. Liquid caustics are preferable, as they penetrate every recess of the wound. At the same time, apply a ligature between the wound and the body, if the location of the wound will allow it, then place the animal in confinement to await developments; one month is considered a long enough period.

If you kill the dog, it prevents the person from knowing whether hydrophobia will develop or not. If it does not mature, the person bitten need be in no way uneasy. No doubt many a valuable, well-bred animal has been killed with the supposition that he was rabid. An antidote for the poison has not yet been discovered, except the attenuated virus of the disease itself, prepared by M. Pasteur, who claims to prevent the development of the disease by inoculation of this prepared virus after infliction of the bite of a rabid animal. No doubt the prophylactic treatment is the only proper one to pursue. Still, Pasteur's method is not as yet universally accepted, but experiments up to the present time have been eminently satisfactory, and will, in all probability, lead to a specific, if not already. Medical treatment consists of nerve sedatives, anti-spasmodics, etc., which are to be given hypodermically, by inhalations, etc.

APPENDIX.

VETERINARY REMEDIES.

Dr. LeGear's

Celebrated Veterinary Remedies

PREPARED BY

DRS. L. D. AND N. G. LeGEAR,
GRADUATES OF THE ONTARIO VETERINARY COLLEGE, TORONTO, ONTARIO.

VETERINARY SURGEONS,

AUSTIN, TEXAS.

These are a line of Stock Medicines we have prepared for the cure of the diseases of stock here in the South. They are not carelessly prepared by unprofessional men, as a great many of the "would-be cure-alls" for stock are that flood the markets, but are guaranteed to be composed of strictly pure drugs, in the proper doses, and compounded with the greatest professional care and skill possible.

We wish to ask all stock owners the following question: "Where are the stock medicines you have been using made?" Your answer will be, "Away up North." Let us ask again, How can men that live five hundred or perhaps a thousand miles from the South and never were down here make up medicines that will cure diseases of stock in this country, as there is just as much difference in the disease of stock and the medicines required in curing them between there and here as there is between the climate in the two places. Our long, hot summers and mild winters give all animals a different temperament and different diseases to what they have up North, therefore it takes specially prepared medicines to cure them. Again, do you know the men who put up these quack medicines? Are they Veterinary Surgeons studying, practicing, and treating the diseases of stock?

No; they are not. They perhaps don't know as much about the diseases of stock as you do, but they have a few formulas from which they are putting up their "would-be cure-alls." Some of these preparations may do to use on stock up North, but they are no good in this climate.

You say "these remedies seem to help our stock." You may think so, but it is only imaginary. We would invite one and all to try Dr. LeGear's celebrated Veterinary Remedies when any of your stock are sick, lame, or injured, and see for yourself how much better they are than any other kind you ever used.

We are preparing these remedies right here in the South after carefully studying and investigating the various diseases of stock and the medicines best suited to cure them.

We wish to say that we are graduate veterinary surgeons, studying, practicing, and treating the diseases of stock here in the South, and that our celebrated Veterinary Remedies are the results of our hard study and later practical work and scientific researches. We ask all readers of this book to carefully read over the following brief description of each of our celebrated Veterinary Remedies and testimonials from the best stockmen on each, for after you read them over carefully and note their superior qualities over all other stock medicines we know you will try them, and when once tried you will use no other.

The testimonials we have on the merits of our medicines are from some of the best stockmen and horse owners in Texas who have thoroughly tested and used them. We have accepted no false or bogus testimonials. All are real and voluntary. If you doubt the reality of any of these testimonials, we would be pleased to have you write to the parties or call on them in person.

HEALING LOTION.

This is without a doubt the very best healing prepartion ever made. It is unequaled in its results in curing sore backs, sore shoulders, saddle and collar galls, barbed-wire cuts, scratches, cracked and greasy heels, sore teats in cows, or sores of any kind on all animals. It has wonderful antiseptic, astringent and healing properties, which makes it such a valuable remedy for sores on stock. Use according to directions on each bottle and you will be highly pleased with its results. Price, per bottle, 50c.

Prairie Lea, Texas, April 14, 1897.

Drs. L. D. & N. G. LeGear, Austin, Texas.

Dear Sirs: I take pleasure in saying that your Healing Lotion, which you gave me, is a sure and speedy cure for all sores on stock. One bottle cured my jack, which had sores on him for one year. Yours truly,

C. POLK, Stockman.

Cameron, Texas, January 20, 1897.

Drs. L. D. & N. G. LeGear, Austin, Texas.

Gentlemen: I have been using your celebrated Healing Lotion for the last six month for barbed wire cuts, sore backs and shoulders, and sores of all kinds on my horses, mules and cows, and find it the best healing medicine I ever used. I can highly recommend it to all horsemen and stock owners. Yours respectfully,

W. K. DICKINSON,

Liveryman, and dealer in Missouri mules and Jersey cows.

LINIMENT.

There are over one dozen different kinds of liniment made and sold for stock, but many of them are of very little good. There is as much difference in liniments as there is in different brands of whisky—some good, and the rest no good at all. In preparing our Liniment, we have used the very best stimulating, penetrating and soothing medicines, therefore, we guarantee it to be one of the best liniments made. It will remove all pain, soreness, lameness and swelling in all cases of sprains, bruises, sore tendons, enlarged joints and glands, inflammatory swellings, sore throat, rheumatism, and all muscular soreness and lameness in horses and cattle, etc. Try it once, and you will use no other. It is a clean, speedy and reliable remedy, and can be used with perfect safety. Price per bottle, 50c.

CONDITION POWDERS.

Nearly all animals, sometime during the year, more especially during the spring, need some good, reliable condition powders to purify the blood, rectify their stomachs and bowels, and tone up the whole system in general; therefore, we offer our celebrated Condition Powders to the public for sale, with the assurance that they will give perfect satisfaction to all those who use them. They are not recklessly prepared by unprofessional parties from cheap, inferior drugs and adulterations, as most of the condition powders are, but are prepared with great care and skill from strictly pure drugs of full strength; therefore, much smaller doses are required, and much more good derived, from one box of our celebrated Condition Powders than from half a dozen packages of the inferior kinds. Our Condition Powders is a medicine, and not a food, and, therefore, it takes only one teaspoonful for a dose, and not from one to three tablespoonsful, as is usually prescribed of the inferior kinds. It is a waste of money to pay medicine prices for feed, as you do when you buy most of the "condition powders" and "stock foods" that flood the market, for they are composed principally of bran, linseed meal, etc. When you buy our celebrated Condition Powders, we will assure you that you are buying medicine, and not adulterations, and when given according to directions will give perfect satisfaction every time. They are especially adapted to keeping horses, cattle, sheep and hogs in general good health and condition, giving them sleek, glossy coats, plenty of life and spirits, renovating the blood, and the whole digestive, muscular and nervous system in general. They are unequaled in their results in relieving hide bound, indigestion, loss of appetite, liver troubles, rough, staring coats, general debility, bad blood, loss of flesh, all chronic kidney troubles, thick, ropy urine, coughs, colds, distemper, epizootic, bladder diseases, etc. A trial will convince you that they are first-class in every particular. Price, 50c.

Giddings, Texas.

Drs. L. D. & N. G. LeGear, Austin, Texas.

Dr. LeGear's Condition Powders for stock have been thoroughly tried by me and I found it to work like magic. It is all that they claim for it, and a good article to have at your barn. I purchased it on trial, to use it for thick, ropy urine, and in a few days the powder had done its good work. It is an exceedingly good appetizer and tones up the system to perfection.

J. W. NORTHRUP,
Publisher Giddings "News."

Luling, Texas, March 1, 1897.

Drs. L. D. & N. G. LeGear, Austin, Texas.

Dear Sirs: Have been using your Stock Condition Powders on my entire herd of Jerseys for past six weeks with entire satisfaction. For animals that are run down, off feed or wormy, the results are marvelous, and it is with a great deal of pleasure that I recommend your stock medicines to breeders of fine stock and the public in general. Have found nothing in my eight years' experience in handling fine stock that acts as promptly and to the point. Wishing you all the success you are entitled to, I am, yours very truly, JAMES A. PRYOR,

Proprietor Oakland Jersey Farm.

COLIC CURE.

There is no disease of the horse that has so many would-be remedies as colic, and nine out of every ten of these remedies are no good, and many of them do a horse more harm than good. In order to prepare a remedy that is safe, sure, and reliable in all forms of colic and all internal pains we have after great study and scientific research compounded our celebrated Colic Cure. It is absolutely composed of the best pain-killers, anodynes, antiseptics and correctives which are needed in the treatment of colic and all those troubles of the stomach, bowels and kidneys shown by pain, cramps, bloating, uneasiness, etc. It is a safe, sure, and reliable remedy for all forms of colic, acute indigestion, flatulency, inflammation of the bowels, diarrhoea, dysentery, irritative kidneys, inflammation of the kidneys, and all internal pain that can be cured by medicine. As colic is a disease that comes on very suddenly without a moment's warning, and is so liable to kill the horse or mule before you can go to the store for any medicine, we will advise all persons owning one or more horses or mules to always keep a bottle of Dr. LeGear's Celebrated Colic Cure on hand, as you will in many instances save the life of your animal by doing so, for "time lost is money lost" in treating colic. We can refer you below to testimonials of stockmen and horse owners who have used and thoroughly tested the merits of our Colic Cure. Another great advantage our Colic Cure has over all others is its cheapness. It is not only the best colic cure on the market, but it is the cheapest. Just think of it, a big bottle of Colic Cure for only 50 cents.

Burnet, Texas, Aug. 2, 1897.

Drs. L. D. & N. G. LeGear, Austin, Texas.

Gentlemen: We have used your Colic Cure for the last twelve months on our horses and find it all O K. It gives ready relief, and is a safe cure for the Colic. Yours with best wishes,

SKAGGS & FOULDS, Liverymen.

Brownwood, Texas, June 17, 1897.

To whom it may concern:

This is to certify that I had a fine mule that had been subject to fits of colic for more than a year, and the last attack he had I gave him up to die. Had tried everything recommended for colic to no avail, when finally Dr. Rufus Payne suggested "Dr. LeGear's Colic Cure," which was given, and to my astonishment the first dose gave perfect relief—not only relief, but a cure, and the mule has not had an attack since. I can unhesitatingly recommend Dr. LeGear's Colic Cure for horses.

J. H. BYRD, a Ranchman.

EYE WATER.

The eye, the organ of vision, is very delicate, and is one of the most important organs of the body, and one that should have special care and proper treatment when diseased. There is no remedy equal to Dr. LeGear's celebrated Eye Water for curing all diseases of the eyes of stock. It is prepared with the greatest care and skill from the best eye medicines known. It is a mild, non-irritating and safe preparation, and is a reliable remedy for all curable diseases of the eyes of horses, cattle, dogs, etc., such as simple ophthalmia, periodic ophthalmia (moon blindness), swelled lids, flow of tears, hooks, cloudiness or milkiness of the eye, inflammation, ulceration, injuries, etc. Don't injure your horse's eyes by putting salt, burnt alum, etc., in them, but use our celebrated Eye Water, which is cheap, safe and sure. Price per bottle, 50c.

Austin, Texas, August 30, 1897.

Drs. L. D. & N. G. LeGear, Austin, Texas.

Gentlemen: This is to certify that I have used Drs. L. D. & N. G. LeGear's Eye Water, and with three applications it perfectly cured my pointer dog's eyes. Very truly,

LOUIS N. BRUEGGERHOFF.

Cameron, Texas, July 29, 1897.

Drs. L. D. & N. G. LeGear, Austin, Texas.

Gentlemen: I have used your Eye Water on quite a number of horses and had splendid results in every case. With best wishes, I am, very respectfully,

W. K. DICKINSON, Liveryman.

Cameron, Texas, July 29, 1897.

Drs. L. D. & N. G. LeGear, Austin, Texas.

Gentlemen: You doubtless remember the condition of my horse's eye, and instructing me how to use your Eye Water. I am glad to be able to state that in a few weeks after beginning its use the eye, instead of appearing like a blind eye, was restored to its natural appearance. Yours very truly,

W. B. STREETMAN.

SCREW WORM POWDER.

Screw worms and flies are such a common annoyance to stock and stockmen that a line of stock medicines would not be complete without some good, reliable remedy to keep flies and screw worms away from sores on stock. Our Screw Worm Powder is a safe, sure and reliable antiseptic protection against the invasion of all flies, screw worms and poisonous germs. It not only keeps out screw worms, but heals all sores very rapidly. It is put very conveniently in tin cans, with little holes in the top, so the powder can be dusted on the sores without any trouble. Try it, and be convinced that this is the best preventive against screw worms you ever used. Price per box, 50c.

Brownwood, Texas, June 18, 1897.

Drs. L. D. & N. G. LeGear, Austin, Texas.

Gentlemen: We have been using your celebrated Screw Worm Powder for the past year and find it to be the best healing medicine for all kinds of sores on stock we ever used. It is also a sure preventive against screw worms, and keep all flies away from sores. We can highly recommend it to all stock owners as an excellent remedy for curing barbed wire cuts or sores of any kind on stock.

G. W. HALL & SON, Livery and Transfer Men.

WORM REMEDY.

You will learn, by reading elsewhere in this book, that there are several different kinds of worms that infest the stomach and bowels of stock, and that they are a very common and troublesome pest. In preparing our celebrated Worm Remedy we have used several different kinds of medicines, which make it the best worm destroyer ever prepared. It not only kills the worms, but aids digestion, tones up the stomach and bowels, cleanses the blood, and conditions the animal in general. It is perfectly harmless to the animal, but sure death to the worms. Price, 50c.

SPAVIN CURE.

This is our favorite blister salve, and it is one of the best blistering preparations made. Don't think, because it is called Spavin Cure, that it is only useful in curing spavin. It is the best penetrating, absorbing and sweating blister that can possibly be made, and, therefore, is very useful in a great many diseases.

A remedy of this kind has a great call for and is certainly much needed wherever horses are owned. We have spared no skill, time or expense in making our celebrated Spavin Cure complete and effectual in every particular to meet the demand.

It is a safe, speedy and reliable remedy for spavin, ring-bone, splints, side bones, curbs, thorough pin, bog spavin, wind puffs, sweeny, all chronic enlargements of joints, all bony or callous tumors or enlargements, navicular disease, chronic founder, and any fever or soreness in the feet. It has wonderful vesicant and absorbent effects, penetrating to the seat of the trouble, and insuring speedy action and sure results in all cases where a cure is possible.

It is guaranteed not to kill the hair when used according to directions. When applied to the feet, it draws out all soreness and fever, softens the hoof, and makes it grow very rapidly. Price per bottle, $1.

Brownwood, Texas, June 15, 1897.

Drs. L. D. & N. G. LeGear, Austin, Texas.

Gentlemen: It is with pleasure that we testify to the merits of your Spavin Cure. We cured one very bad case of enlarged hock-joint in one of our horses which we thought was incurable. It is the very best penetrating, absorbing, sweating blister we ever used, and can highly recommend it to all horse owners who have occasion to use it.

G. W. HALL & SON, Livery and Transfer Men.

Holman, Texas, July 28, 1897.

Drs. L. D. & N. G. LeGear, Austin, Texas.

Dear Sirs: I have sold your line of medicines for stock for about twelve months, and could not get along without them, as they give the most gratifying results among my customers.

Very respectfully yours,

G. W. LEWIS.

Brenham, Texas, July 26, 1897.

Drs. L. D. & N. G. LeGear, Austin, Texas.

Gentlemen: Your veterinary medicines have given entire satisfaction wherever sold. You will notice my orders have been quite frequent during the last twelve months, and the last order showed quite an increase in amount over previous ones. There is a demand for reliable veterinary medicines, and you made no mistake when you entered the field to supply this demand. I shall continue to handle your preparations, knowing that your skill and integrity insure safe and reliable goods. Yours truly,

R. E. LUHN, Druggist

Cameron, Texas, July 26, 1897.

Drs. L. D. & N. G. LeGear, Austin, Texas.

This is to certify that I have been handling Drs. L. D. & N. G. LeGear's Veterinary Remedies for ten months, during which time I have made seven orders. I find them to be good sellers and to satisfy those who use them. Respectfully,

GEO. A. THOMAS.

Brownwood, Texas, July 5, 1897.

Drs. L. D. & N. G. LeGear, Austin, Texas.

Dear Sirs: It is with pleasure that we recommend to the trade and public your veterinary remedies. We have been handling them about one year, and have placed six orders with you. We find them good sellers and give entire satisfaction to the buyer. We can safely say that your Horse Colic Cure is a panacea for colic. Have known of one or two doses instantly relieving some very severe cases. We consider all your remedies medicines of great merit. Yours truly,

R. P. PAYNE DRUG CO.

Georgetown, August 2, 1897.

To whom it may concern:

This is to certify that we have been selling Dr. LeGear's veterinary remedies for over six months and are yet to hear of a case where they have not given perfect satisfaction.

Respectfully,

FLEAGER & WHITTENBERG.

New Braunfels, Texas, August 19, 1897.

Drs. L. D. & N. G. LeGear, Austin, Texas.

Gentlemen: Since you have introduced your celebrated veterinary medicines here, the demand for them has steadily increased, and people who have used them are more than pleased with results.

H. V. SCHUMANN, the Leading Druggist.

INDEX.

HORSE DEPARTMENT.

CATTLE DEPARTMENT.

SHEEP DEPARTMENT.

SWINE DEPARTMENT.

DOG DEPARTMENT.

VETERINARY REMEDIES.

www.ingramcontent.com/pod-product-compliance
Lightning Source LLC
Chambersburg PA
CBHW022113290426
44112CB00008B/664
9783337141202